CAROLINE COURTIER
THE LIFE OF LORD COTTINGTON

MARTIN J. HAVRAN

WITH AN INTRODUCTION BY
A. L. ROWSE

MACMILLAN

First published 1973 by
THE MACMILLAN PRESS LTD
London and Basingstoke
Associated companies in New York Toronto
Dublin Melbourne Johannesburg and Madras

SBN 333 14405 8

Printed in Great Britain by
T. AND A. CONSTABLE LTD
Edinburgh

To my mentors
Joseph Havran
Arvel Erickson
Goldwin Smith

Contents

List of Illustrations

Introduction

A. L. Rowse

Professor Havran has performed a valuable service to studies of the seventeenth century by this biography. We hardly need any more biographies of the primary figures, particularly of kings and queens; we need more studies of the secondary figures to fill out our knowledge of the age and time. This young American scholar has devoted a number of years to careful research among original documents and papers, and he has come up with a convincing account of one of the most important of Charles I's ministers. A difficult task, for, significant figure as he was over a long career, the personality and work of Cottington are by no means easy to make out, in fact were traduced in the party conflict of his time and mis-esteemed subsequently.

Professor Havran is right to point out that historians have paid more attention – and perhaps too much respect – to the opponents of the Crown than to its supporters. It is certainly true that the great Victorian historians were far more favourable to 'their ideological forefathers of the seventeenth century', just as today Leftist historians attach more importance to Levellers and such than they had at the time, or than the facts warrant. The problems of government, always more complex and difficult than those of opposition, attract more adult minds and demand more sophisticated treatment. The best of judges, Clarendon, twice described Cottington as a wise man; but he was by no means an obvious one. He offers a challenging subject.

A West Countryman, of Somerset clothier stock, Francis Cottington came up through the ranks from modest beginnings. It is interesting that this devoted servant of the monarchy should have been a new man, while the Puritan Parliamentarian who displaced him as Master of the Court of Wards (with all its profits),

Lord Saye and Sele, should have been descended from an ancient (and predatory) Treasurer way back in the Middle Ages.

An able career-diplomat, Cottington spent seventeen years in Spain in a crucial post; because he was reserved and reticent, people said he was Spaniolised. In fact, he was not popular in Spain, for he stood up manfully for his country's interests; and he had the courage to stand up to Buckingham over his absurd journey with Prince Charles to Madrid, and again over Buckingham's sudden reversal of the previous peace-policy. More than that could hardly be expected: Cottington jeopardised his career by his courage.

Recalled home, he became an able financial administrator, faithfully serving the interests of the Crown and effective in raising its revenues. Of course he feathered his nest and made his fortune; so did everybody else, except the excessively upright bishops, Juxon and Laud – though they fared no better at the hands of the fanatics when their time came.

Cottington was very unfanatical, cool and good-tempered, patient, persistent and hard-working, with a sly sense of humour – one sees the picture of the trained administrator, giving nothing away, rather uncandid, possibly disingenuous, when most politicians were all too angrily expressive. When faults on both sides brought about the diaster of the Civil War, Cottington lost not only his offices but his fortune, with his estates confiscated. The sainted Saye and Sele, 'Old Subtlety', got Cottington's Hanworth estate, worth £14,000, for £4000; Parliament, to reward its faithful, gave him another £10,000 compensation when the Court of Wards was abolished.

The observant Samuel Butler saw, without illusions, that 'as these Grandees, as they call them, are taken off with bribes or preferment, others start up in their rooms and keep the Party on it'. He concludes philosophically: 'Do what we can, that which is a free government to one Party will be tyranny to another; where every slight Faction and trivial Sect calls itself the Public . . . where every man can teach us how to govern, but nobody knows how to obey.'

And the upshot? – a ruinous, destructive Civil War, at the end of which a compromise was reached which should have been reached twenty years before, and saved all the trouble. By that time,

Cottington, after a long and strenuous life, had died in exile. He had taken life in exile as calmly, and with his exceptional stamina as smoothly, as his days in power. His body was brought home at the Restoration to lie in Westminster Abbey in as resplendent a tomb as he would have had twenty years before, just as if nothing untoward had happened in the interval.

Preface

I VENTURE to suggest that the victors in any contest attract more disciples than the vanquished. Historians customarily have paid closer attention to the critics and enemies of the Crown in the early seventeenth century than to its supporters. This preoccupation with dissent is understandable, especially as it led to the Civil War and a pattern of reform which shaped the subsequent development of English society, but it has had the less fortunate result of creating a distorted picture of the issues and personalities of the epoch. This has been corrected in part since the 1950s by the publication of a number of studies of the monarchy, its servants and agencies of Government. Nevertheless, today we still know somewhat less about the officers of the early Stuart monarchy, particularly those at the second and third ranks of authority, than about the oppositionists in Parliament and in the country as a whole. Francis Cottington is a case in point.

Cottington – the man and the courtier – first interested me more than twenty years ago and has fascinated me ever since. He figured indirectly in my research for an earlier book and has occupied a great deal of my time for a decade. His career of nearly a half-century in the service of the Crown coincided with one of the most volatile periods in English history and was linked closely to those of the leading figures of Caroline England on the Government's side, notably Buckingham, Laud, Portland and Strafford. Cottington participated in or was an eye-witness of many of the most crucial events and issues of his day; indeed Parliament in 1640-1 considered him an issue. He shared with a small number of other self-made men in the Government the distinction of having reached the top without the benefit of solid connections at Court, great wealth, higher education, or other advantages considered essential to success in public life. He stumbled often but rarely lost his balance; like a cat he had the knack of landing on his feet. He was a private man, hard to know and harder to like. Historians have made him a favourite whipping-boy and have held him up as a prime example of what went wrong with Stuart diplomacy and administration. His critics and their admirers have accused him of forwarding schemes which damaged the nation and hurt the King's interests. He has been characterised as a dissembler and an opportunist bent on his own advancement. Yet, for all that, we have known comparatively little in depth about the man and his work these more than three centuries since his death. Such short biographical sketches as we have are cast mainly from a mould made in the seventeenth century by his enemies and competitors. Modern authorities have devoted a few paragraphs to him – usually in reference to Prince Charles's Spanish venture in 1623 and to the nature of Government in the 1630s – but his life as a whole has not been assessed.

Cottington has never lacked critics. The unwavering sameness of this mainly adverse criticism has intrigued me. It has fixed in our minds a sharp image of his personality, character and influence. How we presently perceive Cottington is largely the result of evaluations made by a handful of his contemporaries who, for one reason or another, bore him a grudge or who resisted the claims and actions of the Crown which he defended and represented to the public in key posts at home and abroad. The great Victorian historians were generally in emotional accord with their ideological forefathers of the seventeenth century and extolled their courage and pertinacity in resisting a monarchy based on divine right. They were therefore disinclined to question the harsh characterisation of Cottington which they inherited and readily repeated in their own works. Of course, both groups were hostile witnesses.

On the face of it the standard interpretation looks right. But is it? It seems only fair to ask after all this time whether we, like the ancient Greeks, have been looking at the shadow of the man – at his historical image – and not at the man himself. One of my primary purposes in undertaking this study was to test the accuracy of that interpretation within the context of Cottington's whole life, and not simply on the basis of his work during the years when he served as a principal adviser of King Charles. Indeed, his life before 1629 and after 1641 – the very periods which historians have neglected in treating him – are in some ways more useful in determining his true character and worth. By 1629 he was fifty years old and set in his ways; whereas after 1641, stripped of his offices and most of his influence, he had little else to lose by revealing his mind and heart freely to his associates.

In preparing this biography I have received many favours. I gratefully acknowledge the advice, assistance and encouragement of friends, correspondents and institutions. Two term grants by Kent State University provided relief from my teaching duties and the funds which enabled me to read manuscripts in Great Britain; and a summer grant and a subsidy for typing expenses from the University of Virginia kept the wolf from my door during the final revision of this study.

I learnt long since that archivists and librarians do much more than clean, catalogue and shelve books and manuscripts; they are a fund of information, and scholars in their own right. The archivists at the county record offices of Berkshire, Hampshire, Somerset, Middlesex, Wiltshire and Surrey gave generously of their time and knowledge of local sources, as did others at the Leeds City Library and the Central Library, Sheffield, where I read through the Strafford Letter Books. Extracts from them are made with the kind permission of the Earl Fitzwilliam and his Trustees. The painting of Lord Cottington is reproduced with the permission of the National Portrait Gallery. The staffs of the Public Record Office, the British Museum, the National Library of Scotland, the Bodleian Library, the Archivo General de Simancas, Somerset House and the Folger Shakespeare Library were unfailingly helpful. So, too, were those at the university libraries of Virginia, Northwestern, Alberta, Case Western Reserve, and Kent State.

I have sought advice and assistance from persons with special competence on certain aspects of my subject. Mr J. Francis Mees, Colonel Harry H. Johnson and the late Reverend Kenneth Ashcroft afforded me the benefit of their knowledge of the area where Cottington spent his earliest years, and of its history. Mr A. J. Cooper allowed me to read his B.Litt. thesis on Cottington's political career and shared his insights on him with me in both conversations and correspondence. Messrs M. J. Hawkins and Wilson Hoffman, Professor Joel Hurstfield and the late Professor Harold Hulme answered queries on aspects of Cottington's service in Parliament and as a diplomat and administrator. Mr N. M.

Arnold-Forster welcomed me to his home near Swindon, Wiltshire, where I studied letters in his private collection which Cottington wrote or received in the last months of his life. Messrs Charles F. Kirk and Anthony Mazzaferri helped me with translations of documents. Mrs Barbara Smith and Mrs Adele Hall cheerfully typed the final drafts of the manuscript at short notice. My debts to particular scholars past and present are recorded in the notes while others, anonymous to me, will recognise places where their criticism improved the text and the organisation of the material.

I wish to express my deepest gratitude to Professor Arvel B. Erickson and to Dr A. L. Rowse, both of whom read the entire manuscript and suggested countless ways of improving it. Finally, my dedication of this book to my three mentors, each of whom contributed a great deal to my development as a person and an historian, is made with heartfelt thanks.

Charlottesville, Virginia   M. J. H.
September 1972

List of Abbreviations

Add. MSS.	Additional Manuscripts, British Museum
AHR	*American Historical Review*
APC	*Acts of the Privy Council of England*
BIHR	*Bulletin of the Institute of Historical Research*
B.L.	Bodleian Library
B.M.	British Museum
CCSP	*Calendar of the Clarendon State Papers*, ed. O. Ogle, W. H. Bliss, W. D. Macray and F. J. Routledge (1869-1932)
Clarendon *History*	Edward Hyde, Earl of Clarendon, *The History of the Rebellion and Civil Wars in England*, ed. W. D. Macray (1888)
CJ	*Journals of the House of Commons*
CSPD	*Calendar of State Papers, Domestic Series*
CSPV	*Calendar of State Papers and Manuscripts relating to English Affairs, existing in the Archives and Collections of Venice*
DNB	*Dictionary of National Biography*
EcHR	*Economic History Review*
EHR	*English Historical Review*
Gardiner *History*	S. R. Gardiner, *History of England from the Accession of James I to the Outbreak of the Civil War* (1883-4)
H.M.C.	Historical Manuscripts Commission
Strafforde's Letters	*The Earl of Strafforde's Letters and Dispatches*, ed. W. Knowler (1739)
Laud, *Works*	*The Works of the Most Reverend Father in God, William Laud, D.D.*, ed. W. Scott and J. Bliss (1847-60)
LJ	*Journals of the House of Lords*
P.C.C.	Prerogative Court of Canterbury
P.R.O.	Public Record Office

R.O.	County Record Office
Rushworth	John Rushworth, *Historical Collections of Private Passages of State, Weighty Matters in Law, Remarkable Proceedings in Five Parliaments* (1721-2)
S.P.	State Papers, Public Record Office
S.P.S.	State Papers, Spanish, Public Record Office
Stoye	J. W. Stoye, *English Travellers Abroad, 1604-1667* (1952)
TRHS	*Transactions of the Royal Historical Society*
V.C.H.	Victoria County History
W.W. MSS.	Wentworth Woodhouse Manuscripts, Strafford Papers, Sheffield Central Library, Yorkshire

CHAPTER I

Godminster

FRANCIS COTTINGTON was born probably at Godminster Manor near Pitcombe in eastern Somerset towards the end of 1579. He came from a family of clothiers and small landowners whose principal estate near Bruton had, said Clarendon, 'passed from father to son for many hundred years'. The Cottingtons lived in the borderland of Somerset and Wiltshire where they manufactured a white broadcloth that had long sustained the economy of their district. The organisation of this industry during Francis's childhood centred mainly in the small capitalist clothiers. His grandfather, father, uncles and brothers all raised sheep on the family lands, employed cottagers in the area to spin and weave wool in their own homes, and marketed it locally, in London, and abroad through the great merchant companies. This active production and trade in broadcloth afforded thousands of common folk a livelihood and profited master clothiers and merchant tailors alike.[1]

The village of Leigh upon Mendip lay a few miles west of the Wiltshire border, on the axle of a wheel rimmed by the larger communities of Frome, Radstock, Shepton Mallet and Bruton. In Leigh upon Mendip or near by stood the house of Francis's paternal grandfather, Philip Cottington, a clothier who owned land at Leigh and Coleford and employed dozens of weavers at East and West Cranmore, Nunney, Coleford, Mells, Stoke Lane, Dean and Bruton. Some time prior to 1543 he married Margery Middlecote of Warminster in Wiltshire, into a family of a social and financial position comparable to his own.[2]

Margery Cottington continued to prosper even after Philip's death in 1559; her children enlarged the family holdings and improved themselves through advantageous marriages and education. With their profits they purchased more land; the eldest son,

John, acquired the manors of Egford, Sellwood and Woodlands near Frome. His only sister, Sylvestre, married the promising lawyer John Daccombe, who became a secretary of Robert Cecil, Earl of Salisbury, and later Chancellor of the Duchy of Lancaster. Her brother James took a doctorate in divinity at Trinity College, Oxford, married Helen Bullingham, a daughter of the Bishop of Gloucester, and became precentor of Wells Cathedral. Another brother, Philip, the father of Lord Cottington, settled in 1569 at Godminster Manor. By the 1570s the Cottingtons had begun to extend their influence and connections throughout the region and even to London. It remained for Francis Cottington in the early seventeenth century to raise himself to a position of national prominence and wealth through hard work and long apprenticeship in diplomacy and administration.[3]

The purchase of Godminster Manor, where Francis was reared until early adolescence, consolidated the holdings of the Cottington family in Pitcombe parish. Situated in undulating country astride a shallow valley, this ancient manor was dominated by a fifteenth-century stone house which resembled the larger mansion of Great Chalfield, about twenty-five miles to the north-east. The manor lands spread over some four square miles, in the vicinity of Pitcombe, Honeywick, Castle Cary and Hadspen. About two miles from Godminster house rose the square tower of St Leonard's Church, which figured in the lives of the Cottingtons for seven generations. Philip Cottington was comfortably off, even when the western European market in broadcloth slackened after the onset of the Spanish war. He realised about £200 annually from the manor besides the profits from the family business. He was an upstanding and respected member of his community. On trips to London he customarily did business for friends, who entrusted him with their affairs, and served as a governor of King's School in Bruton for eighteen years before his death in 1615.[4]

It was to Godminster that Philip Cottington brought his bride, Jane Biflete, whom he married at St Leonard's in August 1572. According to Clarendon, she was 'a Stafford, nearly allied to Sir Edward Stafford, who was vice-chamberlain to Queen Elizabeth, and had been ambassador to France'. The marriage improved the status of the Godminster Cottingtons and helped to launch Francis on a career in the royal service shortly after the turn of the century.[5]

Francis was the penultimate son of Philip and Jane Cottington, being one of five children including Elizabeth, Maurice and James, older than himself, and Edward, who was two years his junior.[6] The Cottington children did well by themselves. Maurice stayed on at Godminster and reared two sons who inherited the bulk of Lord Cottington's estate after the Restoration. Edward spent four years at Trinity College, Oxford, but, having been converted to Roman Catholicism, became a Jesuit novice at Rome and died in the Spanish Netherlands in 1602. Apart from the wife and children of John Biflete, his uncle on his mother's side, Edward was the only member of his family to join the Roman Church during Elizabethan times.[7]

The reconstruction of the early life of a national personage in earlier times is often difficult, and Francis Cottington is no exception. An aged Oxford tutor taught the youngest Cottington child, Edward, the 'rudiments of learning' at Godminster and it is improbable that Philip would have denied his other sons a basic education. Clarendon averred that Cottington had been reared during adolescence and early manhood in the household of Sir Edward Stafford, his mother's kinsman and a distinguished diplomat. Since Stafford lived abroad (mostly in France) on assignment after 1578 and did not return to England permanently until 1590, when Francis would have been about eleven, he doubtless remained at Godminster until at least that time. Afterwards he must have spent some years in London, where Stafford mostly resided from 1592 to 1605.

Thus Francis had an opportunity to learn the ways of the aristocracy at first hand in his benefactor's home. Stafford was related to Queen Elizabeth herself, her aunt Mary Boleyn having been his father's first wife. Stafford was also a kinsman of the Poles, the Catholic family of Yorkist descent. Sir Edward married prudently: his second wife, Douglas Howard, was the widow of Lord Sheffield, the mistress of the Earl of Leicester and the sister of the Earl of Nottingham, Lord High Admiral. Moreover, Stafford had identified himself closely with the interests of William Cecil, Lord Burghley, and their friendship continued even after the diplomat lost the confidence of the Queen for allegedly having revealed state secrets in France to the Spanish ambassador. Stafford's connections with the

Cecils and Howards ultimately benefited Francis, who, as a younger
son of a comparatively obscure Somerset family, would have had
great difficulty in trying to launch a career in government on his
own meagre credentials.[8]

The training that Cottington received in the Stafford household
must have been more practical than formal: instruction in the riding
arts, field sports, gentlemanly conduct, the responsibilities of a
courtier and the like.[9] Clarendon, who frowned on Cottington's
Spanish ways, wry sense of humour and modest background,
remarked that 'he was illiterate as to the grammar of any language,
or the principles of any science'. Francis apparently had little formal
higher education, but he was hardly an unlearned man. By the age
of thirty he had mastered Spanish, knew some French and Italian,
and understood Latin well enough to make his way through
financial and legal records; while King James and Robert Cecil
entrusted him with the management of English affairs in Spain.
In his forties and fifties Cottington efficiently administered important offices of the central administration. His long career in diplomacy and government discredits any judgement which questions
his quickness of mind or lack of native intelligence. Cottington's
extensive correspondence shows that he had a facility with the
English language as well as some understanding of botany, astro-
nomy, geography, history, medicine and international relations,
much of which he admittedly picked up in Spain after the age of
twenty-five.[10]

Training in the household of Sir Edward Stafford prepared
Cottington precisely for the career that he subsequently pursued.
Diplomatic service required little formal education, especially at
the lower levels in an embassy. Many Elizabethan and Jacobean
diplomats came from merchant or gentle families and, like Francis,
put their mercantile experience to good use in a period when international trade occupied much of their time. What Francis lacked
in formal education he compensated for in on-the-job training that
was rigorous, lengthy and professional. Senior diplomats, such as
Stafford, Sir John Digby or Sir Charles Cornwallis, who headed
western European embassies, generally acquired their posts through
family connections and patronage. But most 'career' diplomats
came up through the ranks. Service abroad afforded them

opportunities to learn languages, diplomatic procedure, law and business practices, and prepared them for higher office at home in the central administration. Because the standards expected of diplomats were high and the opportunities for advancement quite limited, many younger diplomats spent trying years under adverse circumstances and with little remuneration without ever attaining superior rank. Nevertheless, most continued to hope, like Cottington, that a few years of dedicated service at a foreign capital would promote them to the heights of wealth and prestige at home.[11]

This sort of life awaited Francis Cottington almost to the letter. The death of Stafford in February 1605 robbed Francis of his benefactor and patron, but it also set the stage for his diplomatic career. After two decades of war England and Spain had agreed to make peace, and the embassy of the Earl of Nottingham made ready to depart for Spain. On the eve of his death Stafford had exploited his connections with Nottingham and Robert Cecil to find a modest place for Cottington in the service of Sir Charles Cornwallis, the newly appointed ambassador to the Court of King Philip III.[12]

CHAPTER 2

Secretary in Spain

WHEN Queen Elizabeth died in March 1603, England and Spain had been at war for nearly twenty years. This protracted struggle wore down Spain's strength, but neither side was prepared to yield. Peace was difficult to bring about, but the accession of James I brought a change of attitude towards the war, and created a climate conducive to peace. James was fundamentally averse to things martial. He had on the whole been successful in Scotland in pacifying political and religious factionalism, but his mettle as a diplomat had not been seriously tested. Upon succeeding to the English throne, James believed that he could play a cardinal role in arranging peace in western Europe, whose peoples ached from decades of war and were divided along religious and dynastic lines into essentially two armed camps. So it was that James extended an open hand to Philip III of Spain. He made the right decision, however much his subjects criticised him for it.[1]

King James wasted little time restoring informal diplomatic relations with Spain. He ordered the cessation of hostilities (including privateering) and responded graciously to the overture of peace brought by King Philip's envoy, Count Villa Mediana, in September 1603. In January the Spaniard and the English commissioners, led by Cecil and Nottingham, began preparing an agenda for negotiation. After the Spanish commissioners Alexandro Rovida, Juan Ricardote and Count Aremberg reached England in May, the peacemakers drafted a treaty over the summer. They reached general agreement on the articles by July, by which time the Duke of Frias, Constable of Castile, had arrived in London to discuss the few remaining points of contention.

Notwithstanding their objection to a Spanish treaty, Englishmen had every reason to be pleased with its terms. Except for one concession which they should not have expected to gain – full trade rights in the Spanish territories in the New World – the English won the greatest advantages. The Spaniards wanted England to outlaw the Dutch as rebels, but Cecil skilfully side-stepped the issue, thereby preserving the Anglo-Dutch trade connection and safeguarding a huge debt which the Dutch owed to England and might otherwise have refused to pay. Most important for England, her merchants could do business in Spain or any other Spanish European dominion. For her part, England admitted Spanish merchants into the British Isles and promised to recall her troops helping the Dutch in the Netherlands. The Spaniards as well as the Dutch could recruit volunteers in the British Isles – a minor concession to Spain because only English or Irish Roman Catholics customarily enlisted in His Catholic Majesty's regiments. Few could have foreseen at the time that the treaty would be broken repeatedly by both signatories in the next twenty years, much less that the Spaniards could turn a treaty of primary advantage to England into one which isolated her from military involvement on the side of the continental Protestants.[2]

On 21 March 1605 the Earl of Nottingham assembled a train of five hundred persons for his mission to Spain. King James had commissioned him ambassador extraordinary to witness the ratification of the treaty by Philip III and establish permanent diplomatic relations. With Nottingham went his son Lord Howard of Effingham, the permanent ambassador Sir Charles Cornwallis, the Earl of Perth, Vice-Admiral Sir Richard Leveson, Lords Norris and Willoughby, and many others. Two young men in the entourage were Dudley Carleton, secretary to Lord Norris, and Francis Cottington, clerk to Cornwallis, both of whom were beginning their public careers and were destined to hold high office. The journey which the Somerset man of twenty-five began at Dover on 5 April 1605 launched a diplomatic career that kept him abroad more or less continuously for the next seventeen years. It was an exciting time, and thoughts of the hardships that lay ahead were forgotten as Nottingham's squadron rounded Brittany and the tempestuous waters of the Bay of Biscay, and dropped anchor at Corunna on the north-west coast of Spain.[3]

The Spaniards welcomed the Lord High Admiral with fireworks

and a banquet. These festivities contrasted sharply with the poverty of northern Spain, which struck Englishmen accustomed to their verdant and productive homeland. Always a poor traveller and complainer, Cornwallis wrote to Cecil after disembarking that 'great preparation is made . . . for our Carriages, out of this barren country. The way to Valladolid we understand to be very unpleasant, and exceedingly long.' His apprehension was justified: the roads to Valladolid were wretched, even by seventeenth-century standards, and the Spaniards had difficulty finding food enough for the English a day at a time. Inns were few and beds a luxury. Sir Robert Mansell, an aide to the Admiral, remarked that the land could scarcely support a third of the peasants who lived in hovels surrounded by fields which still bore signs of neglect resulting from an epidemic six years earlier. He looked in vain for cattle or sheep which abounded in England and saw only stunted rye in fields where more nourishing grains might have thrived. The caravan moved slowly by way of Lugo across the mountains to Villafranca, and thence south-eastward over the Esla river through Astorga and Simancas to Valladolid in Old Castile. After twenty days, they reached the Court on 19 May.

The journey taxed the patience of Cornwallis, as did an incident at Corunna involving one of his servants who died soon after disembarking. Cornwallis wanted him buried with Anglican rites, which the authorities refused to allow after two monks failed to see Cornwallis's argument that immortal souls bore no marks of nationality or church membership; he had the body returned to England. He believed that the Spaniards had violated the religious rights of Englishmen guaranteed in the new treaty even before Nottingham had witnessed its ratification by Philip III. This lesson was not lost on Cornwallis, who henceforth rarely trusted Spaniards even when they did not deserve the recrimination he heaped on them.

Cornwallis also worried about the welfare of his staff. He sought to ensure that the Exchequer would adequately support his mission; he realised the hardship that might befall his household in a foreign land gripped by inflation unless allowances were paid on time. He therefore had Cottington write Cecil the first of many letters complaining about the meagre support promised by King James. The Exchequer did have a reputation of underpaying ambassadors, or of not paying them for months at a time, but Cornwallis should not have complained. An Exchequer order warrant dated 10 February 1605 provided him £1,460 annually plus £500 for intelligence purposes. He got more money, in fact, than any of the other English ambassadors at the western European capitals.[4]

If Cornwallis grumbled about what Dudley Carleton called 'feasts and triumphs enough for Stow's chronicle', the other Englishmen enjoyed the celebrations honouring them. Somehow the purpose of the grand mission was forgotten amid the social whirl now that peace had been restored. But finally, on 30 May, the Archbishop of Toledo and the Duke of Lerma presided at the solemn ratification of the treaty. Philip III spoke his promises on his knees, with his hands on a Bible and a crucifix; Nottingham presented the Queen with a diamond brooch with pendant pearls and in turn received gifts valued at 160,000 ducats.[5] On 8 June, Nottingham and most of his party left Valladolid to board ship at Santander for England eleven days later. Some of the travellers, remembering their discomfort on the incoming voyage, elected to go overland across the Pyrenees to Paris and the Channel, a route which most diplomats and couriers subsequently preferred. Cornwallis and his aides remained behind as the permanent English embassy to the Court of Philip at Valladolid, and later at Madrid, to which it moved in 1606.

Apart from the English and Spanish servants, the household included the ambassador and his son, a chaplain, two secretaries and a clerk, among others. English merchants and important tourists sometimes stayed at the embassy from a few days to several months. Walter Hawkesworth served as English secretary, while Nicholas Ousely handled the Spanish correspondence. A native of Bristol, Ousely was the most valuable man in the embassy by reason of more than twenty-five years' service as a merchant and spy in Spain. He understood Spanish affairs, the ways of the Government and the Church, and the problems of the English merchants, but his association with the Jesuits at Valladolid annoyed Cornwallis. It was principally with Ousely that Francis Cottington worked, and apparently from him that he learned Spanish. The chaplain, James Wadsworth, ministered to the Protestant enclave in Valladolid. In the late summer of 1605 he visited the University of

Salamanca for study and conversation with theologians, and afterwards the University of Alcalá de Henares, where he was converted to Roman Catholicism. His apostasy infuriated Cornwallis and embarrassed the English Government. The Spaniards naturally regarded Wadsworth's conversion as a major triumph, and subsequently employed him as a merchant factor, a spy, a religious disputant and English tutor to the Infanta Maria.[6]

By early 1606 the embassy had moved with the Court of Philip III to Madrid. It was situated initially in a small house outside the city. When this house proved unsatisfactory, the authorities found Cornwallis another on the heights overlooking the countryside and, following customary practice, paid the rent. The high cost of living strained the resources of the embassy, as did the expense of supporting merchants who expected hospitality when they visited the capital. Food, particularly meat and bread, was rarely plentiful in the overcrowded and poorly provisioned capital.[7]

Embassy correspondence kept Cottington busy most of the time. He wrote regularly to English merchants at the ports of the peninsula, to other English embassies in western Europe, and to his superiors in London. Cornwallis naturally bore the responsibility for embassy business, but his frequent illnesses afforded Cottington ample opportunity to speak for England at Court. The young man spent two weeks in early 1606 explaining why his Government had executed Father Henry Garnet and others involved in the Gunpowder Plot the previous November, and failed to persuade the Spanish Councillors to identify the English Catholics living in Spanish dominions. Beginning in June, Cottington visited Lisbon for four months to expedite litigation over confiscation of English merchants' property. His encounters with the authorities there convinced him that the Spaniards seemed not to value the treaty which they had welcomed two years earlier.[8]

Cottington returned to Madrid that October to find his associates burdened by sickness. He also contracted the disease and nearly perished in this first of several brushes with death during many years in the unhealthy environment of Madrid. He was unable to resume his duties until January 1607, when he was promoted to junior secretary in place of Hawkesworth, whose death increased his work load even after replacements arrived in the next few months.

The new staff included the courier Walsingham Gresley, who became Cottington's close friend and served in Spain until 1623; Dr Alexander Chapman, Wadsworth's successor as chaplain; and the factotum – possibly clerk – William Resoute, an irascible man without a kind word for Cornwallis or Spain.

English diplomats generally disliked the Spanish mission, and not without reason. Resoute said in September 1608 that practically all the officers and servants who accompanied Cornwallis in 1605 as well as many of their replacements had died or left. By the previous April ten of the ambassador's servants had died, and he himself had 'strangely decayed . . . [even though] he is as regular as any man' in health habits. Since then three more had become seriously ill and returned to England 'to preserve their lives a few days longer'. Little wonder that Cottington often pondered the wisdom of remaining in Spain.[9]

The churlish Cornwallis did little to brighten the lives of his underlings. Resoute complained to Cecil that the ambassador was so stingy that he spent only £1,200 of his allowance for household expenses in the previous year, and turned hungry English merchants away. Worse still, Cornwallis allegedly used a 'shifting manner' to mulct money from the Exchequer, saying that he could not live on his allowance when all along he had actually saved money and pawned the embassy plate to get more.[10]

Whatever one might say against Cornwallis as a person, he served English interests in Spain well considering the problems facing him. His and Cottington's difficulties resulted mostly from the nature of Spanish ways of government and their own misunderstanding of Spanish temperament and culture. England and Spain had had too little direct contact in the generation before 1604 to enable each to form accurate impressions of the other, and the animosity between them since the days of Henry VIII did not help the situation. Catholics from the British Isles had fled to Spain or the Low Countries to escape religious persecution, serve in Spanish armies or study at Spanish seminaries. Some English merchants, and many more Irishmen, had also managed to remain in the peninsula during the war because they were Catholics. Only these Elizabethans had much practical knowledge of the Spaniards and their way of life. A generation of Englishmen had grown up without knowing Spaniards, whom they had been taught from childhood to hate and distrust. Cornwallis, Cottington and other diplomats repeatedly betrayed this bias and thought the worst of Spaniards whenever anything went against the interests of England or her merchants.[11]

If Cornwallis and Cottington misunderstood the Spaniards, they learned not to expect miracles from the officers with whom they negotiated on behalf of the merchants. These officials did react slowly to the ambassador's complaints, but his observations on their inefficiency cannot always be taken at face value. Spanish administrators had to cope with problems that were immensely more important than the welfare of English merchants – inflation, agricultural crises, the Dutch revolt, colonial matters, the ennui or recalcitrance of the aristocracy. The attitude of Philip III did not help matters. He was not indifferent towards his responsibilities as head of a vast empire and a growing bureaucracy, but he disliked a steady diet of business. Unlike Philip II, he habitually delegated his own work to favourites, who were sometimes no more devoted to duty, or used their positions for self-gain. Partly for these reasons the Spanish governmental machinery moved sluggishly, and sometimes broke down for weeks at a time.

The problems of English merchants obliged Cornwallis and Cottington to work with the Spanish Government, which operated through twelve councils. Some councils governed Imperial territories; others managed departments of the central administration, such as justice, finance, the military and the Inquisition. The Council of State, composed of royal appointees selected from the leading noble families, dominated government. Three Councillors of State controlled the administration by the time Cottington became secretary at the English embassy: Don Francisco y Rojas, Duke of Lerma, whom the Venetian ambassador in Madrid thought as powerful as the King; Rodrigo Calderon, Count of Oliva and Marquis of Siete Iglesias; and Don Pedro Franqueza, Count of Villalonga and Villafranqueza. Virtually all important matters of state were decided by these Councillors, who felt no urgency to shorten their consistently long agenda. Thus the fate of persons and policies alike often hung in the balance for months or years at a time.[12]

St Leonard's Church, Pitcombe (Bruton), Somerset
Destroyed by fire since the photograph was taken in 1965

Assessing the character and methods of the Spanish Government, Cornwallis and Cottington became wary of pressing the claims of English merchants too forcefully. Neither the merchants nor the Privy Council fully understood the reasons for delays in negotiations or appreciated the efforts of embassy personnel on behalf of their countrymen. There is a telling dispatch by Cornwallis to the Privy Council in 1607 that summarises his problems. The prolonged absence of the Council of State on progress with the King obliged him to negotiate by letter, and answers were not returned for three or four months. Even then, Cornwallis endured further 'delays . . . to draw any resolution from them . . .'. He described the Council's methods in not altogether fair terms: it was reluctant to settle any question, and was 'apt to take advantage upon any similitude or shadow of any word reprehensible; how desirous to divert when they cannot answer, and how inclinable to stall us with words only, and those, generally, admitting posterns and back doors, to slip out at, when they had no will to perform in effect, what they give a sound of in the generality of their words'. Cornwallis finally sent Cottington to plead English grievances in person. He argued them ably, and the Councillors promised to answer all complaints. At the same time, while professing no intention of dissimulating with Cottington, the Councillors promised no concessions to the merchants. The Privy Council would understand, Cornwallis wrote to his superiors, 'how offensive my importunity for my countrymen is unto them [the Spanish Council], and without that clear it is, that nothing I should effect [can come to a good end] . . .'.[13]

Cornwallis did not question Cottington's ability, but he worried about his susceptibility to Catholic influences. Joseph Creswell, a Jesuit who managed the Society's affairs in Castile and headed the English College at Valladolid, tried to convert Cottington in the knowledge that his brother, Edward, had become a Jesuit novice in 1600. This affront to Cornwallis's religious sensibilities, along with the fact that the former embassy chaplain, Wadsworth, was employed by the Jesuits, terminated a kind of friendly rivalry between Cornwallis and Creswell. Cornwallis thought initially that Creswell, who had powerful friends at Court, might be useful. He cultivated his friendship for more than a year, believing, as he told

Cecil, that the Jesuit was but a misguided Englishman. In the end, the Privy Council ordered Cornwallis to break off relations with Creswell. In the eyes of the Council he was a treacherous man bent on achieving Catholic emancipation in England and overthrowing King James. Cornwallis had Cottington warn Creswell to keep away from Englishmen, but he continued to trouble the ambassador and, after he left, Cottington and Sir John Digby as well. While Creswell had failed to convert Cottington, others tried again in succeeding years until he openly avowed Catholicism and died of that faith in Valladolid.[14]

Cornwallis also believed that the Council of the Inquisition meant to destroy the religious freedom guaranteed Englishmen in Spain by the treaty. From time to time Cornwallis reported attempts by the Inquisition to influence his underlings, and of interference with Protestant services at the embassy and in the homes of English merchants. He had words with the Spanish authorities in 1607 and 1608 over this. In September 1607 the ambassador complained to Lerma of personal insults hurled by the Mayor of Madrid, and demanded an apology. At this Lerma turned on Cornwallis, accusing him of giving scandal to Spaniards by 'public preaching, and exercise of our Religion . . .'. To Lerma's further charge that Spaniards were admitted to Protestant services, Cornwallis retorted that he had often been wrongly accused of such liberties, but that only members of his household attended chapel. This exchange prompted Cornwallis to speak with the Inquisitor, who said that he himself had heard trumpeters summon the community to Protestant services, and that embassy personnel did their best to convert simple-minded Spaniards to Protestantism. Cornwallis denied the allegations and explained that he used trumpets and bells simply to call his people to meals.

Some embassy servants – all Englishmen – had been imprisoned, supposedly on account of religion. In September 1607 a coachman took food to another coachman in a Madrid jail and was himself arrested without explanation. Cornwallis demanded his release and was told that, several months earlier, four grooms of his stable had assisted a felon to escape. Two of these grooms were clapped in irons for a fortnight. Later, when the jailer recognised the visitor as one of those involved in the escape, he was arrested on the spot.

Since the felon had escaped from a prison housing those convicted by the Inquisition, the English were accused of interfering with religion.[15] The English sustained another bruise to their religious sensibilities in August 1608, when Inquisition officers accused embassy officials of scandalising Spanish Catholics employed there by attacking their beliefs in chapel and at dinner. Cornwallis denied these charges to the Constable of Castile, reassuring him that only English Protestants could attend chapel, where sermons and prayers had nothing whatever to do with disputation. The Constable conceded that anyone, Protestant or Catholic, might discuss theology privately, and agreed to study a letter sent with Cottington detailing incidents involving English merchants questioned, imprisoned or dispossessed of books by the Inquisition.

This letter offered an English interpretation of the disputed religious articles of the 1604 treaty, and demanded from the Spaniards a clear affirmation of the right of all Protestants resident in Spain to practise their faith privately. The Spaniards held that only Englishmen on short visits to the country enjoyed religious freedom, while those (except diplomats) who resided more or less permanently had to conform to Catholicism. One question that naturally arose was: did this apply to merchants and their factors who stayed for varying periods of time? After deliberation among themselves and with the concurrence of Cornwallis, the Court of the Inquisition and the Council of State ruled that English Protestants could hold religious services only at the embassy or in their residences, provided no Spaniards were present. But intrusions upon what the English believed to be their rights in religion did not end there. Complaints by merchants continued to pour into the embassy as long as Cornwallis served and afterwards.[16]

If Cornwallis had grounds in the Treaty of London to challenge infringements of the religious rights of Englishmen, he had less success persuading the Spaniards to respect commercial rights. Whether from ignorance of Spanish law or intentionally, merchants broke customs regulations and were brought to law in courts which had a reputation of being corrupt. Local officials had their own interests to protect. If a merchant were convicted of a crime, his goods, and sometimes his ship, were sold and the proceeds divided among the arresting officer, his informer, the judges in the case and the Crown. Even when the merchants appealed to a higher court in Madrid, which generally gave them a fair hearing, they had to bear the cost of litigation. Should a Madrid court require that a merchant be present during the appeal proceedings, he might be kept from trade for months or even years. In the event that a Madrid court reversed the conviction of a merchant in a local court, he still faced the problem of recovering his goods or the money from their sale. Cornwallis and Cottington spent a great deal of time and money trying to expedite the appeals of merchants in the courts, representing their interests at the Councils of State and War, and locating appropriated property or those who profited from its sale.[17]

On the other hand, the deterioration of Anglo-Spanish relations was not only the fault of the Spaniards. English merchants refused to accept the Spanish claim to monopoly in the New World. They engaged in unauthorised privateering against Spanish merchantmen. Customs officers interfered with the rights of Spanish merchants in England. The pursuivants raided the Spanish embassy in London in search of English Catholics attending mass. The Government encouraged the Dutch to recruit volunteers for the continuing war with Spain but did nothing to expedite Spanish recruiting, which violated an article of the 1604 treaty at least in spirit. King James gradually drifted away from close ties with Spain and moved closer to the Protestant states of northern Europe. England accused Spain of harbouring Irish traitors and of actively forwarding their plans for an Irish rebellion. The Spaniards were also annoyed with English diplomats in Brussels and Augsburg, who promoted the candidacy of the Lutheran claimants in the Cleves-Jülich succession question following the death of the Duke of Cleves without an heir in March 1609. Finally, Cornwallis exacerbated relations by over-reacting to pretended insults and quarrelling with Spanish courtiers, who disliked him and showed it in the way they responded to his complaints.[18]

Some English merchants trading to Spain experienced harsh treatment from Spanish officials, despite the intercessions of Cornwallis and Cottington. In 1606-7 the Privy Council and Parliament became concerned that Philip III seemed unwilling to satisfy merchants' grievances. But his and his officers' decisions varied according to circumstances, so that they answered some complaints and ignored others. Early in 1607 Philip could not have been more accommodating, ordering port officials to compensate merchants whose property had been confiscated. He acted promptly in this instance because his ambassador in London reported that Parliament and the Privy Council were angry. In fact there was some danger that England might break off relations with Spain. In June 1606 some merchants' wives, who said that their husbands had been victimised by Spanish port authorities, laid before the Privy Council specific instances of imprisonments and confiscations. James and his Councillors studied them in August, and Cecil, now Lord Cranborne, warned the Spanish ambassador that such actions would not be tolerated. This exchange of views did not appreciably help the merchants. Cottington at first felt optimistic: 'Great show is made here to give our king satisfaction over the grievances of the Englishmen.' But he reported a month later that the Spaniards had seized an English merchantman bound for America, taken the crew to Bayonne and released them half dead. At this King James wrote to Philip III in September 1607, demanding that Spaniards cease such provocative acts. In consequence several merchants received favourable verdicts in their suits. By the time Cornwallis left for England two years later many of the cases had been settled; others dragged on for years.[19]

Perhaps the most celebrated case involved the seizure of the English merchantman *Trial* in the Mediterranean. According to the testimony of Robert Browne – the only member of the crew of fifteen hands and three officers to reach England – the ship departed London early in 1604 for Egypt, with a cargo valued at 40,000 ducats. On orders of the Duke of Feria, Viceroy of Sicily, the *Trial* was seized by Spanish men-of-war while passing through Sicilian waters. Browne said that the vessel was commandeered for two months, used as a privateer against Turkish shipping, and that the Spanish officers treated the crew barbarously. Afterwards, at Messina, the cargo was sold and the sailors imprisoned, tortured and in a few cases executed on the grounds that the *Trial* was a disguised warship transporting contraband to the Turks. Cottington, who spent years trying to secure damages for the shipowners and relatives of the crew, reported on evidence acquired during his lengthy investigation that the sailors had either died on the rack or were poisoned.

Browne's story and the petition of the crew's relatives for compensation touched off a round of negotiations. On orders from London, Cornwallis asked Philip III to examine the case, which he referred to the Council of Italy. It did nothing for three years and then reversed the ruling of a Sicilian court that had allowed the ship and cargo to be sold as prizes, specifying that she should be returned forthwith to her true owners, the firm of John Eldred and Richard Hall. Meanwhile the Viceroy of Sicily had died in 1607. His heir, the third Duke of Feria (grandson of the celebrated English Catholic, Lady Jane Dormer), successfully resisted Cottington's efforts to make him pay restitution. In September 1609, while Cottington headed the embassy in the interval between ambassadors, Salisbury ordered him to deal directly with Philip III, and to return home unless he agreed to make amends. By this time the King had left on progress, so that Cottington negotiated instead with the Council of State. They said they could do nothing, since Feria was in France and could not be reached. Years passed before Eldred and Hall recovered the ship; the families of the crew never received compensation. If this case brought the concerned parties little satisfaction, its forceful prosecution induced the Spanish authorities to be more sympathetic towards the speedier resolution of others that had likewise been pending for months.[20]

A memorandum by Cottington in 1609 discusses in some detail merchant cases involving English nationals who pressed suits in Spanish courts resulting in favourable judgements, partly because of the diligence of Cornwallis and his colleagues and a greater willingness by the Spanish authorities to accommodate them. Sir George Erskine received a thousand ducats for damage to his ship done by a Spanish privateer off Dover. Each member of his crew got five hundred ducats and the widows of others two thousand ducats each for goods lost. Thomas Henryson, a merchant whose vessel was contracted to transport goods for Spain, received fifteen hundred ducats in arrears owing to him and previously withheld. The Scotsman Robert Stockes, like Henryson a carrier for the Spaniards to the West Indies, who sued in a Madrid court for recovery of arrears, lived at the embassy for three years. Cornwallis settled the case for Stockes – who was paid eight thousand ducats – shortly before leaving Spain. Cornwallis and Cottington also helped two merchant factors who were imprisoned and tortured for bringing in counterfeit coins. When one of the prisoners was sentenced to death, Cornwallis got a stay of execution and persuaded the Council of State to reverse its decision. An appellate court eventually exonerated both men. The embassy secured reversals of sentences passed on thirty other merchants trading through Seville and secured the release of seventy-two more serving as galley-slaves.[21]

All this goes to show that Cornwallis and Cottington helped the merchants when they could. Contrary to what Resoute had said about Cornwallis's stinginess in 1608, the ambassador spent a great deal of money – some of it his own – housing, feeding and representing merchants. Furthermore, the Spanish officials – mostly local authorities – sometimes made dishonest profit at the expense of merchants and violated both the letter and the spirit of the Treaty of London. But no administrative system was perfect in the early seventeenth century, and corruption in office was not at all uncommon in western Europe, including England. On the whole the courts and councils of the Spanish central administration dealt fairly and openly, albeit slowly, with the embassy and its clients. Anglo-Spanish relations could not have been expected to run smoothly after so many years of suspension and mutual distrust of each other's motives. Points of contention had to be resolved by a process of trial and error, give and take. In fact, actual or alleged violations of the treaty enabled Cornwallis and his aides to work out an understanding with the Spanish Government. In that sense the treaty stood the test of time until the break in diplomatic relations in 1623, and was renewed by Cottington without much amendment in 1630. In the early years Cornwallis managed to stabilise trade through Portugal and Castile and guarantee his countrymen a measure of legal protection. He also got the Spaniards to permit English trade with the Barbary states of northern Africa in contravention of the original limitations imposed by the treaty, thereby expanding English enterprise in the western Mediterranean.

How effective Cottington had been in pressing the suits of merchants is hard to say. His name appears frequently in the

Cornwallis correspondence in connection with individual cases, but the letters do not generally tell exactly what he accomplished. Cornwallis got credit as the ambassador for the successes and sometimes the blame for the failures. But he relied on Cottington to represent English interests with the Council of State and in the Madrid courts – we have the ambassador's own word for that. He told the Privy Council in September 1608 that he had 'caused Cottington to be present at some hearing of causes and observe them . . .', and mentioned elsewhere that 'the many businesses of my Secretary . . . will not suffer me to be long' in tying him up with official correspondence. Cornwallis was never free with compliments and criticised several aides, but he consistently showed confidence in Cottington, commending his work to superiors in London. Cottington's own correspondence is full of references to his duties as expeditor, courier, intercessor, negotiator and the like. If Cornwallis had been dissatisfied with Cottington's work, he would not have promoted him from clerk to secretary or secured his appointment as chief embassy officer during the interval between ambassadors in 1609-11. The often delicate relations between England and Spain required a firm, trustworthy diplomat in Madrid. Cornwallis and Salisbury obviously believed that Cottington could discharge his duties in one of the most important diplomatic posts in Europe.[22]

The lives of diplomats on foreign assignment could be trying in the early seventeenth century, and the English in Spain had their share of hardship and anxiety. Their health suffered in the dry climate and extreme temperatures of Castile. Crop failures and chronic poverty among the agricultural classes, who ate all they grew, caused food shortages in Madrid and prohibitively high prices. Even when food was plentiful, it rarely pleased English palates unaccustomed to the strong spices used as preservatives. Unlike their counterparts in Brussels and Paris, who operated within a more settled environment in which diplomatic channels functioned smoothly, the diplomats in Madrid had to contend with a less than friendly Government and lived in a religious milieu wherein the Church pressed conformity more assiduously than any other state in western Europe. Most English diplomats at Madrid left their posts sooner or later for reasons of health or hardship, so that the embassy staff changed almost completely every two or three years. Cornwallis and Cottington, and later Digby and Aston, constantly complained about their rigorous lives. Among all those who accepted assignment in Madrid, only Cottington remained more or less permanently from 1605 to 1623.

Cottington was a circumspect and quiet man, not as a rule given to complaining. Nevertheless he became despondent during the early years in Spain. Loneliness bred by lack of English news bore down on him. The Cottington–Trumbull correspondence is illustrative of his feelings. In April 1608 Cottington wrote, 'From England we . . . hear nothing', asking Trumbull to 'write me something of that blessed land'. A week earlier Cottington told his friend to be sure that letters forwarded through Brussels were not delayed, for 'we are here some times six months without hearing out of England, although we write every 14 days'. In February, Cottington reminded Trumbull that three months had passed without word from England, during which time he and his colleagues 'endured most intolerable misery and trouble'. The deaths of a third of the embassy staff that spring and summer and the departure of others upset Cottington. He blamed the 'intemperance of this air, so contrary to an English constitution' for chronic health problems, and dreaded the unbearable heat of summer. The summer was so hot and dry, in fact, that famine stalked the land and peasants refused to bring staples into town, 'so that we had to scratch for bread . . .'. A severe autumn followed the torrid summer; an early frost killed the crops. No rain for five months over the winter and spring of 1607-8 grossly inflated food prices. Cottington himself admitted that he desperately needed 'all things, especially money'.[23]

These were not the least of his troubles. He was imprisoned some time in 1609 prior to 27 September. Cornwallis conveyed his account of the circumstances leading to Cottington's arrest in a note to the Council of State. The ambassador had quarrelled with Sylva de Torres, who disliked him. When Cottington and a bailiff employed by Lerma scuffled over money that the Englishman presumably owed, Torres had him imprisoned and shackled. Cornwallis believed that this had been done as a personal affront to himself, not because of the petty quarrel over a debt. In demanding Cottington's release, the ambassador drew a comparison between

England's and Spain's interpretation of diplomatic immunity. He told the Council about John Ball, an Englishman employed by the Spanish embassy in London, who was accused of treason but allowed to go free during the investigation that proved his innocence. Cottington, on the other hand, had not been formally charged with any crime and should have been treated with the same respect. Cornwallis insisted that the 'law of nations' protected diplomats against arrest for most crimes, and that Cottington had committed no crime at all. Cornwallis also insinuated that Cottington had been imprisoned at the very time that he was pressing the suits of merchants which the Spaniards hoped to delay. This forceful note brought Cottington's release and exoneration, did not ease Anglo-Spanish relations or strengthen the law of diplomatic immunity, and once more demonstrated Cornwallis's bias against Spaniards. But the tactics worked, which after all was what mattered in diplomacy.[24]

English diplomats had the duty of reporting regularly, usually every two weeks, to superiors at home and corresponding as circumstances warranted with other English embassies. These reports covered a broad range of topics, some important, others ephemeral. The Cornwallis–Cottington dispatches commented on changes in Spanish Government personnel, the views and activities of Spanish Councillors, news about Spanish relations with other states and their representatives, the movements of fleets both martial and mercantile, economic questions, visitors in Madrid, the Jesuits, and so forth. The reports have no logical continuity of subject, although major themes do reappear for a few weeks at a time. In 1608 Cornwallis concentrated on the Dutch rebellion because of negotiations then under way for a league of Protestant states that worried the Spaniards. Cottington also wrote long reports containing fragmentary observations on incidental matters of passing interest. However, the reports are on the whole important from another standpoint: they reveal a good deal about Spanish society and culture and the character of diplomacy in the early seventeenth century, and details of the major events of contemporary Spanish history witnessed by an impressionable young Englishman, whose attitudes were sometimes influenced by his experiences.

Cottington's dispatches in 1609 and 1610 described the expulsion of the Moriscos. These descendants of the Spanish Muslims, who had accepted Christianity under duress, were often nominal Roman Catholics, frequently reverted to the practice of Mohammedanism and commonly used the Arabic language, customs and dress in violation of the law. When repeated efforts by the Government and the Church failed to make them conform, they were expelled. It was a massive and barbarous operation, which so preoccupied the Government that it ignored less pressing matters, including English merchant cases. 'Since your lordship's departure,' Cottington explained to Cornwallis in September, 'we have had not one day of justice [for the merchants] in the Council of War, for they are very busy about their Moriscos.' Busy they were; the King had issued the edict of expulsion on 22 September, a copy of which Cottington sent to Salisbury. Except those whose Christianity was beyond question and a few hundred others kept on to train the Old Christians in husbandry, the Moriscos were to be taken to ports of embarkation for transportation to Tunis, Oran and Algiers. Since they had to leave all their possessions behind, the state profited at their expense. Cottington related how the Government had mustered an army to oversee the operation; how thousands of Moriscos fled to the hills to fight; how soldiers joined the guerrillas in battle; and how English merchantmen helped to transport them at seven ducats apiece from Valencian ports. Cottington's account is surprisingly matter-of-fact, even for a seventeenth-century man accustomed to the harsh treatment of dissidents. One might have expected a man who himself experienced trials on account of nationality and religion to have shown a spark of compassion towards more than 100,000 victims of persecution. But the injustice did not trouble Cottington; he agreed entirely with Philip III. It is hard to resist the conclusion that Cottington was already showing signs of becoming the efficient politician, the blind servant of absolutism, the aloof administrator that he was accused of being thirty years later.[25]

Cornwallis left Spain a month before the expulsion of the Moriscos. Dissatisfaction had gnawed at him from the first. Salisbury could not have missed his hints, beginning in January 1608, that he would not object to being recalled. Cornwallis had reason to dislike his post. His solicitations on behalf of merchants brought few results before 1609 and little thanks from them. His conferences with Spanish officials frequently ended in accusations and rejoinders. His health suffered and his temperament did not improve. He worried about expenditure of personal funds. Spaniards pricked his inflated ego. Finally, his superiors in London scolded him for reporting generalities instead of valuable news gathered from informants at Spanish ports.[26]

Rumours of his recall circulated in London and Madrid for months, but official word did not reach Cornwallis until June 1609. The Spaniards apparently interpreted it as a rebuff prompted by their intransigence towards merchant complaints. This may be the reason why cases that had been ignored received attention in the closing months of Cornwallis's mission. There is no evidence that Salisbury intended anything of the sort, however. Cornwallis wished to be relieved and was granted his request. Philip III was away at the time and Cornwallis had been ill off and on since moving into a new house the previous March. When his health took a turn for the worse in the summer, the whole burden of embassy business fell to Cottington, who got a taste of the responsibilities that he would assume for two years. Official farewells at Court were marred by the studied aloofness of both the King and the ambassador, and by Lerma's warning before this final audience that Cornwallis should not embarrass Philip by giving him a book on theology written by King James. On 17 September 1609 Cornwallis left for England. If he had disliked his four and a half years of service, his appointment as Treasurer of the Household of Prince Henry was ample reward.[27]

Since most of the staff returned home with Cornwallis, Cottington was left without much help. His fears over his ability to handle the responsibilities of agent were balanced by the realisation that he had an opportunity to prove his competence to his superiors. He had every reason to be confident. He knew Spanish well and had been at his post longer than anyone else at the embassy. He understood its operations and enjoyed the respect of important Councillors who liked him better than Cornwallis. Experience in the field taught him how to manage delicate questions and compensated for his lack of a higher education. The next few years were crucial in the development of his character and the furtherance of his career.

CHAPTER 3

The Spanish Agent

CADETS of Jacobean genteel families not uncommonly visited the Continent to further their education in much the same way that the Victorians made the Grand Tour more than two centuries later. They generally saw France, Italy and the Low Countries and stayed long enough in one country to learn something of its language and culture. Many fewer travellers got to Spain, not only out of custom established by the Elizabethans, but also because English Protestants feared the possible consequences of exposure to Catholic influences and thought less of Spanish cultural achievements than those of the Italians or French, who had more fully assimilated Renaissance ideas.

There cannot have been many Englishmen of Cottington's generation, apart from the merchants, diplomats and exiles who lived in the Spanish dominions, who knew Spanish or could speak confidently about Spain and her peoples from personal experience. William Cecil, Lord Roos, who left England in 1605 at the age of fifteen to live abroad for nearly seven years, broke tradition by spending four months over the winter of 1610-11 in Madrid to learn Spanish. By all evidence an irresponsible fellow, Roos became an embarrassment to Cottington, who loaned him money and despaired of his meddling in Spanish affairs. If Cottington necessarily put up with a young man with important connections at home (he was a grandson of the Earl of Exeter), he gladly borrowed money on his own credit to ensure Roos's departure for France on schedule.[1]

Lord Roos shared the antipathy of most Englishmen towards Spain. He thought Madrid a backward city lacking attractive public buildings, a university and commercial enterprise. Its architectural eclecticism depressed him, and only the Manzanares river and the

bridge which spanned it – 'one of the fairest . . . I have ever seen'
– merited his praise. His estimate that Madrid contained between
two and three hundred thousand inhabitants was not far off the
mark; it probably had about 200,000 in 1600, and a census in 1646
put the population at 350,000. Like other European cities that had
expanded haphazardly since late medieval times, Madrid had irregular, narrow and unclean streets lined by multi-storeyed houses
and ancient churches. The city was overcrowded. A succession of
agricultural failures and poverty had driven the landless, the poor,
the vagabonds and the idlers into Madrid. They filled the streets
by day and sometimes burgled the wealthy by night. Its teeming
masses, more numerous and dirtier than those he had seen in other
cities on the Continent or in England, offended the sensibilities of
the country gentleman Roos.[2]

Cottington had lived in Madrid for about three years by the
time he became agent in September 1609, and was accustomed to
his surroundings. Since Cornwallis had had to give up the house
on the hill on leaving, Cottington had to find another, more modest
one commensurate with his smaller income and position, which was
difficult in a tight housing market. He lived as simply as he could:

> How poorly myself must live here, keeping a house, a man,
> and two boys with 20s. a day, yourself [Cornwallis] can best
> judge. . . . That I can go on foot, and fare like a good husband-
> [man] I am sure you will easily believe, but I am enforced some
> times (for the good of his Majesty's service) to have convidados
> [guests] at my table and to enter dusty and sweating in the
> summer time, & dirty in the winter (besides the inconvenience
> that may grade unto my health) in those great places where I
> daily go, and you know right well will breed extreme incon-
> veniences. . . .[3]

Cornwallis took the trouble on reaching England to remind Salisbury of the high cost of living in Madrid, where Cottington could
not fulfil his responsibilities without receiving a regular allowance
on schedule. Such an appeal might easily have been ignored considering the dozens of diplomats in similar straits. But the Lord
Treasurer authorised payment to Cottington of 20s. a day in the
customary manner, that is, three months in advance, which was a

third of the allowance that Cornwallis had received and the same amount given to John Dickenson at Cleves-Jülich and William Trumbull at Brussels.[4]

Young men are characteristically impatient and discouraged with the progress of their careers. Cottington was no exception. He had been entrusted with English affairs in Spain – a rare opportunity for one not yet thirty – but he began to doubt the possibility of ever achieving higher office in England and thought his superiors unmindful of him. At darker moments he unburdened himself to his soul-mate Trumbull in Brussels, worrying himself unnecessarily about his finances, health and future. When Cottington heard in 1610 that a permanent ambassador might soon relieve him, he speculated about his next assignment, hopefully in England. 'I protest unto you,' he told Trumbull, 'I do more desire to leave this miserable and unfortunate country than any man did to be freed from an unwholesome prison. . . .' Although Anglo-French relations were strained over the winter of 1610-11 because of the Jülich succession question, Cottington and the French ambassador became close friends. He went out of his way to find the Frenchman a house, and often visited him.[5]

Cottington paid closer attention to the Jesuits and curried their friendship in the hope of learning their plans. Father Creswell realised this, of course, and put his charges on their guard. English refugees, travellers and merchants, some of them Catholics, visited Madrid seeking help from the Spanish Government and the embassy. Some of them stayed with Cottington, who, like Cornwallis, resented spending the money that they cost him. But Creswell welcomed such visitors to his house, partly out of charity and also as an opportunity to proselytise. In April 1610 he opened a hostelry run by an English Catholic innkeeper whom Cottington characterised as a crafty villain. Afterwards Cottington reported that Creswell had turned the hostelry into a 'minor seminary' for youths whom he hoped to make priests. In six months the number of students increased from eight to fifteen. At this Cottington did his best to see that not 'one honest Subject of his Majesty's' entered the hostelry, and somehow managed to persuade the Council of State to close it, forcing Creswell to find lodging for the youths in private homes.[6]

Cottington watched other English Catholics in Madrid because of their notoriety or association with Creswell. The 'sinister junta', the name coined by the agent for this circle of Catholics, included Sir Edmund Baynham, George Gage and Sir Tobie Mathew, among others. With the exception of Baynham, whose oblique connection with the Gunpowder Plot for ever damned him in England, neither Cottington nor the authorities in London had any sound reason to suspect their intentions; all of them were in Spain for innocent purposes. Mathew left England in 1605, spent the next few years in Italy where he became a Roman Catholic, and visited Madrid in the company of Sir Robert Shirley, the self-styled Persian ambassador, for a few months in 1610. He had powerful friends in England, including Sir Francis Bacon and Salisbury, and was never considered a militant Catholic. He and George Gage lodged together in a house rented by the merchant William Calley, a perennial suitor for damages in the Spanish courts. At this time Gage, who later became a priest like his brother, the Dominican Thomas Gage, and went to England as a missionary, was but one of hundreds of exiles living in Spain. Even though Cottington believed Gage's association with Creswell would 'make him a traitor', he had him to dinner at least twice before Creswell forbade him to visit the embassy again. Baynham had been in exile since the summer of 1605, when Father Garnet, executed for complicity in the plot, had sent him to apprise the Pope of the worsening plight of their co-religionists. When the Council of State gave Baynham money and Cottington complained of it, Secretary Arostequi explained that it was his due from lands sold in England during Elizabeth's reign and conveyed to Spain for his support.[7]

Irishmen – some political exiles, some refugees from the recusancy laws, some adventurers seeking a livelihood – had flocked to Spain. Most of them scratched a bare living by their wits; others served in the army or navy. Religion and trade had brought the Irish and Spaniards closer together since the beginning of the Elizabethan war, and some of the Irish who had served with the Spanish Armada[8] or helped with the Spanish invasion of Ireland in 1601 escaped to the peninsula. About eight hundred of them lived in Madrid in the early seventeenth century and were hardly in any position to threaten English interests. Some of them received small pensions, which

Cottington took as an affront to King James. When he asked Don
Diego Brochero about it, the Spaniard replied that his Government owed these Irish a debt because they had honoured their
alliance with Spain by fighting the English and leaving everything
they had behind after the war. Cottington realised, however, that
the Spaniards expected something for their money: 'I've noted that
when they find a man, be he base in nature no matter, who, in their
opinion has ability to serve, he shall have gold & honor; but he
who cannot serve is despised and neglected.' Towards some of
these poor wretches Cottington had compassion as victims of cir-
cumstance. If he denounced two groups of Irish youths who fought
to the death outside his house in mid-1610, he also rescued and
spirited out of the country an Irish boy whom the Inquisition had
tortured and left to die.[9]

In reporting on the Jesuits and Irish, Cottington fulfilled his
duty of keeping the home Government informed of so-called
dangerous exiles. But his principal responsibility remained the
expedition of commerce between the two nations. The enthusiasm
with which he undertook this work after Cornwallis left –
enthusiasm born of the confidence of the young that they could
achieve the nearly impossible by effort alone – turned into
disappointment within a year. Try as he might he could not speed
up the processes of the Spanish courts or do much to increase trade.

The pattern of his responses to the pressures of office are interesting to follow in his correspondence. In February 1610, early on in
his agency, he told Salisbury that 'I am not discontented, for I hope
to get certificates of release [for English galley-slaves] and then the
business will be ended'. He later lost face and got a scolding from
Secretary Prada when caught red-handed reading a document in
the Council chambers at the Escorial that had been carelessly left
out by a clerk. A noticeable change came over Cottington by June,
when he admitted being able to do little for the merchants seeking
his help. His health began to suffer from strain. He developed
stomach pains and had been unable to eat properly for two months,
and indigestion probably induced by nervousness and overwork
robbed him of sound sleep night after night.[10]

The large sums of money involved in several merchant cases
could not have eased his mind. Take the case of the Levant Company

ship *Vineyard* that had been seized in 1605 in the port of Milo after putting in to ride out a storm. The Viceroy of Sardinia maintained that she carried tin and lead to be used for armaments by the Turks, but the captain insisted that she carried only enough metal to make emergency repairs at sea. On reaching Spain after their release, a few crew members contacted Cornwallis, who in turn notified King James. Neither of their protestations to the Spanish Court brought any result, and Cottington pressed the case unsuccessfully during his agency. In the next decade he and Ambassador Digby repeatedly ventilated the question and were as often told that their allegations were unsupported by evidence. Cottington finally sent Walsingham Gresley to Sardinia to locate witnesses, but he was arrested en route, taken to Algiers and released only after lengthy negotiation. The case still had not been settled by the time Digby returned to Spain in 1622 to arrange a marriage treaty. Frustrated by the inability of the diplomats to do anything more, the Levant Company employed James Howell to devote all his time to the recovery of its losses of £30,000 on the ship and her cargo. Then the Anglo-Spanish war intervened until 1629, when Howell asked Cottington to see what he could do about the *Vineyard* during his forthcoming embassy to Spain. But it was too late; after twenty-five years, hope of recovery or compensation was futile.[11]

Cottington lost patience with the Spaniards towards the end of his agency. This is clear from his own remarks on an interview that he had with the Duke of Infantado in October 1610. He apparently had made a nuisance of himself by complaining too often about commercial relations, and the Duke thought it high time to say so. Cottington did not deny the accusation that he had turned in identical lists of grievances on several occasions, as the Duke put it, 'to make a great noise in complaining rather than to seek redress in just and lawful things'. But he took exception when the Duke lectured him about his responsibilities as a diplomat – representing King James and leaving the merchants to fend for themselves. He replied that he knew his duty full well, that it included representation of merchants whose grievances had been minimised by the Spanish Government, and that even a dullard understood how quickly Philip III would lose confidence in a diplomat who chronically lied. The interview ended with both men muttering to themselves as they left the room.[12]

Notwithstanding such unpleasantnesses, Cottington is said by an anonymous writer in 1610 to have achieved four positive results during his agency. He settled a few cases passed on by Cornwallis. The Spaniards agreed not to press English merchantmen into their service without prior payment in cash. He secured the release of countrymen serving on the galleys. Finally, he helped to reverse a decision by King Philip that temporarily stopped Anglo-Spanish commerce.[13]

The most serious interruption of trade since the Treaty of London resulted from a royal proclamation issued in December 1609, closing the peninsula's ports to English shipping. Philip worded it in such a way, however, that ships of other nationals friendly to Spain might land English goods. He acted on advice from his ambassador in London, Pedro de Zuñiga, who reported that English seamen had contracted plague. Cottington believed this to be an excuse contrived to interdict English trade as retribution for real or pretended wrongs, and may have been right.

We know today that the plague epidemic of 1603 had been the worst in England since the fourteenth century as regards the absolute number of deaths. The effects of this cycle continued for a decade. England had never been free of plague in the early seventeenth century, however, and the pestilence had not been as widespread in 1609-10 as it was in 1603-4. But it caused more deaths in 1609 than in any other year until 1630. Even so, it is hard to understand why the Spaniards chose to exclude English shipping in 1609 as against 1607 or 1611, which were also heavy plague years. It is also curious that they admitted English merchandise carried in foreign vessels when the current medical view was that cargo originating in a plague-ridden country was likewise infected. There is therefore some sense to Cottington's reasoning that the Spaniards closed the ports to weaken the English economy by curtailing foreign trade, which in turn affected the Crown's revenue from customs at a time when plague had already seriously interrupted commerce at home. There may also have been a connection between the embargo and Spanish displeasure over England's role with France in helping to arrange the Twelve Years Truce between Holland

and Spain in 1609, or over her support of the Protestant claimants in the Cleves-Jülich question in the same year, neither of which Cottington mentioned.

Whatever the true reason for it, the embargo lasted only about four months. Cottington learned of the proclamation a week after the fact, and Salisbury heard of it from him in early February. By the time Cottington received instructions to seek revocation, two and a half months had passed. Fortunately he had acted on his own much earlier. He persuaded Philip III to end the embargo provided Zuñiga, after consultation with English port authorities, certified the health of English sailors bound for Spain. Meanwhile Cottington got the Council of State to admit all English ships except those whose voyages originated at London. A letter from Zuñiga in late April assured Philip that the epidemic had subsided and he lifted the embargo altogether. Cottington, nervous and ill or not, proved that he could keep a cool head and make the right decision in a crisis.[14]

No diplomat could have attended properly to the problems of hundreds of Englishmen scattered throughout an area as large as Spain and Portugal in which travel was difficult and communications were slow and unreliable. Cottington lived in Madrid, nearly at the geographical centre of the peninsula and a great distance by seventeenth-century standards from such major ports as Lisbon, Cartagena and Barcelona. He employed informants, mostly merchant factors, to forward news, but they could not speak officially for England. The lack of consuls impaired the work of the embassy, and appeals by Cornwallis, Cottington and Digby that they be appointed went unanswered until 1611.[15]

In the early seventeenth century diplomats were not as a rule shifted from one post to another. They served at the pleasure of the King unless they resigned. Cottington was dissatisfied with his post, but he could not leave it without some assurance of securing another, which he did not have. He therefore stayed on much longer than he had anticipated. His career and that of his friend William Trumbull were practically identical and not much different from those of most young diplomats. Trumbull came from a landed Yorkshire family and entered royal service with help from Sir Thomas Edmondes, formerly French secretary to Queen Elizabeth.

In 1605 Trumbull accompanied Edmondes to Brussels, two months before Cottington sailed for Spain. Both Trumbull and Cottington served in turn as clerks, secretaries, and agents during the interlude between ambassadors, beginning coincidentally at the same time in September 1609 with the recall of Edmondes and Cornwallis. Each man expected to be relieved and promoted to higher office in England upon the arrival of a new ambassador, but they remained at their posts years longer. Neither could improve himself significantly without the intercession of a patron at Court.[16]

Cottington had his first hint that he might be recalled when Salisbury ordered him in the late summer of 1610 to determine whether Philip III meant to satisfy the grievances over commerce and the harassment of merchants. Depending on his answer, Cottington should either return to England forthwith or await the arrival of a new ambassador. Excited and anxious at this news, Cottington told Trumbull that he would 'shoot my last arrow and so resolve of my staying or going home'. Philip's favourable response undercut whatever chance Cottington had of realising his hopes. Worse still, King James took an inordinately long time to appoint an ambassador, probably waiting to see if Philip translated promises into action. Finally, in March of the following year, Salisbury sent word of Sir John Digby's appointment.[17]

The arrival of this dispatch coincided with the eviction of Cottington from his residence. He thought the Jesuits responsible, but the Council of State blamed two minor officials who had thoughtlessly cancelled the lease. The Council procured a new house, intending that it should be used by Digby. Cottington found it too small for an embassy of some fifty people, and so had to move twice in two months. Digby reached the Spanish border in early May. On his instructions Cottington left Madrid on the 25th for a rendezvous with him to the north.[18]

Their meeting could not have been a happy one for either man. Cottington thought that he could leave for England soon, but Digby brought a letter from Salisbury ordering him to stay in Madrid indefinitely. Digby also had reason to be glum. He had been detained at the border for nearly a month, first by the Inquisition, which searched his trunks for religious literature, and then by customs officers who would not let him pass without approval from the King, which took weeks to arrive. Moreover, he and his wife were jostled in a springless carriage over rough roads in France and Spain, and became nauseated by the stench of mules and skinners during a journey of thirty-five days, much of it in the rain. The English train then had to wait a week at Alcobendas, north of Madrid, until Sir Robert Shirley vacated the house which Cottington had procured for the Digbys.[19]

Matters did not improve for the Digbys and their associates. The unexpectedly high cost of the trip exhausted the Digbys' allowance so that they had to spend their own money to live until their first bill of exchange arrived.[20] They had another brush with the Inquisition when the Cardinal Archbishop of Toledo sought to prevent the embassy chaplain, John Sanford, from holding Protestant services. Sickness visited the company. Digby developed catarrh and ran a high fever. Lady Digby was delivered of a still-born child and nearly died. Smallpox infected about a third of the staff and a few died of it.[21]

Cottington and Digby struck up a fast friendship in these first months that endured until 1624. They came from different backgrounds and there was some distance between them socially, but Digby, then thirty-one, was only one year his junior. They shared common friends in England and generally viewed their age from a broadly similar perspective. Most important, they liked each other. Cottington described Digby as a civil and kind person whose subordinates could not help but admire him. How sad, he mused, that such a fine man should be 'exiled' to 'this wretched & unhappy country' where no amount of diligence would ensure success in negotiation or earn him the reward it merited. Digby reciprocated his friend's feelings, telling Salisbury repeatedly how much help Cottington had been in those early and trying weeks in Madrid, teaching him all that needed to be known about Spanish affairs.[22]

Having satisfied Salisbury that Digby could handle affairs without him, Cottington was allowed to leave for England in August. He had his last audience with King Philip on 20 July and departed from the city thoroughly disgusted that, against common practice, he had received no present. But it reached him half-way to the Pyrenees – a gold chain worth four hundred ducats. Digby believed that Philip had thought twice before rewarding a man who had made enemies at Court by badgering Councillors with innumerable petitions, and was probably right. It is essential as we reach this point in Cottington's life to realise that he had not taken kindly to Spaniards and their way of life – that, in fact, he had been generally hostile towards them. The point is worth pondering here initially in view of the remarks of his contemporaries later that he had been 'Spaniolised' during his long residence in the peninsula. It remains to be seen as his career unfolds whether there is cause to agree with them.[23]

Cottington wasted no time en route to England, travelling by post-horse and stopping but one full day at Paris to visit John Beaulieu before arriving in London on 22 August. He carried £200 reimbursement from Digby for personal expenses incurred since 1609, and a letter commending his services to Salisbury. 'I have . . . observed in him so great a care and unweariness in all things belonging to his service,' Digby wrote, 'that I shall not only witness what he deserveth . . . but shall be bold somewhat . . . to recommend him unto your Lordship's favor as one whom, if you shall please to employ, I assure myself your Lordship will find him a very useful servant unto you. . . .' What this letter or the future might avail him after six years and four months of service in Spain, Cottington knew not. The answer came soon enough, and not to his liking.[24]

CHAPTER 4

Clerk of the Council

FRANCIS COTTINGTON returned to London in August 1611, hopeful that the Crown or another patron might reward him with a post in England after years of foreign service. He spent four months reporting what he had learned in Spain to the royal family and the Privy Council, visiting relatives in Somerset and awaiting reassignment. His official itinerary can easily be reconstructed, but his personal affairs are clouded at this point in his life when he sought to secure other employment and failed. The necessity of earning a living obliged him to accept a position in Spain, to which he did not wish to return, that carried little prestige but might bring considerable financial reward.

Cottington spent part of August and much of September in conference with Salisbury and the Privy Council and in audiences with members of the royal family. Salisbury was most interested to learn from Cottington how the Spaniards had reacted initially to a proposal introduced by Ambassador Digby for a marriage treaty, and whether there was a chance for greater co-operation in commerce. On 25 August, Cottington journeyed to Hampshire to relay the same information to the King. He remained five days, returned to London briefly, and then attended Prince Henry at Woodstock. Cottington also visited Queen Anne at Oatlands as a matter of courtesy, even though he was anxious to see his family.

Having done his duty to the great ones, as he put it, Cottington spent about two weeks at Godminster in Somerset. He dared not linger longer out of concern for his still unsettled future. Such personal contacts as he tried to arrange in London in October in search of a patron came to naught. Except for a dinner party which Cottington, his cousin Samuel Calvert and others attended on 16 October at the home of Edward Sherburne, one of Salisbury's secretaries, no one of influence in the Government paid him any attention.[1] If Sherburne and Cottington had met previously, they were not close friends. This suggests that Sherburne held the party, probably at Salisbury's request, to ask Cottington to accept the consulship at Seville. Salisbury realised from what Cottington had said over the years that he disliked Spain, and may have thought a meal among friends the best place to broach a delicate matter. Cornwallis, Digby and Cottington himself had told Salisbury of the need for consuls to gather intelligence at the principal ports and help with embassy business. That being the case, and by his own admission under pressure from the Lord Treasurer, Sherburne and 'certain special friends' to accept the post, Cottington had difficulty saying no. He hesitated for about two weeks, and in late October reluctantly half concluded to agree in view of the fact that other avenues seemed closed. The money involved could not be ignored by a man past thirty without land or regular income. The consul would collect 10 per cent of the value of goods imported and exported by English merchants through Andalusia and receive an initial allowance of £100. In addition, he could nominate and superintend any other consuls subsequently appointed. On the other hand, friends warned him that a consulship carried little prestige, certainly less than a position in an embassy. Cottington weighed these factors and accepted the post granted him by royal patent on 8 November. The lean years in Spain taught him that a man cannot live on honour alone – an attitude which was not uncommon among ambitious young men of his class and times.[2]

Consul Cottington did not leave for Spain until 23 December 1611. In the intervening six weeks he made preparations and farewells. To his friend Trumbull in Brussels he confessed anxiety about encountering serious trouble with the Spanish authorities, who had been glad to see him go. He was not sure that the Exchequer would pay his allowance regularly, and worried about meeting his expenses in Seville when he had barely enough to live on in London. This was not entirely true, however. Some time after returning to England he had purchased 'a small cottage' in Suffolk. Why he had bought property in East Anglia, with which he apparently had no previous connection and far from the familiar ground of Somerset and Middlesex, is perplexing. In any event he does not appear to have ever lived there, and sold the cottage in September 1613, a few months after returning again from Spain.[3]

The lackadaisical attitude obvious in his correspondence confirms Cottington's disappointment in having to live in Spain once more. He poured out his thoughts to trusted friends and put on a good face for his superiors. This was characteristic of him all his life, even when he had good reason at times of personal sorrow to betray his feelings. When there was work to be done, he did it; with him, duty almost always came first. He conferred with the Privy Council, received final instructions and set out for Paris, where he spent New Year's Day with Beaulieu. Cottington could have reached Madrid from there in a week, but he did not arrive until 14 January, obviously being in no hurry to return to the scene of unpleasant years. In line with his orders he planned to stay with Digby until the end of March in order to allow the Spanish Government time to approve his appointment.[4]

Digby responded to the news of Cottington's appointment with mixed feelings. The ambassador had supported the enlistment of consuls but had not expected Cottington to become one. Nor had he known that a consul would be given such a large share of the fees arising from trade. Diplomats in Spain customarily grumbled about the nuisance of merchants in trouble, yet they profited from the gratuities or fees from such cases. Now the consul at Seville, one of the busiest ports in the realm, not the ambassador, would benefit from the legal and commercial transactions of the merchants there. Furthermore, Digby knew that Cottington had few friends at the Spanish Court, so that regardless of his 'serviceableness and industry', another man would have been more suitable. By the time Digby told this to Salisbury, Cottington was already on his way, and nothing could be done for the present about the appointment.[5]

Digby continued to press his point after Cottington arrived. The arguments that Digby advanced to the Lord Treasurer made sense. What irritated Digby most was that the new line of authority gave Cottington jurisdiction over English trade in much of the peninsula. As Digby pointed out, 'unless great care be exercised . . . [the merchants and other consuls] will only address their services to him [Cottington] on whom they have dependency, and I shall have but cold correspondency from them in his majesty's service'. That being the case, Digby argued, how could he keep abreast of English affairs for which he was ultimately responsible? And what could he do if Cottington or another consul chose to ignore his duty, embarrass the embassy or challenge its directives? Digby therefore asked Salisbury to instruct Cottington to respect the authority of the ambassador and not nominate other consuls without his consent.

Salisbury did not honour the request, but it made no difference. The Spanish Government refused to accept Cottington as a consul, although he may well have had some of the fees promised him in the royal patent. There is no indication that he knew about Digby's correspondence on his appointment or that, if he did, it had any effect on their relationship. In fact, Digby worked hard in favour of Cottington's approval by the Spaniards. They remained fast friends and close associates for another decade. When the House of Lords considered a charge brought by the Duke of Buckingham in 1624 that Digby had been responsible for the collapse of the marriage treaty negotiations in the previous year, Cottington said nothing to hurt his friend, though they gradually drifted apart afterwards.[6]

Why had the Spaniards frustrated efforts by the English Government to place consuls at Seville and other ports? The English contended that they had an unequivocal right to appoint them, subject only to the *pro forma* approbation of the Spanish Crown. But the Council of State refused to accept Protestant consuls, dislodged Hugh Lee at Lisbon, prevented Cottington from being consul at Seville and placed English Roman Catholics in their place. Since each nation resented the pressure brought by the other to achieve its goals concerning consulships, the issue could not help but strain relations and hurt efforts by the embassy to meliorate the problems of the merchants.

Hugh Lee, an elderly merchant who had been at Lisbon since 1605 as an informant for the embassy, was appointed a consul. His patent authorised him to collect fees of one ducat for every English ship that put into Lisbon and 4 per cent of the value of English goods traded through Portugal. Lee held office officially for only four months, until April 1612, when he surrendered it to a Spanish appointee named Baynes on threat of imprisonment or deportation to Africa. Digby challenged Baynes's appointment, since by implication the dismissal of Lee made every English appointment in Spain subject to Spanish approval before it had been firmly established in diplomatic procedure that a host country might properly do so. Digby's complaint brought Baynes's removal in May, and Lee once more took up his duties for about a year. Meanwhile the Council of State reconsidered and reaffirmed the rule that all foreign consuls must be Catholics. On this account the Spaniards appointed Wadsworth, the former embassy chaplain and factotum of Creswell, consul at Seville in juxtaposition to Cottington, who was still technically the consul in English eyes by reason of his patent. Digby remonstrated, Wadsworth was removed, and everything was back at square one.[7]

Further negotiation failed to reverse the Council's ruling. Spanish intransigence may well have been related to broader questions of commerce. Salisbury became so annoyed with infractions of English privileges that, shortly before Cottington returned to Spain in December 1611, he warned the Spanish ambassador in London not to be surprised at Digby's recall, the rupture of diplomatic relations and issuance of letters of marque against Spanish shipping unless the Spanish Government showed a greater willingness to co-operate. Cottington thus arrived at a time of worsening relations, when the Council of State was disinclined to indulge the English. Furthermore, since Cottington had held an important position in the embassy and now returned merely as a consul, the Spaniards suspected him of coming to spy. Then there was the matter of Cottington's unpopularity at Court. Since Digby had managed to certify Lee's appointment at Lisbon, albeit for a short time, and had overturned the appointments of Baynes and Wadsworth, his inability to serve Cottington equally well may have been due more to the Spaniards' dislike of the Seville consul than to their opposition to Protestant consuls in general, who could impede the work of the Church and civic officials at the ports. On the other hand, the open hostility to his becoming consul as much as confirmed their respect for him as an efficient and uncompromising defender of English interests. The Spaniards surely would have welcomed him whole-heartedly if, as his critics later insinuated, he had gone over to their point of view.[8]

The meagre Cottington correspondence for 1612 tells next to

nothing of his work at the embassy. But it is inconceivable that Digby would have permitted a man of his experience to remain idle for more than a year while awaiting decisive word on the consulship. In the event that the Spaniards said no, he planned to leave after the expiration of the period of grace in April. On the eve of his departure, however, the Council of State suddenly moved his case to the top of its agenda, and this induced Cottington to delay his trip. 'Within a few days,' he advised Trumbull, 'I shall know what will become of me. . . .' The days became weeks and then months and still the Council failed to act. Don Pedro de Zuñiga headed for England as special envoy to prepare for the arrival in the following year of Diego Sarmiento de Acuña, later Count Gondomar.[9]

Cottington languished in Madrid over the winter of 1612-13, his royal patent aborted by the inaction of the Council of State. The answer that he had awaited finally came in November: he might be consul provided he became a Catholic. It surprised no one, much less Cottington. His letters to the Privy Council made light of his disappointment; but in three telling sentences his pique is unmistakable. He spoke of the arrival of the West Indian treasure fleet which carried silver, silk, hides and cochineal worth twelve million ducats. Such evidence of wealth embarrassed him in the company of Spaniards whose jeers that England traded only in 'trifles' like wine, tobacco, sugar and fruit cut deeply into his national pride. What he should have realised is that the English economy, though as seriously inflated as Spain's, benefited from a thriving international trade, while her competitor absolutely depended on her treasure troves in the New World to sustain a lavish Court, meet the needs of empire and war, and satisfy the foreign bankers from whom she had borrowed heavily to pay current bills.[10]

At long last the Privy Council summoned Cottington home in May, none too soon considering his personal finances that he said had suffered from nearly two years without any living allowance. His recall coincided with the embassy of Sarmiento to England and was almost surely connected with the urgency of having someone of his expertise at hand to advise the Privy Council on Spanish affairs. No one had better credentials in this regard than Cottington: he was the only member of the embassy of 1605 still in Spain who knew from experience what had transpired there. Among his packet of letters was one from Digby to Robert Carr, Viscount Rochester, the favourite of James I. As he had done in 1611, Digby again recommended Cottington as a person of honour, industry and experience who might be useful despite 'his many years a breeding', a telling comment on his lack of promotion. The King and Privy Councillors closeted themselves with Cottington immediately upon his arrival on 10 June. About the same time Londoners showed how they felt towards Spain by crowding menacingly around Sarmiento's carriage and trying to burn down his house.[11]

The popular feelings aroused by Sarmiento's arrival and rumours that the King hoped to arrange a new Spanish treaty initially worked to Cottington's advantage. The notoriety that he had gained from his rejection as consul broadcast his name at Court not long after the administrative organisation built by Salisbury had been fractured by his death. Salisbury had so dominated affairs in his twin capacities of Principal Secretary and Lord Treasurer (not to mention his Mastership of the Court of Wards and Liveries) that even the meanest clerks in his office felt the weight of his personal influence. Several clerkships opened up soon after Salisbury died. It was believed that the King meant to appoint junior diplomats to them in order to strengthen the hand of the Privy Council in the stepped-up negotiations with Spain and other western European powers. Trumbull heard this news and it is not likely that it escaped Cottington.[12]

If Cottington had known what lay ahead before reaching London, he would have told the world in no uncertain terms. That is why his appointment as a clerk extraordinary of the Privy Council assigned to Rochester's office must have come as a complete surprise. His Spanish expertise and Digby's recommendation at the right moment undoubtedly helped him to get the post, but otherwise we are in the dark as to why Rochester picked Cottington; the documents are dumb. Soon after King James returned from a progress, Cottington took his oath of office at Whitehall on Thursday, 22 July.

His appointment out of the blue had been fortuitous considering the competition for the two clerkships. Trumbull apparently had had a good chance of winning one, but he waited too long before making his feelings known in the right circles. He believed on hearing of the possible recall of Ambassador Edmondes that he might lose his secretaryship in Brussels. He wanted a clerkship but could not decide the best way of going about securing it. If he did so personally and directly, he risked embarrassment. Without his knowledge, however, the Privy Council decided in the interval that he should remain in Brussels, since Ambassador Winwood – normally stationed at The Hague – was on extended leave in England and it was thought imprudent to leave the Low Countries without an experienced diplomat in the event that Edmondes also left. His indecisiveness and changes in diplomatic assignments excluded Trumbull from one of the clerkships and opened the way for Cottington's first opportunity at service in the central administration.[13]

Six clerks extraordinary normally served the Privy Council. They held secure positions and could move up, in the event of a vacancy, to one of the four clerkships in ordinary. Ordinary clerk Sir William Waad had held office for some thirty years since being appointed about the same time as his better-known colleague, Robert Beale. Civil servants sometimes occupied more than one office simultaneously; Waad was both an ordinary clerk and the Lieutenant of the Tower. He surrendered the lieutenancy after falling into disgrace in May 1613. The Privy Council then pressed him to relinquish his clerkship, which he held for life by royal patent and sought to sell at something above the current market price of approximately £300. Since the patent could not be purchased without Rochester's consent, Waad had to negotiate its sale through him. Cottington purchased the patent with Rochester's approval in late September. What is peculiar about the transaction is that Cottington paid £400 even though Waad was obviously in a poor bargaining position. Cottington must have thought the inflated price worth paying in view of the income attached to a clerkship in ordinary. In addition to an annual salary of £50 and the privilege of hospitality at the Principal Secretary's table, Cottington might expect fees and gratuities amounting to at least £1,500 a year. With this went a good deal of personal security, since Cottington's patent (dated 24 September 1613), like Waad's, granted him the office for life.[14]

The precepts of monarchic absolutism and the constitution under the early Stuarts discouraged the clear definition of many royal servants' duties. Customary practice and the personality of the office-holder generally dictated the manner in which he performed his tasks, and the extent of his authority depended on how much latitude his superiors allowed him. Duties usually performed by the Elizabethan principal secretaries, for instance, had sometimes been relegated to one or two clerks of the Privy Council. Clerk Beale assumed the responsibilities of Secretary Walsingham during his frequent illnesses and his embassies to Scotland and France. On the other hand, Salisbury tolerated little independence among his staff, so that it was unusual for any officer – great or small – to burst the bounds of his customary duties. His clerks therefore did merely clerical and other perfunctory work.[15]

While Viscount Rochester, later Earl of Somerset, enjoyed the King's confidence and exerted influence over him, he never managed to control the central administrative system. The favourite had no inclination to work hard and no ability. His correspondence reveals a lack of leadership or command of all situations that is unmistakable in Salisbury's letters. Moreover, Rochester had the King's favour only for about four years, which was insufficient time in which to fashion an administrative clique loyal to his interests, especially in view of his dependence on the Howards. None of the principal secretaries under King James, except Salisbury, made a mark as superlative administrators.[16]

The same can be said for the Jacobean clerks in ordinary, who no longer played decisive roles in administrative business connected with the Privy Council. The precise duties of the Jacobean clerks are not easily defined. Generally speaking, each of the four clerks in ordinary attended the Privy Council in rotation, serving a month at a time. They drafted correspondence and kept such records as the Council registers and copies of outgoing and incoming letters. They were secretaries to the committees created by the Council, and often ran errands in England and abroad. The oath of office which Cottington took as clerk tells practically nothing of his responsibilities and authority, since it was nearly identical to that taken by the Privy Councillors themselves. Councillors and clerks both swore allegiance to the King, promised to notify the Council of anything prejudicial to the Crown, and agreed to keep whatever was discussed at Council meetings confidential.

But Cottington had special talents that the Privy Council put to use; indeed, they were probably the rationale for his appointment. He was entrusted with much of the diplomatic correspondence with Spain and her European dominions. He and his aides translated or decoded letters, sifted out matters worthy of the attention of the Privy Council and the King, and drafted replies to letters addressed to Lake, Rochester and others. Cottington also performed numerous clerical duties by direction of the Councillors. Given his situation of close contact with them, he enjoyed a measure of prestige that petitioners sought to exploit. It may safely be presumed that his beneficiaries rewarded him appropriately. At the same time, the practice of rotating the clerks' terms of service allowed Cottington time to do other work to his financial advantage.[17]

Cottington's work with the Privy Council and in Spain permitted him to learn more about the ways of the aristocracy. In olden days gentlemen smote each other with broadswords and maces to avenge injured pride. While the civilising early Tudors put an end to outright feudal combat in satisfaction of chivalric honour, those who put stock in an exaggerated code of personal honour still needed a way of punishing an insulting rival. Duels, which served this purpose nicely, persisted into Jacobean times, despite three royal proclamations aimed at stopping them. The third proclamation (February 1614) was based on research in which Cottington participated by invitation of the Earl of Northampton, commissioner for the office of Earl Marshal. It was Cottington's job to describe duelling in Spain and learn from Sarmiento what sort of punishment Philip III meted out to offenders. Cottington reported that the penalties for duelling in Spain were so harsh – excommunication from the Church, imprisonment, dispossession of property and possibly execution – that it was practically unknown, or at least repressed. His report, incorporated into Northampton's study, helped to convince King James that Spanish penalties were too severe for Englishmen, and for this reason the proclamation which ensued provided for arbitration proceedings, house arrest for contumacious duellists or, at worst, banishment from Court and prosecution under the common law.[18]

His duties as clerk also sharpened Cottington's awareness of national politics and exposed him to the differing views of the Crown and its critics in Parliament and the Church on basic issues. Since he was beholden to Rochester and others and obliged to carry out their orders, he tended at first to accept their judgement uncritically, and afterwards to support the interests of the Crown out of loyalty and habit, so that in the years 1613-15, even more than before, he identified himself with the administrative system that provided him with a comfortable living and bestowed status upon him. Neither at this time nor later did he associate with opposition-ists to royal practices and policies. This one-sided relationship could not help but warp his perspective towards current events. It surely was significant that King James chose Cottington to burn the twenty-four-page rejoinder by Sir James Whitelocke, M.P. for Woodstock, to impositions following the dissolution of the Addled Parliament (1614). The deep-seated division between the House of Commons and the King over the continuance of this archaic prac-tice could not have escaped the clerk. He was also present in the Tower to take down questions and answers made at the interro-gation of the Somerset rector, Edmund Peacham, who had in a set of private, unpublished notes for a sermon criticised the bene-volence, suggested the possibility of rebellion against the King's collection of unparliamentary taxes, and seemed to presume the imminence of his death. Confession under duress was hardly new to Cottington after six years in Spain, but he nevertheless made the point in his account of the examination that it was conducted 'before torture, in torture, between torture, and after torture'. What he did not say was that such procedure was not unusual in cases involving suspected traitors, and that Peacham died in Somerset county jail.[19]

Cottington had meanwhile become involved in the plans of the Spanish faction of the Privy Council. Salisbury's death left a vacuum of strong, effective leadership in the Government, which King James personally tried to fill. Virtually all the great offices held by Salisbury were left temporarily vacant, and the resultant scramble for power never quite came out in favour of any single Councillor until the meteoric rise of the Duke of Buckingham later in the decade. The decision of James to be his own man while permitting the Treasury commissioners to handle finance, calling in Rochester's service and Sir Thomas Lake's industry, clogged the wheels of administration and split the Privy Council. Northampton, one of the Treasury commissioners, led the Spanish faction which had the King's ear more often than not, especially on foreign affairs. With Northampton stood other Howards by birth or marriage – Lord Admiral Nottingham; Lord Chamberlain Thomas, Earl of Suffolk; his son-in-law William, Lord Knollys – as well as Lake, Edward, Lord Wotton, and Edward, Earl of Worcester. Since this faction included several Roman Catholics – professed or covert – and supported with the King a stronger, peace-keeping alliance with Spain, an opposing faction hostile to Catholicism and Spain, in tune with Elizabethan goals, took shape. The leadership of this Protestant faction included William Herbert, Earl of Pembroke; the Archbishop of Canterbury, Abbot; Lord Chancellor Ellesmere; and Henry Wriothesley, Earl of Southampton.

King James hoped as early as 1611 to arrange a marriage treaty with Spain which would become a part of his plan to gain a foot-hold in both the Protestant and Catholic camps on the Continent and enable him to preserve peace throughout western Europe by acting the honest broker with each. The Spanish party of the Privy Council supported him in this aim and also worked to forestall the possibility of an Anglo-French or Franco-Spanish alliance. James met part of his objective by giving his daughter Elizabeth in marriage in 1613 to Frederick V, Elector Palatine and the fore-most Calvinist prince in Europe. Sarmiento, in England since mid-1613, likewise supported an English treaty to prevent England and France from joining forces against Spain. But he was in a delicate position. He could not openly solicit a marriage treaty without permission from Philip III and dared not alienate the French, with whom his Government had already concluded an informal agree-ment for a marriage between the older Infanta and King Louis XIII that was fulfilled in 1615. All Sarmiento could do was try to dis-courage an Anglo-French alliance and learn what he could about English conditions for a Spanish treaty. Neither the Spanish faction nor King James realised at the time, however, as Sarmiento himself may not have either, that Spain had no intention for the present of making a new treaty.[20]

C

In 1614-15 the Spanish faction employed Cottington as a go-between with Sarmiento, since none of the Councillors could themselves properly do so. They wished Sarmiento to know the strength of their feelings and had Cottington sound out his views. Who better to do this work than the clerk? He knew the current state of Spanish thinking and could speak in detail of things Spanish that might ingratiate him with Sarmiento. The meetings between Cottington and Sarmiento began in early 1614 when Rochester, taking advantage of the cordiality of the ambassador in sending him a wedding gift, had Cottington visit him several times, asking him to promote the Spanish treaty and assuring him that overtures for one would be graciously received at Court. But Sarmiento would commit himself or his Government to nothing.[21]

Somerset tried again unsuccessfully through Cottington in the succeeding weeks to force Sarmiento's hand. Nevertheless, he and Cottington developed a relationship of mutual advantage. From Cottington the ambassador weaned choice bits of news, and encouraged his co-operation by giving him small amounts of money. Nothing like dishonesty or treason should be insinuated from this. What information he gave to Sarmiento hardly threatened the security of England or divulged anything that his superiors themselves might not have revealed. It did not hurt his reputation with King James or the Spanish faction that Sarmiento took a liking to him.[22]

Cottington had evidently been dishonest with both his own people and the ambassador in late 1613, however, but gained nothing in the bargain. On 5 October, Sarmiento informed Lerma that the English embassy in Madrid had learned the contents of their correspondence and other state secrets, possibly through a spy, whether English or Spanish he did not know. Sarmiento suspected that Cottington, who handled much of his Government's Spanish correspondence, was somehow implicated in this espionage. But he dared not mention it to Cottington for fear of silencing him – and ending their fruitful relationship – or tipping his own hand to the English. Sarmiento finally narrowed the suspects down to three persons, none of whom was in high office. Cottington got word of this business and, together with Sir Charles Cornwallis, offered to reveal the spy's name to Sarmiento for a price, saying at first only that they had employed him themselves in Spain. A few days later Cottington told Sarmiento that the spy was a Scotsman named Morey. But Cornwallis came up with a different story, from which the ambassador concluded that they had each purposely lied to conceal the spy's true identity. In the end Sarmiento wormed everything out of Cornwallis: the agent was John Eston, one of Digby's servants at the embassy. While this whole matter is clouded by conflicting reports, what Cottington apparently tried to do was to enrich himself by duping the ambassador and, at the same time, increase his stock with the Spanish party to whom he confided only that he was guarding the spy's identity and refusing bribes to tell it. Neither the Councillors nor Sarmiento were fooled by this amateurish deception and simply let the matter drop.[23]

In these same years Cottington saw his benefactor Somerset become embroiled in a scandal and trial that ultimately cost him his honours and freedom. By 1609 Somerset had fallen into an adulterous relationship with Frances, Lady Essex, daughter of the Earl of Suffolk and grand-niece of the Earl of Northampton. The King supported her successful suit for a divorce from her husband, who had married her while they were both very young. She soon married Somerset and thereby drew him more closely into the arms of the Howards and the pro-Spanish party. In September 1613, shortly before she was granted the divorce, Sir Thomas Overbury, Somerset's erstwhile friend and a lieutenant of the Protestant party in the Council, was found dead of poison in the Tower to which King James had had him committed. Two and a half years later, in 1616, Somerset and his wife were convicted on circumstantial evidence of poisoning Overbury and sentenced to death, but the sentence was commuted to imprisonment for life.

The misfortunes of Somerset likewise became a misfortune for his client Cottington. The times were dangerous. The young and handsome George Villiers took his first steps towards power and wealth greater than anyone would have imagined him capable of achieving with good looks and not much talent. With Northampton dead, Somerset in prison and Nottingham a weak old man, and with Suffolk, Lord Treasurer since mid-1614, holding on to what remained of the Howards' influence, the anti-Spanish Privy Councillors began to make louder noises against a Spanish marriage and for a new Parliament that might stop the folly of England's consorting with papists. If the King and the Spanish party embraced the idea of a treaty, an early draft of which Philip III sent to Sarmiento for James's consideration in May 1615, the country at large had little good to say about one; there was even talk of war with Spain to prevent its consummation. Through all these machinations at Court, Cottington kept his counsels to himself – wisely so. At least indirectly, he had by entering royal service on the side of the Spanish party identified himself with its interests and now faced the possibility of losing out because of this association.

For the time being, at least three years before Suffolk's fall and the collapse of the Spanish party, Cottington had no way of knowing that he had taken a wrong turn that would cost him nearly everything he had achieved since 1605. In 1616 the Spanish treaty was still possible of realisation, but it was stalled by religious and political impediments that batteries of diplomats and theologians in London, Madrid and Rome were either anxious or loath to have removed. In this indecisive situation the Privy Council sent Cottington to Madrid in January – he thought for a short spell – to fill in for Digby, whom King James had recalled to report on the progress of the negotiations. Secretary Sir Ralph Winwood, realising that Cottington had departed from London in the midst of the investigation into the poisoning of Overbury, sent him word of Somerset's conviction. When his fall resounded even in the halls of the Escorial, Cottington could not have been unmindful of its significance for his own career.[24]

CHAPTER 5

Babylon Revisited

FRANCIS COTTINGTON launched the third phase of his diplomatic career at the age of thirty-seven on returning to Spain in January 1616 as *chargé d'affaires*. He retained his clerkship of the Privy Council *in absentia* until 1622, but surrendered certain financial and personal advantages connected with that office. Of most importance in retrospect was his great distance from England during the years when the Spanish party weakened and was replaced by a new configuration of power dominated by Buckingham. If he reshuffled the places in the Council with the King's consent and ultimately created an administrative system dependent on himself, he did not basically change the goals of foreign policy pursued more or less consistently since the Treaty of London. That policy still turned on a stronger alliance with Spain resulting from a marriage treaty, and on the preservation of peace on the Continent. James followed this policy even after the outbreak of the Thirty Years War, which began as a revolution in Bohemia and escalated into a much wider war involving the major powers. Since Cottington served for about six years at the capital of probably the strongest military power in Europe – one which played a crucial role in the war that touched England only indirectly – his became a difficult and, in some ways, dangerous assignment. During it he remained a prisoner of English Court politics and the servant of pro-Spanish interests about whose true motives he was at best only inadequately informed.

That he followed orders more out of duty than conviction in the wisdom of retaining Spanish friendship is clear from his personal correspondence during 1616-22. And although he regretted being away from England, far from the vortex of power and intrigue, his absence actually was fortunate, because he thereby avoided personal

involvement in Court politics and picked his way almost blindly
to safety. His residence in Spain also allowed time to sharpen his
administrative talents, to foster the trust of superiors at home in his
reliability and, through obedience and accomplishment, to attain a
certain prominence that led to the honours that he craved.

The decision of the Privy Council in December 1615 to recall
Digby to report on his negotiations and to send Cottington as
chargé d'affaires left him little time to prepare for what he believed
would be a short sojourn abroad. Within three weeks he was on
board ship bound for San Sebastian. Heavy seas and cold made the
voyage a nightmare during which he was seasick for one of the
few times in his life. Deep snow on his journey by mule through
Castile delayed his arrival in Madrid until 23 January, when Digby
first learned of his own recall, the decision in London having been
taken so quickly that Cottington reached him sooner than the mail.
Cottington found Digby strained and desperately short of money;
the ambassador could not think of leaving until he had arranged
for a loan from merchants at Seville, paid his respects to Philip III
and helped his wife prepare to follow him. He reached England in
March, and Lady Digby and their children joined him two months
later, having lost most of their possessions and nearly their lives
when half her pack mules plunged into a ravine in the mountains
en route to the Spanish coast.[1]

Cottington took up his duties with confidence born of diplomatic and administrative experience and maturity. His position
vis-à-vis the Spanish authorities had been strengthened by the un-
spectacular but solid achievements of Digby in the preceding three
years. The ambassador had by and large upheld English treaty
rights, although, like his predecessors, he had had his share of
wrangles over seizure of merchandise and his countrymen's imprisonment. He had come close to persuading the Council of State
to establish a special tribunal to hear English suits-at-law and made
progress promoting a joint Anglo-Spanish expedition against the
Barbary pirates in the western Mediterranean, neither of which
proposals was implemented after his departure. Whether Digby
could keep the marriage treaty alive in the face of a similar one
concluded between France and Spain, it was still too early to tell.
But his patient negotiation and that of Sarmiento in London had

helped to reverse the downward cycle of Anglo-Spanish relations that had coincided through no fault of his own with the agency of Cottington.[2]

If the Privy Councillors had rushed Cottington off to Spain with unconscionable haste, they all but ignored him for months afterwards. For the moment the main negotiations had shifted to London, where Digby cooled his heels while Sarmiento pondered the English reaction to the latest intelligence on a Spanish treaty. In Spain there was news of a different kind. A drought in central and southern Spain – Málaga had had little rain in over a year – stunted the crops and drained grain bins nearly empty. Grain shortages were often catastrophic in the marginal economy of the early seventeenth century because western Europeans subsisted mostly on a diet of bread. Even the well-to-do felt the effects of the crisis: Cottington could not find sufficient food from April to June to feed his household adequately, and only his repeated appeals to the President of Castile got them what they absolutely needed. Even then, hungry townspeople thronged outside Cottington's door demanding bread which he did not have to share. With drought came an epidemic that killed thousands and infected the embassy. Cottington had graves dug for three servants in his cellar and buried a footman in the garden because only Catholics could be interred in city cemeteries.[3]

It is instructive of his developing character to watch his calm reaction to such a crisis, and to compare his correspondence with that written before 1613. He usually couched his earlier letters to superiors in polite, almost apologetic language; those written now were bold, demanding, clearly expectant of results. He wanted his allowance and asked for it unashamedly. But was he being entirely honest about his financial straits? Spend some of his own money he surely did before arrears due to him came through a year later. Yet he evidently had enough to see him through lean months: a man pressed for money would not have wasted any on gifts of bacon and wine that he sent to Secretary and Lady Winwood in 1616. He also had had money to invest in property – something a man without surplus capital does not do. In 1613 he had purchased the cottage in Suffolk. A year later he paid £600 for a share of the revenue of Baltonsborough (Somerset) rectory. Two years after that he acquired leases to the lands of Blueberry (Berkshire) and Kennington (Surrey). In April 1615 the Crown granted him the goods and chattels of Thomas, Lord Grey of Wilton, who died in prison eleven years after conviction for involvement in the Cobham Plot (1604). He had enough property and income in England by 1616 to need the services of a business agent, Alexander Stafford, with whom he was associated for nearly thirty years. These acquisitions easily provided sufficient income to sustain him and a small household for a year or so, and laid the basis for much larger property holdings that made him a wealthy man by the 1630s.[4]

He could more easily handle finances than international disputes that contributed each in their own way to a potentially explosive situation on the eve of the Thirty Years War. His orders obliged Cottington to use England's good offices to try to end the war in Italy between Spain and Savoy that eventually involved Venice and Naples as well. England had no vital interests to protect in that area. She traded with both Spain and Venice, but the war did not jeopardise her commercial operations in the western Mediterranean any more than did the Turkish or Barbary pirates. Even so, King James tended to regard any conflict involving a great power as potentially capable of escalation into a bigger war that it had always been his concern as peacemaker to avert. The war went against Savoy, and she made peace at Asti in 1615 only to break it soon afterwards with help from French Huguenot mercenaries. Cottington reached Spain not long after this violation of the treaty. He at once undertook a round of talks with the Councils of State and War and with the Venetian ambassador in Madrid, Pietro Gritti. The Spaniards insisted that they wanted peace, but that the Savoyards and Venetians had resumed hostilities and refused to compromise.[5]

Perhaps no diplomat could have hoped to mediate a war involving the vital interests of Spain in western Europe – the disputed Valtelline connected both ends of the supply route between northern Italy and the lower Rhineland – but Cottington's powers of persuasion in this situation are not impressive. The arbitrator had to be a distinguished and strong personality whom both sides respected. The man whom King James sent as ambassador in the autumn to help make peace, Lord Roos, did not meet these qualifications. He was no stranger to Latin Europe, or to Cottington, alas! He knew some Spanish, next to nothing about diplomacy, and a great deal about the pleasures of aristocratic life. Roos wasted weeks following his arrival at Lisbon in merrymaking as the guest of the Viceroy of Portugal. After agreeing to meet Cottington on Christmas Eve at Toledo, Roos postponed the rendezvous in favour of more hospitality. Cottington finally got Roos down to business in Madrid for five weeks after the New Year. He accomplished nothing, of course. As they had told Cottington earlier, the Spaniards promised to honour the terms of the Treaty of Asti provided Duke Charles Emmanuel of Savoy evacuated Piedmont and accepted mediation. In the end English intervention had little to do with settling the war. Worse still from Cottington's standpoint was Roos's financial irresponsibility: he spent his entire allowance in Lisbon (even though the Viceroy paid most of the bills of his entourage of 150 persons in Portugal), relied on Cottington to raise money on his own credit to meet expenses, and left behind a huge debt from which Cottington and Digby finally extricated him two years later.[6]

Meanwhile Cottington had had to deal with a far more important question involving England's interests directly. The expedition of Sir Walter Raleigh to the Orinoco in Spanish South America to dig for gold reflected badly on England and ended disastrously for him. King James allowed Raleigh to go provided he personally assumed full responsibility for his conduct. Raleigh hoped in this risky venture to free himself from the taint of treason and long imprisonment, and regain the favour of the Court. For his part the King speculated that Raleigh might bring back a fortune in gold, stake a territorial claim for England in South America and, by daring to intrude upon the Spanish commercial monopoly there, strengthen his hand in Spanish relations.

The Spanish Government knew of Raleigh's plans before he undertook the expedition and followed its progress closely. Gondomar had seen a copy of his deposition and sent the paper to Philip III. Yet the Spaniards acted as if news of the expedition came as a complete surprise. They repeatedly worried Cottington by demanding explanations of England's intentions from Raleigh's sailing to his return. Cottington was in an awkward position because, although James had instructed him to explain the purpose of the expedition to the Council of State, no one bothered to tell him very much about the circumstances that led to it. Cottington took the line that since Englishmen were constrained by no legal or moral impediment from visiting Latin America, Raleigh or any other Englishman had every right to do so. At the same time he appreciated that the Spaniards were making a fuss in order to impress on the English their claim of monopoly in South America. It was doubtless for this reason that they brought up other supposed acts of aggression committed by Englishmen, such as an engagement near Mozambique between four East India merchantmen and a Portuguese carrack en route to Goa, which ran aground and was scuttled. The Spaniards also complained after their countrymen killed a number of Raleigh's crew, who had gone ashore in the Canaries to take on water, an incident caused in their eyes by English provocation.

The news of skirmishes between Raleigh's men and Spanish colonials near the Orinoco river broke like thunder in Madrid in May 1618. Once more Cottington bore the brunt of invective. Secretary Lerma, brandishing the copy of Raleigh's deposition in front of Cottington, denounced the adventurer and demanded that King James punish him for piracy. Cottington did not know what he should say in reply, for the Privy Council had not kept him abreast of the progress of the expedition or instructed him how to justify its results. Left to his own devices, he wisely blamed Raleigh and exonerated King James of complicity in the affair. King Philip demanded satisfaction and got it when Raleigh was executed. It then became Cottington's duty to convince the Spaniards that he had been put to death as a mark of England's good faith towards Spain, which she might reciprocate by removing the impediments to a marriage treaty that had been hanging fire for many years.[7]

The idea of a marriage had first been suggested by Queen Anne during the negotiations for the Treaty of London, and again, in 1605 and 1607, by Spain. In each case England balked at the condition that Prince Henry should become a Roman Catholic and be educated in Spain. But James embraced the proposal of a marriage made by Ambassador Velasco in 1611, and Salisbury laid a basis for further discussion between the Council of State and Digby following Sir John's arrival in Spain in May of that year.

The Spaniards could not have been surprised by the offer of a marriage between the Prince and the Infanta Anne brought by Digby, but they acted as if they had never heard of the idea. It was not until the following August that Digby understood why they had evaded his and Cottington's overtures: Philip had secretly consented to the betrothal of Anne and Louis XIII of France. The assassination of Henri IV in 1610 had helped to thaw the cold war that Spain and France had waged since the Treaty of Vervins in 1598. Marie de' Medici, Queen Regent during the minority of her son Louis, trusted the talented Spanish ambassador, Inigo de Cardeñas, and even admitted him into her secret council. It was Cardeñas, Sully said, who had by arranging this marriage assured his monarch that France would not threaten the territorial integrity of the Spanish Netherlands or ally with England. Having done so, Spain could afford to put off England.

James was furious over the Franco-Spanish arrangement. Digby demanded an explanation of Philip III. Ambassador Zuñiga hurried to London to try to explain away the French treaty, was greeted by cold indignation, and scoffed at when he suggested the possibility of another marriage between his widower King and Princess Elizabeth. Afterwards Philip offered England the hand of his younger daughter, the Infanta Maria, six years old. Digby read this offer as a palliative to James. He was right; soon the Spaniards contrived reasons why even this marriage should be postponed indefinitely – Maria was still too young and Henry was not a Catholic. At that the matter was dropped.[8]

If James occasionally entertained the idea of a marriage treaty with another Catholic state – France, Tuscany or Savoy – such speculation came to naught. We saw earlier how Cottington served the Spanish faction in 1614-15 as go-between with Gondomar, who embraced their proposal for a Spanish match and promoted it in Madrid and Rome. Philip III and the Pope at first thought it senseless to reintroduce the religious articles that England had already rejected repeatedly over the years. Moreover, the Papacy frowned on an alliance between Spain and Protestant England. Then, with further encouragement by Gondomar, they reconsidered. James might just accept the religious articles, in which case the conversion of Prince Charles (Henry having died) might restore the faith in England, or the English recusants might be unburdened of their

troubles on account of the penal laws. Failing that, at least England
could be prevented from assisting the anti-Habsburg forces on the
Continent. In this spirit the Spanish Government drew up articles
for a treaty and sent them to London. They called for suspension
of the penal laws, papal approval of the marriage by dispensation,
freedom of religion for the Infanta and her household, education
of her children as Catholics and other privileges. James balked,
waited six months, and finally told Gondomar that he accepted the
articles as a basis for discussion. From this proceeded Digby's sudden recall and Cottington's departure for Spain in December 1616.

How Cottington felt about a Spanish treaty at this point is hard
to say positively, though there are clues in his correspondence. In
all his letters but one – a crucial one for our purposes – he professed
his unreserved support for a treaty, telling Buckingham and others
in glowing reports of his confidence in the success of the negotiations.
He could hardly have said otherwise in view of the King's interest
in the treaty and his own dependence on the goodwill of the Spanish
faction which favoured it. But Cottington told Sir Thomas Lake –
one of Suffolk's lieutenants on the Council – something else. In a
carefully constructed paragraph he cautioned Lake not to expect
success in Digby's forthcoming talks in Madrid, for it was doubtful
either that the Spaniards would compromise on the religious articles
or, even if they did, that James could accept them. 'As far as I am
concerned,' Cottington concluded, 'I am less confident now than
I was 2 months ago. Let no one know you have this letter from
me – burn it.' Was he warning his benefactors of danger ahead?
At least he admitted in a back-handed way his own reservations
about the treaty.[9]

The new round of talks between Digby and the King commenced
in September at Lerma, in north-central Castile, where Cottington
had also gone to help. They got off to a poor start and made little
progress. Philip was staying at the Duke of Lerma's castle, but
Digby was not asked to join them, lodging instead at a decrepit
inn in the town that could barely accommodate the lesser Spanish
officials, much less the large English train. The slight to England
could not be missed. A succession of grandees – Lerma, his son
the Duke of Uceda, the King's Confessor Luis de Aliaga, and
Secretary Juan de Ciriza – each assured Digby of Spain's honourable

intentions and worked hard to convey the impression that the religious impediments could be overcome with a little patience and understanding on both sides. Even now, they told Digby, Philip III awaited favourable word from the Pope on the dispensation. Cottington knew that they were lying: the papal nuncio in Madrid had told him that the Pope was dead set against the marriage and would never consent to it – an opinion shared by the Spanish theologians and bishops.[10]

Digby suspected from the first that he had gone on another wild-goose chase, but he was obliged against his better judgement to proceed as instructed. What neither he nor his superiors realised, however, was that only full English compliance with the religious articles would satisfy the Spaniards, and that they intended to use denial of papal approbation as an excuse to delay the negotiations indefinitely in the event of English intransigence or their own change of heart. Should the English become impatient and threaten to break off the talks, assurances that the papal dispensation was expected momentarily, or that it was in doubt, would prolong them a little longer. Such strategy kept England on the defensive, dangling like an overwrought suitor and over-anxious to please for fear the treaty might fail.

There was another side to the question, one which posed a nearly insurmountable obstacle to a Spanish match. Even if both sides agreed to the religious articles, King James faced an uphill battle persuading some of his Councillors, Parliament and the country to accept them at the cost of Protestant scruples. Digby said, not entirely honestly, that apart from the King and himself only Lake whole-heartedly supported the treaty; the rest of the Councillors either opposed it or were indifferent. Assuming that the much-withered Spanish party and the King consented to a treaty, Parliament would still have to be consulted because only it could legally rescind the penal laws as Spain expected. Considering the differences between James and Parliament over foreign policy and religion, its co-operation was unlikely.[11]

As winter approached, the conferees had moved only slightly off dead centre. Both sides wanted a recess: Philip III continued on his progress and Digby and Cottington returned to Madrid. Meanwhile Secretary Winwood had died, and his successor, Sir

Robert Naunton, needed time to familiarise himself with Spanish affairs. Once talks were resumed in January, Digby put his heart and soul into them, conferring principally with the King and Lerma, while Cottington met with other Councillors of State. That the two Englishmen achieved little is understandable in view of the disadvantages under which they had to negotiate. First, Raleigh had left for the Orinoco in the summer of 1617 and his expedition gave the Spaniards a stick with which to beat the English during the talks that autumn and winter. Second, the theologians whom King Philip had asked to study the religious articles reported that they were unacceptable. Now the Spaniards expected immediate repeal of the penal laws, refused to allow the Infanta to leave or pay her dowry until that was done, and insisted that Prince Charles come for her himself. King James could not comply with these conditions and for once resisted Gondomar's cajolery. Digby therefore went home empty-handed, having, as Cottington said, 'concluded nothing, but left all to the wisdom of his majesty who is still so free as he may accept or leave [the new articles] at his pleasure'.[12]

The negotiations remained deadlocked for two years. King James and Digby, now Baron Digby of Sherborne, conferred with Gondomar regularly until he returned to Spain in July. There Gondomar and Cottington occasionally discussed the marriage before Philip III sent the ambassador back to England in late 1619. Another round of conferences, this time primarily with Buckingham and Prince Charles, brought England and Spain no closer to agreement by 1620.[13]

Portentous news broke in Madrid in May 1618, only weeks after Cottington once more assumed responsibility for embassy business. First came reports of Raleigh's skirmishes near the Orinoco, already mentioned. Then couriers brought word of an insurrection in Prague touched off when two Habsburg royal governors of Bohemia had been flung out of a window of the Hradschin Castle. Seen from the perspective of Bohemian–Habsburg relations, the revolution was the final desperate attempt by the Bohemian feudal nobility to preserve their prerogatives against further encroachment by the absolutist, centralistic Government in Vienna. The revolution widened in the months following as the Austrians and Bohemians stepped up the fighting and sought to enlist allies.[14]

The Bohemian revolution occurred at a time when neither England nor Spain wished to plunge into the miasma of central European politics. But they could not afford to ignore them. The revolution also came shortly after the two states had once more become deadlocked over the marriage negotiations, so that neither could be certain of the other's goodwill or how the other might respond to the crisis. It was fairly certain that the historical bonds of family and religion would draw Spain and the Habsburg Empire together in the event of a larger war. This James realised and hoped to prevent, since Spain's entry into the war would be matched on the other side by the entry of Protestant states. Would England then honour her ties with the Protestant Union by dispatching troops and supplies to its aid? Seeing this possibility, Philip out-manoeuvred James by inviting him in the summer of 1618 to mediate in the conflict in the Habsburg eastern dominions and to promote peace in the major European capitals. James took the bait, thus assuring Spain that, at least for a while, England would not enter the war. The Habsburgs dishonestly accepted the offer of good offices extended by Sir Henry Wotton in the Empire and by Sir Edward Conway in the Spanish Netherlands, while James Hay, Viscount Doncaster, visited other European princes in search of peace. None of these missions succeeded because no one except the English took them seriously. Besides, the Habsburgs were winning the war in Bohemia, and Bavaria and Spain had preparations on foot to attack the Palatinate in the absence of its Calvinist prince, who had impetuously accepted the dubious honour of becoming monarch of a fractious people.

English public sentiment at every level ran overwhelmingly in favour of Frederick, the Protestant David confronting the Catholic Habsburg Goliath. At Court, sentiment was bolstered by the fall of the Howards and their replacement on the Council by Lionel Cranfield, Naunton and others who, in union with the anti-Spanish Protestant party, clamoured for war against the Catholic League or at least wanted to put an end to collaboration with Spain once and for all. Even Buckingham and his *alter ego*, Prince Charles, beat the war-drums. But James shut his ears. If his daughter's becoming a queen and her husband a king momentarily thrilled him, he soon thought better about lending military support to

revolution against divinely constituted monarchy. Going to war
would betray his deepest convictions against it, perhaps end for
ever what chance remained of concluding a Spanish match after
nearly ten years of negotiation, and probably drive the Spaniards
into implementing their rumoured intention of invading the
Palatinate.

So James allowed himself to be influenced by Gondomar into
believing that only through a policy of neutrality would the
Habsburgs be persuaded to spare the Palatinate and rescue his
children. He would allow the Protestant Union to recruit troops
in England, but nothing else would he do to advance its cause or
England's by force of arms. Frederick's defeat at the Battle of
White Mountain in 1620 and his exile at The Hague confirmed
most Englishmen in the conviction that James had taken a wrong
turn and been humiliated by Spain. James now tried to extricate
his wayward children from their predicament by asking Philip to
help persuade the Emperor to permit Frederick's restoration in the
Electorate. The plan failed because it flew in the face of Spanish
and Imperial war aims and the realities of international politics.

It became Cottington's duty at first to persuade Philip III to use
his influence to isolate the Bohemian conflict. At the same time
Cottington warned his Government that Philip would probably
lend military support to the Emperor, and predicted general war
unless James took steps to prevent it. Cottington advised Philip
that, while England did not condone revolution, James hoped that
neither Spain nor the Empire would punish the Bohemians inordinately. They had acted hastily and illegally, Cottington contended,
but they had done so out of misguided patriotic zeal and to protect
their religious rights. Philip should await the results of the peace
missions that James had dispatched before doing anything rash.
Philip answered that freedom of religion was merely an excuse
trumped up by the Bohemians to shroud their intention of
overthrowing Imperial authority and electing a Protestant
Emperor.[15]

Cottingon continued his efforts to discourage Spanish entry into
the war even as the Council of State authorised 300,000 ducats
towards strengthening the army, while heavy fighting took place
in Bohemia, and English diplomats searched for peace in the

European capitals. Gondomar, the Duke of Uceda and Secretary Ciriza reassured Cottington that their Government meant to see the results of these missions before determining whether or not to support Ferdinand, and hinted that a new treaty with England would soon be forthcoming. In fact Spain had already promised to assist her German allies and made plans to renew full-scale war in the Netherlands. In order to strengthen its case with England, however, the Council of State showed Cottington copies of dispatches to two Spanish diplomats, Julian Sánchez and the Count of Oñate, ordering them to assist Doncaster in mediating in the Bohemian crisis. This fooled Cottington: he assured his Government that Spain would honour her promises. He had no way of knowing, though a shrewder man would have suspected it, that Spain had no intention of doing so.[16]

Over the next few weeks Cottington fell under the influence of Gondomar, who charmed him as he had King James, and reported that the ambassador would leave shortly for London via Heidelberg, where he would help Doncaster. This was in March 1619. But Gondomar left instead directly for London in November. Meanwhile the Court went on progress and Cottington contracted a disease which kept him in bed for seven weeks. News of Ferdinand's election as Emperor and Frederick's accession to the Bohemian throne reached Madrid towards the end of Cottington's convalescence.[17]

In September the Privy Council sent Cottington papers explaining to King Philip England's ignorance of Frederick's enthronement before the fact. Cottington translated them and hurried to intercept the King at Tomar, north-east of Lisbon. He remained with the royal train for a month as it moved into Estremadura, and left Guadalupe with Philip's assurance that he held James blameless of any complicity in Frederick's actions. Although Cottington suffered a sharp relapse after returning to Madrid, reports that Philip had fallen gravely ill constrained him to travel another seventy miles to visit him. Then Gondomar left for England in such haste that Cottington raced miles to bid him a proper farewell. Snow delayed the ambassador's journey for weeks, but it also held up an English courier bringing word that Cottington would shortly be replaced by Sir Walter Aston.[18]

In the weeks that followed this good news, Cottington reflected on his work during the last four years. Much of what he had done was routine, part of the everyday duties of a diplomat. The pattern of commercial relations and attendant merchant problems had not changed appreciably from earlier years, although procedures had been worked out to expedite the settlement of grievances. Cottington appears to have exerted himself more strenuously on behalf of the merchants than either Cornwallis or Digby, but then this was one of his particular assignments in the embassy in the years when he served under them.[19]

Under the best of circumstances Cottington found life in Spain arduous and lonely. It was therefore with particular delight that he rode several leagues north of Madrid to meet Ambassador Aston, formerly a Gentleman of the Privy Chamber. Imagine his disappointment when he learned that he should remain indefinitely! A steady hand was needed at the wheel while Aston studied the roll of the sea. He had much to learn. By his own surprising admission (for an ambassador), he feared the responsibilities of office. 'I must confess,' he told Sir George Calvert, 'I enter rather with careful fear into my master business [the marriage treaty] than with a secure presumption, but I hope though no time can make me too secure, that shortly I shall have less cause to fear.'[20]

On Aston's arrival Cottington retreated into the background, quietly assisting him at every turn until he became familiar with embassy business. The King had charged the ambassador with three major objectives, which neither Digby nor Cottington with all their experience and skill had been able to achieve. First, Aston should speedily complete the draft marriage treaty. Second, he should arrange the withdrawal of the Spanish garrisons from the Palatinate. Third, he should renew talks with the Council of War on the joint Anglo-Spanish fleet to suppress piracy. In addition, the King expected Aston to establish cordial relationships with the Spanish royal family; report the actions of the papal nuncio and other diplomats; faithfully represent English mercantile interests; guard against the intrigues of the Jesuits and Catholic exiles; and keep London informed of the movements of men, money and ships to and from the ports. Little wonder that Aston's stomach turned sour.[21]

There are periods in Cottington's long life of seventy-two years in which his activities are shrouded; the two and a half years from Aston's arrival in February 1620 to Cottington's departure in September 1622 is one of them. Aston scarcely mentioned him in dispatches, and when he did, little specific was said. Occasionally we can catch a glimpse of him, as when he made one more effort to persuade the Spaniards to accept Protestant consuls and failed. Even as these negotiations were grinding to their inevitable conclusion, Cottington wrote to a man designated to become consul in Andalusia, telling him from experience that the post would bring him a hatful of rain and barely £500 annually in fees and gratuities, out of which he would have to pay his own expenses.[22]

There was a hint of cynicism in this letter. Cottington had written repeatedly to his superiors in the year after Aston's arrival, but no one bothered to explain why he had not been recalled as promised. At forty-two and with sixteen years of service behind him, he felt cheated of success and spurned by his Government. Depression consumed him in 1621, and a succession of minor illnesses weakened him. The only evidence he had that he had not been completely forgotten came in March, when Buckingham arranged for the immediate payment of arrears due to him since 1617. He seized the chance to thank Buckingham in such a way as to ingratiate himself with his potential and much-needed patron. This explains why Cottington spent his own money purchasing and shipping choice Algerian stallions to Buckingham, who was Master of the Horse.[23]

A rumour reached the embassy in late October: the secretary to Prince Charles, Thomas Murray, who openly opposed the Spanish match and was ordered from Court to reconsider his indiscretion, was to be replaced by Cottington. In December his old friend, Lady Digby, who described him as a 'gentleman I much love and respect . . . especially for being an honest man', noted the probability of Cottington's recall and preferment to higher office. Months passed while he waited anxiously. Some time in the early spring of 1622 he got the thrilling news that he should return to England upon Digby's imminent arrival and become the Prince's secretary. It was Buckingham himself who had made the decision.

Cottington's long and faithful service meant something after all, as did his usefulness at Court on the eve of what the Privy Council believed would be the final stages of negotiation leading to the marriage treaty. His exile in Babylon was over. The promised land lay just ahead.[24]

CHAPTER 6

Secretary to the Prince

FRANCIS COTTINGTON and his aide, John Dickenson, left Madrid in late September 1622, six months after his nomination as secretary to Prince Charles. His departure had been delayed initially by the late arrival of Digby, now Earl of Bristol, who had been to Vienna and back on a peace mission; then by the tardy decision of the College of Cardinals in Rome that the treaty must guarantee the full religious liberty of the Infanta, her suite and all English Catholics; and finally by Bristol's serious illness during the latter part of the summer. Personnel changes at the highest level of government had been made in Spain during the last eighteen months of Cottington's service. The succession of Philip IV in 1621 brought a new order fashioned by Gaspar de Guzman, Count-Duke of Olivares, who destroyed the old clique headed by the Duke of Uceda and Rodrigo Calderon and strove to bolster the economy before it undermined the Spanish war effort. Faces had changed in the Privy Council as well. The Howards and their allies – Suffolk, Lake, Knollys, Nottingham and others – had long since gone and the grasp of the Spanish party had been broken. Buckingham had received practically every dignity at the disposal of the King and organised a new administration of efficient bureaucrats, including Lionel Cranfield, Earl of Middlesex; Secretaries Sir George Calvert and Sir Robert Naunton (soon replaced by Sir Edward Conway); Keeper of the Great Seal John Williams, Dean of Westminster and afterwards Bishop of Lincoln; and Chancellor of the Exchequer Sir Richard Weston.[1]

These were the powerful men with whom Cottington associated as an adviser on Spanish affairs and an administrative assistant in the next few years. He brought from Spain messages from Digby and Aston on the Pope's uncompromising attitude on the treaty's

religious articles and on the intransigence of the Spanish Government respecting the occupation of the Palatinate. In discussions
with the King, Prince Charles, Buckingham and the Privy Councillors, Cottington advised them that the Spanish Government
seemed indignant towards the Pope, unbending over the Palatinate,
but apparently willing to continue negotiations on the treaty,
provided these two obstacles could be overcome. Cottington felt
that the Spaniards would never withdraw from the Palatinate until
the treaty had been concluded to their and Rome's satisfaction, but
that they probably would come around more to England's way of
thinking rather than risk her military intervention on behalf of
Frederick and the Protestant Union.[2]

His duty fulfilled for the moment, Cottington gratefully set aside
business to accept the congratulations of friends on becoming
secretary and to enjoy his formal installation to that office in mid-
October at St James's Palace. His thoughts naturally turned to the
fees and gratuities attached to the secretaryship and the nature
of his new responsibilities. It carried with it an allowance for
clothes and personal needs, meals and lodging in the Prince's
Household at the Palace and, most important for a person of
Cottington's modest social origins and high aspirations, the chance
to mix with the leading persons of the Government and to win
their trust. His duties were not constitutionally defined, so that
what Cottington did depended largely on what the Prince and
others expected of him, and what he himself believed he should
do. He wrote most of the Prince's formal correspondence, and
managed his daily schedule by arranging appointments and fending
off unwelcome suitors and the like. He also accompanied Charles
on progress, making sure that his needs were met, and generally
handled his personal finances apart from the general Household
expenses. Cottington was frequently employed as well in affairs
not directly related to the Prince, such as committee work arising
from Privy Council business. Such duties gave him additional
experience in the everyday operations of the central Government,
which he put to good use later in his career. He was much in
demand for what he might do through his personal influence at
Court. In December 1622 Chamberlain wrote that 'Cottington is
much with the King, and in great request, as having been so long

conversant and well seen in Spanish affairs, and knows the bias of that Court to a hair'. His friend Beaulieu said that 'Cottington prospereth apace in the Court & groweth very inward in the Cabinet'.[3]

Now secretary, Cottington sold his life patent as a clerk in ordinary of the Privy Council. The sudden death of Sir Clement Edmonds of a stroke and his own appointment to the Household of Prince Charles created two vacancies in the four clerkships. Sir George Calvert secured a temporary one for John Dickenson on Cottington's recommendation, and he disposed of his own clerkship through Buckingham's help to Sir Thomas Meautys. He paid £450 for it, £50 more than Cottington had given William Waad in 1613.[4]

All this time Cottington had another matter on his mind – a beautiful young widow named Anne Brett (*née* Meredith), not to be confused with the lady of the same name, the daughter of James Brett and a Villiers cousin who married Lionel Cranfield.[5] The widow had considerable wealth, an impressive lineage and connections at Court. She was descended from two respected families, the Palmers and the Merediths, many of whom became civil servants in the early seventeenth century and owned estates in Kent, Suffolk, Denbigh and Gloucestershire. Anne's great-grandfather, Sir Henry Palmer (d. 1557), had purchased monastic lands at Wingham in Kent and served as Master of the Ordnance. Her great-grandmother was a Windebank, a family which achieved prominence during the secretaryship of Sir Francis Windebank in the 1630s. In 1627 Jane Meredith, Anne's sister, married Sir Peter Wyche, later ambassador at the Porte. Their uncle Sir Roger Palmer married into the Porter family of Gloucestershire and served in King Charles's Household. Another uncle, Sir James Palmer, was attached to the King's Bedchamber. Sir Henry Palmer the Younger, a cousin, became Comptroller of the Navy.[6]

Cottington may have known Anne and her husband, Sir Robert Brett, for some time, since he had sent him books from Spain in 1620 shortly before his death. The courtship must have been a whirlwind affair, however, because Cottington returned to London only five months before his marriage in the second week of February 1623. Sir Robert had had only one child by a previous marriage, who predeceased him, so that he bequeathed almost all his property and wealth to Anne. Her inheritance included a house near Charing Cross in London,[7] jewels, a fourth of the household effects and plate, and £1,000 in cash. A codicil to Sir Robert's will also guaranteed Anne an annual jointure of £500 from the income of Brett lands in Kent. All this goes to show that Cottington did well by his marriage, both socially and financially; in fact, he married somewhat above his own station in both respects.[8]

Fortune continued to smile on him. On 15 February, a few days after his marriage, he was made a baronet. In his case he was doubly fortunate in that he was not obliged to pay the customary fine and fees for it, but received it in reward for long service.[9]

In Stuart England there were two sides to the common coin of patronage – services to be returned for favours – as Cottington was reminded soon enough. The security and prospects of practically all royal servants depended ultimately on the wishes of Buckingham, the grand dispenser of royal largesse, to whom Cottington was twice indebted for the secretaryship and the baronetcy. While Sir Francis put his new household in order, Buckingham was secretly scheming to bring the marriage treaty to a dramatic conclusion. Either the Prince or Buckingham had asked Bristol on the eve of his departure for Spain in the previous year whether he believed it prudent that the Marquis should visit Philip IV to speed matters along. Bristol answered Charles: 'As for my Lord of Buckingham's coming into Madrid I doubt not but Mr Cottington will have represented all the inconveniences and difficulties thereof. . . .'[10] This was Bristol's respectful way of saying no. Before this letter reached London, and without consulting anyone but the Prince, and possibly Gondomar,[11] Buckingham shocked King James with the proposition that he and the Prince should visit Madrid at once to win over Philip IV, sweep the Infanta Maria off her feet, and bring her back as Charles's bride. Buckingham believed that he alone could arrange in a few weeks what neither Bristol, Cottington nor Aston could achieve in years of frustrating negotiation. It took a man of his incomparable vanity, naïveté in diplomacy and ignorance of Spanish social conventions to concoct such a bizarre and perilous adventure.

Bewildered and distraught at this news, James summoned Sir Francis, who awaited his master in an adjoining chamber. James told him that he had always been trusted as an honest man, and asked him to answer truthfully a question of the gravest consequence. 'Cottington,' said James, 'here are Baby Charles and Steenie, . . . who have a great mind to go by post to Spain to fetch home the Infanta, and will have but two more in their company, and have chosen you for one. What think you of the journey?' Now, suddenly, Buckingham's generosity was explained to Cottington in a way that a man of his intuition could not have misunderstood. A moment passed. Buckingham glared at Cottington and whispered something into Charles's ear. The Prince stood motionless, characteristically placid, and mumbled. Cottington turned pale, began to tremble, and spoke haltingly in full realisation of what the favourite expected to hear. No one had crossed him except at grave risk; Sir Francis knew that too. Yet he replied courageously that the idea struck him ill; that the trip would nullify everything that had been achieved thus far in the negotiations; that, with the Prince in their clutches, the Spaniards would impose new demands. Charles mustered up a grimace. James threw himself on a bed, and screamed that he would lose his son. Buckingham, blood in his eyes, berated Sir Francis for forgetting his place by discussing matters of policy when he had been asked only for his opinion on the best route to Spain. Whereupon James scolded Buckingham for abusing an honest man who had done only what was asked of him. Cottington left the room, Buckingham never forgot the seeming impudence of his client, and before that fateful day ended James had reluctantly agreed to let Steenie have his way.[12]

Impudent or not, Buckingham needed Sir Francis and instructed him to make preparations at once for the journey. On 17 February, Charles and Buckingham – disguised in cloaks, oversized perukes and beards as the merchants Tom and Jack Smith – left the King at Theobalds for the favourite's house at Newhall in Essex. Next day they crossed the Thames at Tilbury and aroused the suspicion of a ferryman by paying him with a twenty-shilling piece. En route to Rochester the odd couple passed Sir Lewis Lewknor, who was accompanying the French ambassador to London, and reached Dover that evening. Sir Henry Manwaring, Lieutenant of Dover Castle, was forewarned by Lewknor's messenger of the approach of strangers, intercepted them and nearly arrested them before the

Marquis doffed his beard to prove his identity. Meanwhile Cottington and Endymion Porter, grandson of the linguist Sir Giles
Porter who had served with Sir Francis in Spain, had procured
passage.

The party departed from Dover on the morning of the 19th
and disembarked at Boulogne shortly after noon. They left by
horse for Paris via Montreuil and arrived on the morning of the
21st. All lodged at an inn on the Rue Saint-Jacques and spent that
day and the next seeing the city and the French Court. All along
Cottington feared the worst, trembled when the Prince fell from
his horse, and slept fully clothed each night like a dog at the foot
of Charles's bed. The travellers resumed their journey on the 23rd
and in six days reached Bayonne near the Spanish border. On the
night of 7 March, with Sir Francis and Porter lagging half a day
behind, Charles and Buckingham alighted at the gate of the English
embassy in Madrid.[13]

Their unexpected arrival shocked Bristol, who made the mistake
of showing his annoyance and later criticised Buckingham to his
own eventual misfortune. Bristol wrote to Carleton of the 'sudden
and unthought of arrival of the Prince's Highness', and that 'had
I notice thereof I should have used all the dissuasions I had been
able to have hindered it . . .'. He noticed a change of attitude in
King Philip, Olivares and the Councillors. It is said that Olivares,
rubbing his hands gleefully, awakened Philip to the news that Spain
might now dictate whatever terms she pleased. They were exultant
at the reality of the heir to the English throne within their grasp;
whereas they had been somewhat more accommodating than usual
before he arrived, afterwards they rejected every English attempt
at compromise. In the following August, when the marriage seemed
arranged and Buckingham and Olivares parted enemies for ever,
Bristol reminded King James how Spain had deceived England
from the first and never intended to go through with the treaty.[14]

The first weeks passed happily enough for all concerned. Charles
and Buckingham exchanged visits with the King, Gondomar and
Olivares and were entertained at bullfights, banquets and the
theatre, throughout which the Spaniards scrupulously prevented
the Prince from saying more than a few words to the Infanta, with
whom he fancied himself in love. Meanwhile James poured out his

heart in letters to his boys and sent courtiers, servants and clothes to ensure their comfort and impress the Spaniards with the dignity and opulence of English royalty. On the face of it both parties strove to exceed each other's pageantry and cordiality. Beneath this icing, however, each manoeuvred and connived to win concessions at the conference table at the other's expense.[15]

Buckingham and Charles were terribly naïve about Spanish motives. However much they believed that they could turn Spanish faces smiling towards them by charm and expensive gifts, they were mistaken. Whatever they did, Spain meant to continue her support of the Empire in the war and only conclude a treaty provided England agreed not to enter it and accepted the provisions laid down by the Pope and the Spanish theologians. So that while Buckingham paraded his magnificence at Court and Charles cooed from afar at the Infanta, Olivares and Gondomar strove to convert Charles, secure his promise to repeal the penal laws, and bury the issue of the Palatinate. It was not until nearly the end of their visit that Charles and Buckingham began to suspect the Spaniards. Olivares tipped his hand during a conversation with Buckingham: 'Let us dispatch this matter out of hand and strike it up without the Pope.' Buckingham agreed and said, 'But how is it done?' Olivares replied: 'The means are very easy. It is but the conversion of the Prince, which we cannot conceive but his Highness intended upon his resolution for this journey.' When Buckingham blinked, the Count-Duke retorted: 'Then we must send to Rome [again for reconsideration of the religious articles].' It is unlikely that Olivares really believed that Charles could be converted, but he put him and Buckingham on the defensive by letting them think that the only alternative now to the collapse of negotiations was their agreement to the Spanish terms. The anxiety of King James over the safety of his boys strengthened Olivares's hand, since, as Beaulieu observed in reflection of opinion in London, 'You can imagine what a fair game those men have now that they have our Prince in their hands'. In June the English Court had bristled with optimism that the treaty would soon be concluded; by July everyone was worried about the Prince's safety.[16]

Cottington watched with increasing apprehension as Charles and Buckingham played the principal roles in the drama unfolding at Madrid. Sir Francis opposed the venture, but Buckingham took him none the less from his wife of only a week to lead the party over familiar ground to near-calamity. There had been time to write to Anne only once during the journey, from Paris, and to catch some fitful sleep between furious daily rides averaging sixty miles. In Madrid he gratefully turned over to Bristol responsibility for the Prince's safety and lodged at the embassy. Sir Francis usually accompanied Charles wherever he went, and served as his translator and amanuensis. His duties became heavier in May when Buckingham, newly created a Duke, virtually ostracised Bristol after quarrelling with him, and put Cottington on the joint committee which drew up the final terms of the treaty. The newest version of papal terms reached Madrid in late April and served as the basis of negotiation. The Pope specified that the Infanta should supervise the education of any children born of her marriage until they were twelve years old; that the Catholics in England should be permitted to substitute a new oath, written by the Pope, for the objectionable Oath of Allegiance (1606) that obliged them to renounce transubstantiation and papal supremacy in England; and that Parliament must accept the treaty in its entirety, including the religious articles.[17]

In mid-May the Duke ordered Sir Francis to make ready to leave for England. He should only await the preparation of documents on the articles for King James and the Privy Council, and yet another opinion by the Spanish theologians on the propriety of the 'mixed' marriage. On the 23rd they decided that the Infanta should remain in Spain for at least a year after her marriage; that the penal laws should be suspended during this period; and that King James, Charles and the Privy Councillors should each solemnly swear never to reimpose them. When the Spaniards delayed forwarding these documents to the embassy, Buckingham sent Cottington on his way without them. He and Gresley left Madrid on 31 May, charged to give James a full account of the conditions laid down by the Pope and the theologians.

Sir Francis reached the Court at Greenwich on 13 June and immediately conferred with the King and Secretary Conway for four hours. James responded: 'My sweet boys, your letter by Cottington hath struck me dead . . . [I beg you] to come speedily away if you can get leave and give over all treaty, and this I speak, without respect of any security they can offer you except you never look to see your old dad again.' James wrote again on the 15th, saying that if they could not rescind what they had already promised for a treaty, he would willingly accept any terms to ensure their safe return home. It may be safely assumed that Cottington told him that the situation in Madrid was critical for the Prince and for England.[18]

Sir Francis remained with the King at Greenwich as an adviser in talks with the Spanish ambassadors, Inojosa and Coloma, and kept up a regular correspondence with Charles and Buckingham. At the same time he coped with suitors who took advantage of his brief visit to secure favours from the Prince through him. He also ran errands and paid bills for friends in Spain, and took time to bring Katherine Villiers greetings of the strangest sort from her husband: the Duke, Cottington was told to say, wanted her to know that he would not touch a woman until he saw her again. Even as Cottington did these things in England, in Madrid Charles accepted on 7 July each of the Spanish proposals, provided he could marry the Infanta in September.[19]

Cottington accompanied the King to London in July and counselled him after news arrived of what Charles had promised. In concert with Secretaries Conway and Calvert, Sir Francis advised that there was now nothing to do but honour the agreement; he was also careful to point out that James alone made the decision. On 20 July, the day before setting out on progress, James took solemn oaths at Whitehall in the presence of Cottington, the Spanish ambassadors and the Privy Councillors to abide by the articles and conditions laid down in the treaty. After dinner that same day, with only the ambassadors, Sir Francis and one or two others present, James promised secretly in the Council Chamber to try to persuade Parliament to repeal the penal laws.[20]

Since he realised that he would soon have to return to Spain with copies of the oath taken by the King, Cottington rushed to finish a number of tasks. He conferred again with Inojosa, translated letters brought by Lord Andover from Spain, waited on Secretaries Calvert and Conway, and attended to Charles's finances. While his agent Stafford negotiated bills of exchange for £4,000 that the Prince had charged against them, he himself secured a loan of £1,600 to pay for expenses incurred during the hurried journey to Madrid and for gifts to Spanish courtiers.[21] He even had to bother about the care of animals sent by Buckingham from Spain – 'Four asses . . . two hees and two shees. Five camels, two hees and two shees, with a young one; and one elephant' – making sure they would be fed and stabled in St James's Park. There was a little time, too, to spend with his wife in London before Sir Francis joined the Court at Andover on 21 July. Three days later, at Hanworth House in Middlesex, Lord Carlisle gave a banquet in honour of the Spanish ambassadors and to celebrate Charles's official signing of the treaty in Madrid the next day. Cottington doubtless attended, in which case he saw the house and gardens of a property that he subsequently purchased and from which he took his title as Lord Cottington of Hanworth in 1631. Either that evening or the next morning he left for Spain.[22]

By the time Cottington reached Madrid on 5 August, Charles and Buckingham had already made plans to leave for England the next month, following the wedding. Then, almost overnight, the situation changed. Both parties to the treaty – Englishmen and Spaniards – became suspicious of the other's dissimulation. Why this happened is not entirely clear. Clashes between Buckingham and Olivares had something to do with it – 'a public professed hatred and an irreconcilable enmity' between them. Buckingham's vanity had been bruised, and by late spring he had begun to doubt the wisdom of concluding a treaty with Spain that did not guarantee the withdrawal of her garrisons from the Palatinate. As for Charles, he lost interest in the Infanta, who upon closer examination was not as desirable as his blind infatuation for her had at first led him to believe. Finally, each side accused the other of trying to convert its courtiers. Olivares sent priests to discuss theology with Charles and Buckingham, but the English had only smuggled in a few Spanish translations of their prayer-book.[23]

About mid-August 1623, shortly after Sir Francis had made his third trip in five months between London and Madrid, he fell ill and nearly died. Friends described his malady variously as ague, a fever, terciana and a *dolor de las tripas* – all general terms of little use in guessing at the nature of his sickness. Bristol called it a sharp

attack with seven or eight 'fits' followed by two relapses that pros-
trated Sir Francis for a month. Cottington is said to have feared
for his life after the usual bleedings and purges failed to help.
According to Francisco de Jesús, Cottington summoned Fray Don
Diego de la Fuente, Gondomar's confessor, to his bedside, where
this priest is said to have received him into the Church of Rome.
When he recovered, he emphatically and repeatedly denied it.

Whether or not Cottington actually became a Roman Catholic
is problematical. Newsmongers in England took his conversion to
be incontrovertibly true and chortled it as the alleged reason for
his subsequent disfavour at Court. Yet except for one letter by
Aston, who cannot be established to have been with Cottington
and Fuente in the sick-room, not a single dispatch mentions the
supposed conversion. Cottington himself had reason not to mention
it, of course, provided that he had apostasised, for in all likelihood
it would have meant the end of his career. Bristol may have kept
silent out of loyalty to his friend. But neither Charles nor Buckingham need have had any scruples about revealing the truth. As will
be shown later, there were other reasons why Cottington temporarily lost favour at Court. Afterwards he lived practically all his
life openly as an Anglican, and raised all five of his children in
that religion. Nor did he betray in the 1630s the crypto-Catholicism
that the Laudians accused him of trying to conceal, perhaps to
impugn his trustworthiness and thereby undermine his influence
in the Government, which they sought to control. The stigma of
apostasy marked Cottington throughout his public life after 1623
and does so even yet. His contemporaries snickered over it behind
his back, and Restoration Englishmen exaggerated the apocryphal
tale that he became a Catholic whenever he fell dangerously ill.
Since then pro-Parliament authors, grasping at straws to strengthen
their case against the Caroline governmental system, have likewise
maligned Cottington partly on religious grounds. It should only
be emphasised here in general that he conformed outwardly to the
Established Church, and that he did not openly embrace Catholicism
until a few years before his death in Valladolid in 1652. Only then
can it be said categorically that he was Roman Catholic.[24]

While Cottington lay near death, his masters wearied of trying
to arrange the withdrawal of Spanish troops from the Palatinate

and of the further delay in the arrival of the papal dispensation without which Philip IV would not permit his daughter to marry. Charles and Buckingham left Madrid on 29 August for Santander and England, giving Bristol a proxy for the marriage that should take place ten days after receipt of the dispensation. But at Segovia, Charles sent back new orders for Bristol: he should not execute the proxy before further instructions came from London. Thus Charles and Buckingham began to unravel the knots that bound England and her royal family to an awkward and unwanted alliance with Spain. The arrival of the Prince and Duke at Royston on 6 October cheered the Court and set off celebrations throughout the country. But Buckingham burned with anger. He believed that the Spaniards had treated him shabbily and had prevaricated shamelessly in the marriage and Palatinate questions. He took the first steps towards rupturing diplomatic relations with Spain by instructing Bristol and Aston to delay the proxy marriage set for 29 November, and by persuading the King to summon Parliament, which would surely vent its strong anti-Spanish feelings and arouse the country to war.[25]

In Madrid, Bristol sensed that his recall was imminent and that it foreboded dire consequences for England as well as for himself. Sir Francis recovered his health sufficiently by late September to undertake the journey to England in a mule litter.[26] What disturbing thoughts rumbled in his brain will never be known. How the Court would receive him he could not predict.

CHAPTER 7

Eclipse

PRINCE CHARLES and Buckingham returned to England in October 1623 in an ugly mood. They had agreed to a treaty on Spanish terms which conflicted with the political and religious axioms of a Protestant nation and failed to provide for the restoration of the Elector Palatine. Now they strove to disengage themselves and England from the obligations that they had foolishly promised to fulfil and to heap the blame for their own mistakes on others. The Spaniards had not been entirely honest and had dragged their feet during the negotiations, but Buckingham had been arrogant and contentious, so that both parties had contributed to the strained atmosphere which characterised the last two months of the talks in Madrid. In order to exculpate himself from blame in the eyes of his critics, especially in Parliament, the Duke made scapegoats of the Spaniards, maligned the Earl of Bristol and impugned the integrity of Cottington. Such casuistry eventually led to war with Spain and very nearly ruined the careers of two loyal diplomats.

Bristol and Cottington were made to pay a price for their part in the abortive negotiations, not because they had neglected their duty, but for doing precisely the opposite and at the cost of scruples and personal sacrifice. For years they had followed instructions – including Buckingham's – in trying to arrange an alliance acceptable to the Spaniards and consistent with the goals of England, Frederick and their allies. That they failed was clearly no fault of their own. Both diplomats harboured serious reservations about the treaty and on occasion voiced them privately to friends. But it was not the province of diplomats to question the policy of their Government, only to carry it out.

The decision taken in London to delay the execution of the proxy put Bristol in an impossible situation in Madrid. He weathered

D

the crisis of 29 November, the date set for the wedding, and afterwards skilfully put it off time and again by pleading that his
Government needed time to reconsider the Palatinate question.
Meanwhile he began to realise the danger of his own position. In
October he wondered aloud why Buckingham had criticised his
work during the previous summer. He wrote long letters to the
Duke, to Charles and to the Privy Council protesting his trustworthiness and loyalty and inquiring why opinions to the contrary
were being entertained at Court. He knew the answer, of course.
He had offended Buckingham, first by supporting Olivares's suggestion that the Elector's son should marry the German Emperor's
daughter as the best way of resolving the Palatinate issue, and later
by informing King James that Buckingham's insolence towards
the Spaniards was hurting the negotiations. Afterwards, even as the
Duke demanded war with Spain, Bristol tried to salvage the
alliance. James recalled him to England, received him coldly, and
ordered him confined to his estate at Sherborne in Dorset.[1]

These were worrisome weeks for Cottington as well. Talk of
his supposed apostasy continued after his return in October.
Chamberlain said that Charles and Buckingham found Sir Francis
'faulty [and they] complain and have no good opinion of him, so
that he is like to be discarded from the Prince's service . . .'.
Matthew Nicholas, the brother of future Secretary Edward Nicholas,
advised him not to bother approaching Cottington for a favour
from Prince Charles because he no longer had influence at Court.
Even playwrights capitalised on Cottington's damaged reputation.
Ben Jonson, author of the libretto of a masque entitled *The Fortunate Isles and their Union*, represented Cottington as the character
Proteus. He described Proteus as the 'father of disguise', an obvious
double entendre, and had him say towards the end of the masque:
'Yet now, great Lord of Waters and of Isles [James I], Give Proteus
leave to turn unto his wiles.' Such aspersions on Sir Francis's
integrity doubtless echoed the insinuations of Buckingham. They
helped to create an impression that Cottington was devious, not
to be trusted. This characterisation still has credence today, even
though it began as a result of his putative conversion to Catholicism,
which cannot be proven to be true.[2]

Neither Charles nor Buckingham gave any indication in the

months following his return that they blamed him for his conduct in Spain. Sir Francis continued to serve as secretary to the Prince until the death of King James, at which time he surrendered his post, not because he had offended Charles or Buckingham, but for at least two other reasons. First, there was no Prince to serve after he became the King. Second, Buckingham came to dislike Cottington and could dictate who would and would not serve in the royal Household. The Duke and the royal family initially continued to employ Cottington's services in matters relating to the interests of the Crown and secured a place for him in Parliament. Buckingham subsequently took exception to Cottington's apparent pro-Spanish bias after such an attitude became anathema at Court. The degree of Buckingham's distrust of him intensified as his repeated expressions of preference for a Spanish over a French alliance conflicted with the favourite's plan of forming an Anglo-French alliance against Spain. Cottington's opposition to this alliance reminded Buckingham in turn of his earlier criticism of the Spanish trip and of his willingness to accommodate the Spaniards when the negotiations verged on collapse. These divergent views of Buckingham and Cottington on English policy in western Europe tended to accentuate the seriousness of their personal clashes which culminated in 1625 in a quarrel in which Cottington stood up to the Duke at the cost of his security and favour at Court.[3]

Cottington resumed his usual secretarial duties after returning from Spain. Charles continued to entrust Cottington with the management of his personal finances and had him arrange for the transportation and safeguard of jewels given to Philip IV, who returned them following his refusal to withdraw his garrisons from the Palatinate. Cottington likewise continued the correspondence with Bristol and Aston on behalf of the King and Charles. In 1624, when the Spanish ambassadors in London accused Buckingham of plotting against James, he had Cottington and Conway question the Spaniards.[4]

The death of King James in 1625 worked to Cottington's disadvantage: it meant at the very least the loss of his position as secretary to the Prince. If he presumed that he would be given another place at Court, he miscalculated. Nothing could be presumed in the light of Buckingham's fickle temperament, long

memory and influence over King Charles. There is a hint that
Cottington sensed he was in some danger. On 30 March 1625, only
three days after the death of the King, he wrote to the Palatine
Princess Elizabeth saying that he no longer served her brother as
secretary. Shortly after Cottington wrote this letter, one of the
Principal Secretaries told him that his attendance at Court was no
longer required. The words crushed him – not his services, but his
attendance. He realised that only the Duke could have made such
a decision. He went to Court looking for an explanation and acci-
dentally ran into Buckingham, whom he asked what might be done
to restore confidence in him. The favourite answered that far from
ever trusting Sir Francis again, he would do all he could to ruin
him. In that case, Cottington replied more out of anger than good
sense, the Duke would oblige him by reimbursing the £800 that
he had spent in Spain on a suit of hangings for him. Buckingham
nodded and the next day it was done. Without any forewarning –
indeed, in the face of apparent cordiality towards Cottington – his
exercise of independent judgement in arguing in favour of a Spanish
alliance against the wishes of his patron had been avenged. This
seems the only explanation for Cottington's ostracism from Court.
Charles himself cannot have shared the Duke's feelings, for it was
not long before the King granted Sir Francis lands worth £400 a
year and an annuity of £200 as compensation for his loss of office.[5]

The rebuff sustained by Cottington at the hands of the second
most powerful man in England might well have disheartened a
person of less resilience. All that he had striven for during the
preceding twenty years now seemed pointless, or so his friends
believed. But he himself absorbed the crushing blow of being
eclipsed at Court without admitting that it necessarily meant the
end of his career. If beneath his well-known placidity disappointment gnawed at him, he did not show that anything bothered him.
He had made his way from the obscurity of a rural Somerset childhood through a succession of increasingly responsible offices
without the benefit of solid connections at Court, wealth, higher
education or other advantages considered essential to success in
public life. It is true that important men had pushed him along
at crucial points, but their patronage alone would have availed
Cottington little in the long run without the added impetus of his

own ability and ambition. All these factors, plus an advantageous marriage, had helped him to achieve the status he enjoyed in 1625. He had done well for a man of his background in twenty years, which was not a long time to fashion a career.

The Court had found Cottington the courtier wanting, but Cottington the clothier's son had many kindred spirits in the House of Commons. By the time he had lost the secretaryship at the age of forty-five, he had served in the Parliament of 1624 as a member for Camelford in Cornwall. His disfavour at Court did not preclude his sitting for Bossiney (Cornwall) in the 1625 Parliament. Saltash (Cornwall) returned him to the Parliament of 1628-9. In these five years Sir Francis gained experience quite different from his work in diplomacy and administration; he stood in the mainstream of national political life and felt the currents of those troubled times swirling round him. He gained some understanding of the tension existing between the supporters of the royal political and ecclesiastical policies and their critics. The Court found him particularly useful in Parliament because his expertise in Spanish affairs could be exploited at a time when England and Spain verged on war and then entered it.

In 1624 Sir Francis sat in the Commons with such North Country men as Sir Thomas Wentworth, Sir John Radcliffe, Sir Henry Slingsby, Sir Arthur Ingram and others with whom he would associate more closely in the 1630s. Speaking generally about the election of 1624, Beaulieu said that it had been hotly contested and that the Crown had had considerable difficulty overcoming objections to its nominees in different parts of the country. This probably had been the case with Cottington, whose identification with the marriage treaty negotiations and supposed apostasy could not have increased his popularity among his heavily anti-Spanish and anti-Catholic countrymen. A reason for his nomination to Parliament by Buckingham soon became apparent to Cottington. While the Duke had little trouble fanning the flames of anti-Spanish sentiment in the Commons, he still had to justify his own actions in Madrid. On 24 February he recounted to a delegation from the Commons and the Lords assembled at Whitehall what in his view had transpired there the previous summer. He did so in a way calculated to shift the blame for the dismal failure of the negotiations on to the Spaniards and whitewash himself. Three days later Sir Richard Weston reported the gist of Buckingham's remarks to the full Commons. Cottington and Secretaries Conway and Calvert assisted him. Weston did most of the talking and Cottington made occasional comments by way of elaboration and clarification. Cottington knew that Buckingham and Weston emphasised certain facts and concealed others to convey the desired impression. He kept silent except on trivial points, and at the end of Weston's speech stated that the Spaniards had contrived new articles and conditions which forced the Prince and the Duke to break off discussion and leave Madrid. In the sense that he did not tell the whole truth, he lied. Worse, he betrayed his old friend Bristol.[6]

The following week the House of Lords heard more on Spanish relations and accepted what Buckingham had told their representatives at the Whitehall meeting. The Lords gave Buckingham a vote of thanks and recommended that the treaty with Spain should be disregarded, never admitting that Charles had signed it. Meanwhile the Commons appointed a committee that included Cottington to consider what advice should be given to the Lords on the treaty and to meet with the Upper House in the Painted Chamber to draft a joint statement to the King. Although James had told Parliament earlier that he welcomed its advice on Spanish relations, he reacted to it angrily, accusing Parliament of exceeding its authority. Nevertheless, Buckingham explained away the King's harshness and saw to it that the treaty was aborted unilaterally. All the while Cottington kept his counsel to himself, tacitly approving everything that Buckingham did. Sir Francis also served on a number of committees of the Commons relating to domestic questions.[7]

Not long afterwards Cottington became involved in the investigation of Lord Bristol's conduct, instituted by Buckingham. King James himself appears not to have had anything against Bristol, but when Buckingham expected Bristol to admit to all the insinuations made against him, he insisted on being judged solely by Parliament and refused to concede that he had done anything wrong. While at home in Sherborne the following July Bristol was asked to answer a long list of questions on every aspect of his embassy. The questions had been phrased in such a way as to show his favouritism towards Spain, impugn his loyalty and stress his failure to press for the restitution of the Palatinate. He did not fall into the trap; instead, he insisted that he had only done his duty on orders from superiors and had given advice consistent with the best interests of the King.[8]

Friendship and common decency dictated that Cottington should have spoken out on Bristol's behalf, but their correspondence in the summer and autumn of 1624 suggests that Sir Francis sensed his own insecurity at Court and said nothing which Buckingham could use against him. On 1 June, Bristol told Cottington that he could not understand why Prince Charles had apparently taken offence at his conduct in Madrid and asked him to make sure that Charles was fully apprised of the facts. Cottington merely sent Bristol a brief note, advising him that the Court had decided that he should remain at Sherborne until September to give him time to reach a better understanding with Buckingham, which was another way of saying that he should admit to the charges. Meanwhile Bristol had learned with considerable misgivings about Buckingham's account of the Spanish negotiations to Parliament and Cottington's corroboration of it. Sir Francis's concern to protect his own interests at the expense of Bristol's friendship availed him nothing, for in April 1625 the Duke sent him packing from the Court. That spring he watched events from the sidelines. The stately funeral of King James occurred on a rainy day in early May. Preparations were on foot for the war with Spain. The collapse of Count Mansfeld's expedition to the Low Countries shocked the nation. Marriage by proxy at Paris had united King Charles and Princess Henrietta Maria, sister of Louis XIII. On 18 May, only a few weeks before the opening of Parliament, the vicar of St Martin-in-the-Fields, Dr Thomas Mountford, baptised the Cottingtons' child Frances, their first-born.[9]

Cottington had once more been returned to Parliament, this time by the Cornish borough of Bossiney. Sir Richard Weston had previously held this seat and used his influence as Chancellor of the Exchequer to procure it for Cottington. Thus began a relationship between these two men that was of great importance to Cottington's career and that endured until Weston's death in 1635.[10]

It was but a short walk from Charing Cross to Westminster Hall, and Cottington had no other serious responsibilities to distract his attention from debates in the morning and committee work in the afternoon. His name is mentioned only a few times in the *Journal* for 1625 and not a single speech of his, if he made any, is recorded. This should not surprise us. The Crown was in no position to expect his services, and those of a mind to question the Government's policies could not have been anxious to admit into their counsels a person reputed to have been a papist, friendly towards Spain, and recently separated from the administration. So Sir Francis stood in the shadowy middle ground, a stranger in both camps.

The apparent finality of the break between Cottington and Buckingham should have excluded him from Court for as long as the favourite controlled the administration. Surprisingly, this was not the case. Sir Francis began to employ the stealth and ingenuity of which he was capable in the most critical situations to insinuate himself back into favour. The remarkable regeneration of his career in the four years from his dismissal to his appointment to the Privy Council can be followed by piecing together odd bits of information. In these years the King, Buckingham and the Privy Council began to re-employ Sir Francis in a variety of assignments. He served the Council as an unofficial adviser on Spanish affairs. He also helped the Crown with proceedings against the Earl of Bristol. Cottington visited him in the Tower at least twice, first in July 1626 and again the following February, by which time the Earl's illness was construed as sufficient excuse to postpone indefinitely his trial in the Court of Star Chamber. Walter Montagu, with whom Cottington was negotiating a fine on behalf of the Privy Council, described him as a man 'who is indeed their [the Councillors'] mouth, and that shrewd stickler . . .', a statement which confirms that he was a skilled negotiator whom the Council trusted. He served in 1627 on a royal commission that reckoned the annual value of certain lands in the Duchy of Cornwall in answer to a petition for their lease by Thomas Carey, a Gentleman of the Bedchamber. Business for Buckingham took Cottington to South Wales for a fortnight in September of that year in connection with the disposition of the Dutch merchantman, the *Loper* of Edam, and her cargo, a share of which accrued to the Duke in his capacity as Lord High Admiral. This errand would suggest that Buckingham and Cottington frequently conferred, that they had by then become more or less reconciled.[11]

Other evidence shows that Sir Francis improved himself financially in 1627-8. He was named Keeper of Freemantle Park in the county of Southampton, which led in 1629 to his being granted by royal patent this property worth £60 annually. In June 1628 the Crown granted Cottington and Philip Palmer, his wife's cousin, jointly for life the office of Keeper of the King's Game and Wildfowl in or about Hampton Court and Hounslow Heath, which brought fees of 2s. a day and an annual allowance of 26s. for livery. Another notable indication of royal favour towards Cottington is seen in his acquisition by lease in several stages of the manor and park of Hanworth, Middlesex. Next to Fonthill Gifford in Wiltshire, which he acquired in 1632, Cottington prized Hanworth most. He proudly described the gardens at Hanworth and improvements made there in a letter to Sir Thomas Wentworth in 1629. 'My wife', he wrote, 'is the principal contriver of all this machine, who, with her clothes tucked up, and a staff in her hand, marches from place to place like an Amazon commanding an army.' She had a brick wall built around the grounds to enclose game, and a garden house with a fountain and a gallery decorated by 'the hand of a second Titian'. Over the new walks trod the 'old porter with the long beard', who collected fees from villagers who came to marvel at the grandeur. The Cottingtons lived comfortably at Hanworth, and Anne bore her third child there. At the parish church of St George, situated on the manor lands, the King, Buckingham and the Marchioness of Hamilton witnessed the baptism of Charles Cottington on 21 July 1628.[12]

The presence of the King and Buckingham leaves no doubt that Sir Francis had by that time recovered their confidence. Indeed, the year 1628 was in many ways his *annus mirabilis*. A dangerous period in his life had passed without permanent injury to his career in the Government. In the same year he had been returned once more to Parliament, this time by the Cornish borough of Saltash, located across the harbour from Plymouth. Crown candidates had found it hard going in the election, except in the close corporation boroughs where sympathetic nobles and councillors had the right of nomination. Only three Privy Councillors secured seats, and Weston, who had sat in every Parliament since 1614, did not even offer himself. Cottington encountered substantial opposition to his candidacy but prevailed in the end with help from Sir James Bagg, Vice-Admiral of North Cornwall and M.P. for Plympton, and from the borough officers of Saltash. The mayor, judging by the charge of malfeasance brought against him by the Commons, had apparently been up to something in countering the opposition to Cottington of the other M.P. for the borough, Sir Richard Buller.[13]

Cottington took little direct part in shaping the events of the Parliament of 1628-9. So far as the records reveal, he made no speeches and served on only a few committees. Whether he exerted much influence as a spokesman for the Crown is doubtful. On 20 March he was appointed to an important committee of eighty-eight members to examine records and hear testimony on elections, returns and privileges of the House. Two months later, beginning on 23 May, he served on another committee to draft a bill to confirm the old King's letters patent to Lord Bristol, whose cause the Commons took to heart as one way of thwarting Buckingham.[14]

Buckingham's assassination at Portsmouth in August set the people wondering what his death might mean to the patronage system that he had largely controlled, to the power structure at Court, and the war with Spain. Edward Osborne sensed the dangers and opportunities of the moment: 'What change this will work God knows', he wrote Wentworth, 'but I would ... you were here to play your own cards.' Cottington surely asked the same question. This much he knew from experience: Buckingham had been a man who could turn against a friend in an instant. While Sir Francis had done the nearly miraculous by regaining his favour, he could not say how the Duke might react another day under different circumstances. It seems unlikely that Buckingham would have allowed Cottington to move up in the administration or ingratiate himself with the King. With the favourite out of the way, Cottington could exploit other connections that he had made without serious opposition from any quarter.[15]

Lord Percy, writing to the Earl of Carlisle, assessed the political situation at Court following Buckingham's death: 'It is thought the

Treasurer [Weston] will have the greatest power with the King, then consequently the Popish faction [read 'pro-Spanish'] will be much exalted (for he will bring in Arundel, Bristol, and Sir Francis Cottington his great friend) without they have great resistance.' Buckingham so dominated the power structure that it took some time after his death for anybody else to begin to approach the level of authority which he had exercised; in fact, nobody ever could match it for the remainder of the reign. A distinction can be made between royal favour and political importance by reason of high office. The Earl of Carlisle, Groom of the Stole in 1631-6, never held an important office and yet was recognised as one of the most influential men at Court. William Laud, Bishop of London and a Privy Councillor, did not become Archbishop of Canterbury until 1633, but his influence over Charles was considerable before Buckingham's death and grew steadily until he became predominant in Charles's counsels by the middle of the decade. Laud helped Charles over a difficult period of grief following the assassination and, because of the virtual abdication of power by Archbishop Abbot, he dominated the Church long before he became its constitutional head; thus he, next to Weston, shaped policy most. Weston had risen rapidly, and in 1628 became Lord Treasurer and one of the commissioners administering the office of Lord High Admiral. He did not step out of line so long as Buckingham lived, and it took some time before he could organise anything like his own clique on the Privy Council. It was even longer before Weston, Cottington and their supporters began to conflict openly with the Laudians.[16]

Buckingham's death on the one hand and the friendship of Weston and Cottington on the other suggest why the second half of his *annus mirabilis* proved no less exciting for Sir Francis. Weston wanted him for his Chancellor of the Exchequer, but first had to clear several office-holders out of the way, including the incumbent of that office, Lord Newburgh, who was persuaded to accept the Chancellorship of the Duchy of Lancaster. On 30 March 1629 King Charles authorised a grant to Cottington of the offices of Chancellor and Under-Treasurer of the Exchequer for life, apparently without his having to pay for them.[17] About five months earlier, on 12 November, Cottington had been sworn a Privy Councillor. If the excitement of the moment when he took his solemn oath caused him to recite the words unthinkingly, he had ample reason in the next two decades to reflect upon what it had cost him to speak his mind fully in accordance with his conscience and to defend the Crown against enemies at home and abroad. For the present, however, he took pleasure in his success, all arranged by Weston, who strengthened himself more than he imagined by acquiring the assistance of a firm ally with an artful tongue, a quick mind and administrative talent. The importance of this connection, later matched by another between Laud and Wentworth, was not lost on contemporaries.[18]

Cottington's appointment to the Council increased the number of Councillors in the Commons to four during the second session of Parliament which convened in January 1629. He took a somewhat more active part in the business of this session because of his position in the Government and his membership on the Council Committee for Trade. He was particularly involved in negotiations between the Crown and the Commons over illegal trade with Spain in war-time. A committee of the House on which Cottington sat learned that the Crown had licensed certain merchants to transport foodstuffs to Spain, and the House charged Cottington to investigate. Despite the embarrassment of the Government in admitting to such underhand dealings with the enemy, he reported back on 29 January. He said that at least three ships bound for Spain carried cargoes of grain and other provisions, but added that the King permitted this trade so as to realise a profit of £100,000. Cottington neither tried to apologise for the Crown's action nor criticised the Commons for questioning this apparently illicit commerce. Rather, he concluded: 'how much of it [the profit] will advance the King in these times of necessity I leave it to this House to consider'. Was this a back-handed way of reminding the Commons that it had neither adequately supported the war effort nor authorised the King's collection of tonnage and poundage?[19]

If that is what Cottington meant, he struck a nerve. The decline of English foreign trade and the depredation of pirates since the onset of the war worried both the Crown and the Commons, since Charles tried to increase revenue in part by levying tonnage and poundage without the consent of Parliament and prosecuted merchants caught evading the duties. This is a complicated story that strained relations between Parliament and the Crown and culminated at the end of March in the adoption of resolutions which infuriated the King. He believed that he had the right to collect the duties whether or not Parliament approved, for that was his prerogative. On the other hand, the Commons saw no difference between an unparliamentary levy of impositions, supposedly illegal since the King's assent to the Petition of Right, and an unparliamentary levy of tonnage and poundage. The Commons therefore instructed Cottington and others to remind the Barons of the Exchequer of the fact. The House based its argument partly on the grounds that one of the merchants whose goods had been confiscated for not paying duties, John Rolle, was an M.P. and had tried to recover them by replevin. The Commons contended that the privileges of M.P.s extended to their property as well as to their persons. Charles rejected the argument and assumed personal responsibility for the confiscation of goods, thereby relieving Custom House officers and Customs Farmers of persistent pressure brought by the Commons through interrogation. But the Commons was unable to resolve this issue because the King dissolved Parliament and afterwards did as he pleased.[20]

The dissolution of Parliament in March 1629 coincided with the end of Cottington's five years as an M.P., during which time he had recovered almost unbelievably from the near-calamity of dismissal from Court and gone on to become a Privy Councillor and Chancellor of the Exchequer. At the age of fifty he had achieved the status and financial security that he had dreamed of twenty-five years earlier upon first entering royal service. After all this time his country was still entangled disadvantageously with Spain and faced a situation not unlike that which obtained in 1603 – involvement in a war that had greatly increased expenditure and hurt commerce at home and abroad. The two overriding and inter-related problems of war and finance required immediate attention in 1629. Cottington soon became intimately connected with the resolution of both problems.

CHAPTER 8

Ambassador Extraordinary

THE Crown had gone increasingly into debt in the early seventeenth century, and the irregular and rather lame efforts to reduce
costs and raise revenue had not been successful.[1] King Charles
inherited a large debt and saw it rise sharply during the first few
years of his reign, to a considerable extent because of the French
and Spanish wars that also hurt revenue from foreign commerce.
With no immediate prospect of the authorisation of extraordinary
taxes following the dissolution of Parliament in 1629, and with
much of the country in the grip of a depression, there was a clear
need to cut expenditure. One obvious and not altogether unpopular
means of doing so was to end the wars with all deliberate speed.
The French war of 1627-9, a misadventure from first to last, was
concluded by the Treaty of Susa.

Making peace with Spain proved to be a more delicate task to
which Sir Francis Cottington devoted himself for nearly two years.
A surge of anti-Spanish sentiment had engulfed the nation and
magnified the seriousness of the issues that divided the belligerents.
Moreover, the more strenuous English Protestants, who identified
their interests with those of co-religionists on the Continent in
the Thirty Years War, discouraged talk of peace. So too, for
strategic reasons, did the diplomats in London from the United
Provinces, France and Venice attempt to prevent its realisation.

The peacemakers prevailed in the end because the Spaniards
wanted peace as much as most Englishmen. Spain had succeeded
so well in isolating England from direct military involvement on
the Continent since 1605 that war with her might have been
averted twenty years later but for the insistence of Buckingham
and the reluctant compliance of King James. Both countries soon
realised that they had made a mistake. Indeed, early in the war

Buckingham began to make peace overtures through his agent in Brussels, Balthazer Gerbier. There Archduchess Isabella, sister of Philip III, employed Peter Paul Rubens as her unofficial liaison with England. Rubens and Gerbier, both artist-diplomats from Antwerp, conferred intermittently about peace. In January 1627 Gerbier proposed on Buckingham's behalf that England, Spain, Denmark and the United Provinces should make a general truce, but the suggestion failed when the Savoyard Abbé Scaglia persuaded Isabella that the English and French intended to ally against Spain. This was a remote possibility, of course, but that and other circumstances delayed peace for almost three years. Philip IV rightly saw in Buckingham his greatest enemy in England, feared an Anglo-French military alliance, and hoped to discourage further English support of the Dutch against whom he still warred. The assassination of Buckingham and peace with France in the following year increased the chances of ending the Spanish war.[2]

Neither Spain nor England had been involved officially in the Gerbier–Rubens talks. On the eve of his death in August 1628, Buckingham was making plans at Portsmouth to lead an expedition to La Rochelle and continue on with Cottington to Spain. A month earlier the Spanish Government decided to promote negotiations openly, and summoned Rubens to Madrid for consultation. He and Endymion Porter, who arrived about the same time in September, confirmed England's eagerness to discuss peace. At this Rubens was sent to England in April 1629 to arrange a truce preliminary to an exchange of ambassadors.[3]

Philip IV made a felicitous choice in Rubens, whom King Charles admired as a painter and whom Cottington had met long before in Spain. The mutual admiration between these men eased discussion of such hard realities as the exclusion of Frederick from the Palatinate, the possibility of including the Dutch in the peace settlement, and the full acceptance of English commercial privileges under the old treaty of 1604. The familiarity of Cottington and Rubens with Spanish culture, recalled in exchanges of anecdotes and pleasantries, helped them to work closely for several months and reach an understanding.[4]

Rubens reached London on 6 June and lodged with his friend Gerbier, who had retired from diplomacy following Buckingham's death. Charles summoned Rubens to Greenwich and immediately began to specify the essentials of a peace treaty, even though the agent insisted that he had no authority to discuss it. Honour, faith and conscience dictated that the treaty should settle the Palatinate question, Charles told Rubens, but since Spanish forces occupied only part of the Electorate, he would be satisfied if they alone were withdrawn and the rest of the treaty were based on the terms of the Treaty of London. When Rubens again reminded Charles that he had come to arrange a truce and nothing more, the conference ended in confusion and mutual dissatisfaction.

By this time the King had appointed Cottington, Portland, Carleton (now Viscount Dorchester) and William Herbert, Earl of Pembroke his peace commissioners. In the week following the conference at Greenwich, they and Rubens exchanged views at the Lord Treasurer's house in London. Rubens told them that the King seemed so surly in raising questions beyond his own authority to resolve that it might be best for him to leave at once rather than jeopardise the peace. But Portland and Cottington assured Rubens that Charles had spoken out of enthusiasm for peace and without understanding the proper way of resolving differences through patient negotiation. Indeed, they told the agent that England's acceptance of terms which would restore only part of the Palatinate would forfeit any claim Frederick had to the rest of it. On hearing this, Rubens became even more disillusioned and very nearly left London there and then.[5]

It was not only the King's attitude and the differences between him and his peace commissioners that worried Rubens; several Privy Councillors wished to continue the war and favoured a French alliance. The French Ambassador, Châteauneuf, no sooner reached London than he undertook to capitalise on such sentiments to sabotage peace. Rubens learned of his intentions from the Marquis de Mirabel and was kept abreast by Cottington of the talks between Châteauneuf and the Earl of Holland, one of the anti-Spanish spokesmen in the Government. When the Councillors learned that Charles was willing to accept the partial restitution of the Palatinate, the anti-Spanish faction unjustly reprimanded Cottington. These Councillors warned that accepting such terms was precisely the sort of compromise Spain craved, because it would ease her military obligations without forcing her German and Bavarian allies to surrender any ground. They need not have been alarmed, however; the Venetian ambassador reported from Madrid that Philip IV desired peace so desperately that he would willingly pay a heavy price for it.[6]

Charles had already decided in late June to send Cottington to Spain as ambassador extraordinary. The King understandably chose Sir Francis over others including Aston and Carlisle: Cottington was not only the most experienced diplomat in high office, he was also the strongest exponent of peace on the Privy Council. Moreover, he had been intimately involved for two decades with Anglo-Spanish commerce and the deliberations over the Palatinate, subjects which would have to be renegotiated for the new treaty. He did not wish to go, however. Long service in Spain had taught him that concessions might be extracted from the Spaniards only after the most exacting negotiations, regardless of their stated intentions.[7]

Cottington had other reasons for not going to Spain. First, he worried whether Portland could effectively handle negotiations with Plenipotentiary Don Carlos Coloma in England; Rubens concurred that the English phase of the talks might collapse without Cottington's presence, so dependent was Portland on his judgement. Second, Cottington had recently accepted the most challenging position of his career. As Chancellor of the Exchequer he was preoccupied with demanding problems of state and did not wish to be interrupted, and he was actively promoting his own commercial and landed interests. He felt that he needed time to make a decent start in his new duties. Politics had to be considered too; his place in the still fluid power configuration at Court was by no means secured. He appreciated that failure to arrange a favourable treaty, or returning home without one, might well work to his disadvantage. Finally, he thought it a bad bargain to exchange a year or more in Spain for the pleasure he enjoyed with his family in England. He worked exceedingly hard, but he also lived well. He entertained so generously at Hanworth that Rubens, who had enjoyed the comforts of the aristocracy while decorating the churches and palaces of European capitals, was astonished by Cottington's lavish style of life.[8]

None of these considerations altered the decision that Cottington should leave on schedule in August. Then complications arose. The firmest anti-Spanish Councillors unwittingly played into the hands of Olivares, who would have preferred to deal with a weaker man such as Aston, by seeking to curb Cottington's authority. They thought to further their own views on a treaty by having the Earl of Rutland, Buckingham's father-in-law, and Sir Henry Marten, Dean of the Arches, accompany Cottington as advisers on German and legal affairs. Rubens reasoned that Carlisle made this suggestion knowing that Rutland would be rejected, thereby leaving the way open to go himself as ambassador. Portland adroitly side-stepped it by assuring his colleagues deceitfully that Cottington would not try to settle the Palatinate until after the treaty had been signed.[9]

Cottington and his party finally left London on 26 October and a week later boarded the *Dreadnought* at Portsmouth. She and the merchantman *Lion's Whelp* slipped out with the tide on 5 November but were forced that night into Falmouth by a storm. While riding it out, the ships were fired upon harmlessly by the garrison of a hilltop castle who mistook their flags for the enemy's. On resuming the voyage, the ships encountered such heavy weather that they did not reach Lisbon until 5 December. Cottington's aide, Sir William Gardiner, was amazed at how joyfully the townspeople received the ambassador. It was evident that the Portuguese wanted peace. Forgetting their natural reserve on seeing Cottington's coach wind through Lisbon's crooked streets, the women threw off their veils, ran beside it shouting words of welcome, rang bells and kissed his outstretched hands. Until 17 December, when he left the city, the commonalty toasted his health, England and the traditional friendship between her and Portugal.[10]

Gardiner was able to assess the impact of the war on Lisbon by comparing its economy in 1629 with his recollection of it eighteen years earlier, when he had accompanied Digby. In 1611 he had seen warehouses packed with sugar, spices and other commodities from India, the East Indies and America. But in 1629 the storehouses and cellars of merchants contained only poor wines from the region. Formerly wealthy businessmen now were either reduced to selling coarse sugars and wild Brazilian tobacco or had gone bankrupt.

The captains of four English merchantmen recently arrived at Lisbon could locate only enough good merchandise to fill one ship on the return voyage.[11]

Since Cottington knew that Philip IV had left Madrid with his sister for Saragossa on the first leg of her journey to Hungary, he could take his time covering the hundreds of miles to the capital. On reaching it on New Year's Day, tired and dirty, he avoided a party of courtiers led by Olivares who had ridden out to meet him, and slipped into the city after dark. But he had been seen, and within half an hour the Count-Duke whisked him off to the royal palace and kept him up talking until past midnight.

The following afternoon Sir Francis had audience with his old adversary, King Philip, under somewhat more favourable circumstances than in former years. So many courtiers attended the ceremony that it took Cottington a quarter of an hour to make his way from the back of the hall to the dais. Thus began a succession of royal audiences and meetings with the peace commissioners – Olivares, the Duke of Oñate and the King's confessor – that kept Cottington busy for thirteen months. His reception, the enthusiasm of the crowds and his entertainment at Madrid all bespoke the strong sentiment for peace and set the tone for the generally harmonious negotiations which ensued.[12]

King Charles had instructed Sir Francis to settle a broad range of issues. He should first determine whether Spain genuinely wanted peace and, if so, write a treaty containing the commercial provisions of the aborted Treaty of London. He should also bargain for the restoration of the Palatinate with any interested parties, whether Spaniards, Germans or Bavarians, and help to resolve any other problems relating to Anglo-Spanish relations, the pacification of Europe and the Dutch war. His superiors trusted him and proved it by intruding hardly at all in his deliberations. He in turn kept them fully informed and remained scrupulously within the scope of his authority so as not to be blamed later for negligence.[13]

Although the satisfaction of English goals depended ultimately on a solution of the German problem, which Cottington hoped to make a formal part of the treaty, his early discussions with the peace commissioners confirmed his fears that Spain would consider the issue only after peace had been concluded, and then only with the consent of her allies. Olivares wasted no time in telling Cottington that difficulties would arise if England persisted in pressing for general peace in western Europe as a prerequisite of a treaty. He answered that his instructions required him to conclude a treaty within the context of the Palatinate, and that no true understanding could be reached between their countries unless Spain persuaded the Empire and Bavaria to withdraw from the Palatinate and she herself came to terms with the United Provinces. King Charles was pleased by Cottington's progress, because he had skilfully forced the Spaniards to open discussion of the Palatinate and the Dutch war. He told his ambassador to remain at his post, assess the situation in a few weeks, and make up his own mind whether to stay or leave. But Charles became so anxious by April to conclude the treaty that he ordered Sir Francis to remain until King Philip answered two questions: (1) Would Philip try to persuade the Imperial Diet to evacuate German and Bavarian troops from the Palatinate, thereby showing that Spain genuinely wanted peace? (2) Would Philip permit England to mediate a truce between Spain and the United Provinces?[14]

These instructions had been sent to Cottington in reply to his dispatch of 3 March in which he reported the unwillingness of the Duke of Bavaria and the Emperor to send representatives to Madrid for joint talks on the Palatinate. Since Cottington had gone to Spain on the understanding that he should refuse to sign a treaty unless Spain agreed to withdraw her troops, he felt that he should leave immediately. The refusal of the Germans and Bavarians to send peace commissioners reinforced his suspicion that the Spaniards had discouraged their participation so as to prolong the war and at the same time side-step the attendant issue of Frederick's restoration.[15]

About mid-April he received ill news from Endymion Porter and Dorchester. In December 1629 Anne Cottington and her three children had moved from Hanworth to their house near Charing Cross in crowded London. With the approach of spring, plague visited the city. Two of the children, Elizabeth and Frances, aged four and five years, died of it in early March, and the third, Charles, very nearly did. The only surviving Cottington letter for the month following the news of his children's deaths is a request to Porter to do what he could to help Anne. Stricken with sorrow, Sir Francis temporarily suspended negotiations and received the condolences of the Court at an audience with King Philip. Characteristically, Cottington soon recovered his equanimity. Meanwhile Sir Robert Anstruther, English resident in Denmark, and Sir Henry Vane, Comptroller of the Household, had been sent to Vienna and The Hague for consultations with the Habsburgs and the Dutch.[16]

On the basis of new instructions[17] Sir Francis concluded discussion on the thirty-one articles in about five weeks, despite the fact that the Spaniards raised new questions and threatened to amend articles that had been more or less resolved. English trade with the West Indies set everyone wrangling, and they also quarrelled over fixing a date from which prizes taken at sea by both belligerents could be kept without paying compensation. The Spaniards wanted restitution of prizes made retroactive to the beginning of the war, but Cottington refused in part because he could not see how his Government could compel privateers to whom it had given letters of marque to return ships and cargoes captured in war-time. In the end both sides agreed to leave the date to the two Kings.

Other contentious issues likewise lengthened the negotiations. One involved the right of ships of one nation to refuge and protection in the ports of the other. Cottington readily conceded this point while making sure that it was worded in such a way that England was not put in a position of helping Spanish ships at the expense of those of the Dutch. Another question arose over the imposition of inordinately high customs duties charged upon English, Scottish and Irish exporters of Spanish wine, oil, fruit, tobacco and hops. Cottington thought the duties excessive, since exporters from other nations not protected by the treaty were charged the same rates. He therefore asked that the English merchants be given preferential rates as guaranteed in the old treaty and since discontinued. But the Spaniards were disinclined to lower the tax because the English Government required all foreign merchants, including Spaniards, to pay double the duties charged upon its own nationals. When neither party accepted the proposals of the other, King Philip ruled not to raise duties on English exports, and set

them at about 30 per cent of the assessed value of the goods. English
merchants could recover their money provided they transported
the merchandise directly to ports in England or the Spanish
Netherlands.[18]

Olivares expected Cottington to sign the treaty that was completed
in mid-August, but he refused. Such a matter was too important
to decide for himself at the risk of offending King Charles. On 25
August a courier left for England with a copy of the treaty, Cottington's request that a ship be sent promptly to fetch him, and his
recommendation that Sir Arthur Hopton be appointed agent in
Spain until the arrival of a new ambassador. This worried Olivares,
who feared, as in fact happened, that the Privy Council and Charles
would amend the articles. They studied them on 7 September at
Wanstead, concluded that certain ones weakened English commercial privileges guaranteed in the old treaty, and sent Cottington
back to the conference table for several weeks more. He signed the
treaty on 5 November and arranged that Philip and Charles should
take oaths to abide by it on the same day, 7 November, in London
and Madrid.[19]

Cottington understandably felt satisfaction in successfully ful-
filling his assignment, and boasted of it. 'Ask the bearer' of this
letter, he bragged to Wentworth, President of the Council of the
North, 'how I rode to the palace the day of the oath, and then tell
me when I come home if the President of York used to make such
entries and sit with kings under the cloth of state.' His vanity may
perhaps be forgiven under the circumstances. There is no gain-
saying that he had done well to extract a few concessions from the
Spaniards. How much was there really new in the treaty, however?
On comparison, the treaties of 1604 and 1630 look much alike; in
some instances the articles are nearly identical.[20]

S. R. Gardiner saw little difference in the two treaties and implied
that Cottington only managed to accommodate his Government's
minimal goals in making peace.[21] Is this entirely fair? Does such a
comparison take into account dissimilarities in the climate of international affairs in 1629-30 as against 1604? Although the Elizabethan
war had ended in something of a stalemate, the English had won
some victories which allowed them to bargain from a position of
considerable strength. But Cottington had no victories to flaunt at

a humiliated adversary in 1630. Thousands of English seamen had died; nearly three hundred English merchantmen were lost to privateers; expeditions to the Low Countries and Cadiz had been failures; and serious damage to the domestic economy of East Anglia and to the export trade, especially in the new draperies, had widened the effects of the depression. Moreover, the tripartite occupation of the Palatinate, the complications generated by the Thirty Years War, the refusal of the Germans and Bavarians to co-operate with Spain and England, the continuing struggle by the Dutch, and forces at work in England to sabotage peace greatly complicated Cottington's task. In addition, although Spain welcomed peace in 1630 as fervently as she did in 1604, she did so for different reasons. She had greater military and financial obligations in 1630, even though she worried a good deal more about the capabilities of the English navy at the end of Elizabeth's reign. So the situation overall was more complicated in 1630 than in 1604. It is true that the new treaty did not settle the Palatinate question or effect a truce between Spain and the United Provinces, as Cottington and Charles had hoped. The question is, could any Englishman have resolved these issues in view of the unwillingness of the Government to employ military force sufficient to achieve its goals, the Crown's financial straits which crippled the war effort, and the righteous indignation of the Dutch? All things considered, Cottington's work in 1629-30 merits somewhat more commendation, or at least recognition, as a genuine diplomatic achievement than Gardiner and others have admitted.

King Charles officially revoked Cottington's commission as ambassador extraordinary on 27 September, and sent two ships to bring him and his party home. Everyone expected him by Christmas, but an unexpected development delayed his departure by two months. Whether England or Spain first proposed that they conclude a military alliance against the United Provinces is unclear. In the previous May Charles had instructed Cottington to drop the hint that England might be receptive to such an idea as a way of forcing the Dutch to come to terms with Spain. He may also have believed the suggestion helpful to Cottington in persuading the Spaniards to withdraw their garrisons from the Palatinate. No one gave it much thought until Olivares brought it up again in December.

After only a few conferences the secret treaty was drafted and signed by Cottington on 2 January 1631. The offensive and defensive alliance obliged the signatories to invade the United Provinces jointly and re-subject them to Spanish rule. England promised to pay three-quarters of the cost of the war. Spain promised to pay England 100,000 crowns a month so long as the war lasted and cede the island of Zeeland to her, provided King Charles granted its Roman Catholics religious liberty and continued to fight until the Dutch capitulated. For reasons best explained later, the alliance was never implemented.[22]

His work done, Cottington's train left Madrid in the depths of a Castilian winter for Cadiz, where the *Convertine* and the tenth *Lion's Whelp* awaited them. They sailed on 22 February and saw the familiar quays and warehouses of Portsmouth eleven days later. The accomplished man of fifty-two could think of little else but his family, which plague had reduced by half. He saw Anne again, and the graves of little Elizabeth and Frances. Soon he was back at the Exchequer and in the Council Chamber, attending to business as usual. Gradually the memory of his lost children and of the nation he had just left, he thought for ever, faded.[23]

CHAPTER 9

Baron Cottington of Hanworth

THE return of Sir Francis Cottington to London in March 1631, after nearly seventeen months abroad, stirred the imagination of his countrymen. They welcomed the news of the treaty that he had skilfully concluded with an old adversary, at a time when spirits were damped by plague, food shortages and high prices. King Charles, merchants and financiers greeted him all the more enthusiastically for having also made a financial arrangement with King Philip IV that helped the Crown and its creditors through a period of fiscal stringency, continued to increase royal revenue for the remainder of the decade and encouraged trade with Spain. Cottington had passed through the streets of London to the Tower followed by twenty cartloads of silver bullion. This bullion, which one reliable source valued at £100,000 and another at 200,000 crowns, was the larger part of an initial shipment worth about 500,000 ducats that Spain permitted England to import for partial transhipment to the Spanish Netherlands to help finance the Dutch war. Cottington had arranged that a third of this shipment, and a third of all subsequent shipments of bullion, could be minted into English money and paid for through bills of exchange drawn on Antwerp.[1]

This benefited both England and Spain. Under the old Spanish system of bullion transfer to the Low Countries, Genoese financiers had transported the silver in their own or in Portuguese ships, which Dutch or other privateers readily attacked. The new system afforded greater protection for the bullion in heavily armed English merchantmen that privateers were less likely to attack in the English Channel near the English coast. English merchants and financiers gained an immediate advantage through wider opportunities for trade and manipulation of money. An example of how

the English transportation of Spanish treasure benefited businessmen can be seen in the case of the East India Company, an exporter
of large amounts of bullion and specie. The Company no longer
had difficulty procuring Spanish reals for export trade payments,
since reals could readily be purchased in the London money market
that was developing into a centre of international exchange. The
Crown also profited in at least two ways: it minted silver coins in
sufficient quantity to ease the shortage of specie in circulation, and
the Crown increased its revenue from seigniorage by thousands
of pounds a year. On the other hand, the flow of so much new
money into the economy further stimulated the inflation that had
been eroding the real value of money and raising prices for most
of the century.[2]

Cottington had even greater reason to rejoice in the successful
completion of his Spanish embassy. King Charles created him
Baron Cottington of Hanworth on Sunday, 10 July 1631, in the
main hall of the Queen's House, Greenwich, which Inigo Jones
had recently designed along Italianate lines.[3] The ennoblement of
Cottington was the major triumph of his life; from his humble
beginning in a Somerset family of yeomen and master-craftsmen
he had pulled himself up by his boot-straps to a position in society
attained by fewer than four hundred persons in the nation. His
elevation also inaugurated the most active decade of his public life.
Until the death of Weston in 1635 Lord Cottington managed to
sustain, even to raise, the level of political influence that he had
built up since the assassination of Buckingham. Afterwards, when
he gradually gave ground to the Laudians, he remained one of the
King's closest advisers on finance and foreign affairs. His admission
to the baronage therefore signified not only a reward for achievements and services, but opened doors to political and financial
opportunities of which he took full advantage.

Cottington was already well on his way to becoming a wealthy
man. He knew as well as others with a good head for business
that in their inflationary economy it was a sound and profitable
investment to acquire land. He had purchased considerable property
before assuming high office, including Hanworth Manor and smaller
parcels of land, such as the park and woods of Freemantle in Hampshire and Blueberry in Berkshire. In 1630 he bought a share of

unspecified lands in Derbyshire, Leicestershire, Staffordshire and Shropshire when the owners, John and Philip Draycott, compounded with the Crown for recusancy. Cottington spent a great deal of money on land in 1631, undoubtedly in consequence of his financial windfalls in this lucrative year. The Crown reimbursed him for extraordinary expenses of £3,838 18s. that he had incurred during the Spanish embassy. He reportedly profited by 50,000 ducats (say £12,500) from his percentage of the merchandise traded in Portugal by the London merchants who accompanied him, and from one or two other smaller commercial ventures there. King Philip made him a present of silver gilt worth 1,000 crowns. In October the Crown discharged Cottington and Stafford of their liability for a debt of £50,027, which they had 'taken up and disbursed' in 1623 during Charles's trip to Spain. Cottington had raised most of the money on his own credit and loaned the Prince of Wales the rest of it. Instead of taking repayment in cash, he had the debt applied towards part of the purchase price of his new estate of Fonthill Gifford in Wiltshire.[4]

To these moneys Lord Cottington added the income from his properties, for which there are no figures, and from his wife's jointure of £500 a year from Brett lands in Kent. He also had fees from lesser offices, such as the Keepership at Hampton Court and Hounslow Heath, and a half share with Weston of the farm of fines on licences and recoveries out of Chancery. His principal offices of Chancellor of the Exchequer and Under-Treasurer brought him more in salary and fees, although the extant documents do not reveal how much. In 1627, as Chancellor of the Exchequer, Weston had received an annual salary of forty marks plus a livery allowance of £12 6s. 4d., while the Under-Treasurership carried a basic fee of £173 6s. 8d. in addition to £4 6s. 8d. for livery. Of course, the fee of any higher office in the Government bore little relationship to the amount it actually brought office-holders in fees and gratuities. Finally, his work in royal finance afforded Cottington access to information on potentially profitable investments, such as the availability of Crown lands for sale or lease. A man in his position had no trouble getting credit at favourable interest rates with which to speculate.[5]

All this goes to show why Lord Cottington had the means to

purchase lands or interests in them in the 1630s. In October 1631 he bought for £3,500 the property variously called Brewham Lodge, Braham and Brewcombe Walk, which was situated in Sellwood Forest near Bruton, Somerset, close to his ancestral home. In the same year Cottington acquired lands and tenements in the manor of Battle, described as part of 'the meadows at Reading' in Berkshire. In 1632, perhaps with the 'gift' of £2,000 which he had received from an unnamed source in August, he paid £1,400 for a lease of twenty-one years of Feltham Rectory and Parsonage that lay to the south of the main road from Hounslow to Staines, near Hanworth. With the lease went the right of patronage to St George's Church, its glebe lands, tithes and emoluments. To this property Cottington soon added a farm called Haubergers, near Feltham. The acquisition of Ashell's Wood in Wiltshire, including part of the manor of Tisbury and some land in neighbouring Dorset that had formerly belonged to a knight convicted of a felony, is an example of how Cottington increased his holdings through information gained in the course of his work at the Exchequer. His interest in speculation in land is seen in his purchase of 145 acres of drained fenland in south-eastern Lincolnshire from a syndicate headed by the Earl of Lindsey and Sir William Killigrew. Two of his agents, Lawrence Squibb and Anthony Manning, arranged not long afterwards to buy for Cottington an additional 60 acres of fenland from Sir Anthony Thomas and John Norsopp. He profited handsomely from these lands: in 1639 he was renting part of his fenland for 8s. an acre, a shilling more than the other owners were getting for comparable land in the same district.[6]

Cottington's most prized possession was the mansion and park of Fonthill Gifford, near Tisbury in south-western Wiltshire, which he acquired from the Crown in 1632. The rich ploughland and forest of Fonthill had sustained its inhabitants since the days of the Conqueror, whose man, Berenger, held the manor then called Fontel. The Giffards had resided there from the early thirteenth century until Reginald de West took possession two centuries later. The 2nd Earl of Castlehaven had purchased Fonthill Gifford in 1611; twenty years later he was tried by the House of Lords and executed for gross sexual offences. For his felony he forfeited his lands; the Crown disposed of Fonthill to Cottington. Three houses stood there since the early seventeenth century, the first of which was destroyed by fire. The second mansion, called Fonthill *redivivus*, is said to have been partly reconstructed by Cottington. It too was gutted in 1755, some ten years after Lord Cottington's great grand-nephew, Francis, sold it to William Beckford, later Lord Mayor of London.[7]

One visitor, the Rev. George Garrard, who stayed with Cottington at Fonthill in September 1637, described the estate and some improvements recently made to it:

> It is a noble place both for seate, and all things about it, downs, pasture, arable [land], woods, water, partridge, pheasant, fish, a good house of frieze [coarse] stone; much better by some additions he [Cottington] hath newly made to it; for he hath built a stable of stone, the 3rd [finest] in England, Petworth and Burleigh on the hill only exceed it; also a kitchen which is fairer and more convenient than any I have seen in England anywhere, £2000 [annual income from the] land he hath about it; and while I was there his park wall of square white stone, a dry wall, only lopped at the top was finished, which cost him setting up £600 a mile, but it is but 3 miles about. . . . He lived then like a great don of Spain; and I was used as a grandee by him, though I am one of his most humble servants.[8]

Lord Cottington enjoyed staying at Fonthill more than anything, but it was a hundred miles or so from London, a long trip for a middle-aged man whose responsibilities tied him down almost continuously. When he did visit the estate, as in 1632-3 and 1637, he could only afford to stay for a few days at a time. Upon sur-rendering office in May 1641, he lived at Fonthill Gifford for more than a year before joining King Charles at Oxford.[9]

Garrard also emphasised that Fonthill was 'the finest hawking place in England, and [had] a wonderful store of partridge . . .', in which Cottington took particular delight, for he had a passion for hawking. He had taken it up as a boy at Godminster and regularly enjoyed it afterwards, both in Spain and England. The Restoration antiquarian, John Aubrey, told how in Spain Cottington always consulted shepherds before going into the fields to learn whether it would rain, and when to expect the mists to rise.[10] He shared a passion for field sports with Englishmen of all classes in his day, when vast open stretches of virgin country lured them after game. Wentworth liked to go hawking as much as Cottington, and they teased each other about it. In November 1633 Wentworth commiserated with his friend in having to leave Fonthill unexpectedly to attend to urgent business in London, and complained about having to teach sparrow-hawks to fly at blackbirds for lack of partridges around Dublin. Weston once remarked that Cottington counted falconry as 'more weighty' than public affairs. No outdoors man himself, Weston was annoyed with his lieutenant because he had gone to inspect Fonthill when he should have stayed at his desk. The remark was unkind; Cottington probably worked harder than all the other Privy Councillors with the exception of Laud.

The country always had greater appeal for Cottington than busy London. He took pride in his estates and spent money freely on improvements, mostly at Hanworth and Fonthill Gifford. He prized his aviary of hawks and boasted of them to friends. 'I have certainly the best hawks . . . in England,' he told Wentworth, 'but no time to see them. . . .' When the Lord Deputy bragged that nearly two hundred riders had accompanied him on a hunt outside Dublin, Cottington answered: 'I'll tell you, when I was last in Wiltshire, there were so many gentlemen attended me into the field, as hath made my Lord Chamberlain leave chasing, and courted me ever since.' It was not often that he could upstage the Earl of Pembroke and Montgomery, his near-neighbour at Wilton, and an enthusiastic huntsman whose sport was riding to deerhounds.[11]

For all the pleasure he derived from his estates, Cottington was by no means uninterested in the income they provided. He continued to add to his holdings after acquiring Fonthill in 1632, but the surviving records of his purchases and leases are scanty. Near the end of his life, in 1650, the Derby House Committee appointed commissioners to reckon the annual value of his sequestered estates, but they failed to take into account property which had been alienated in other ways during the previous decade. They estimated that his former lands in Middlesex, Kent, Berkshire, Hampshire, Wiltshire and Somerset returned £2,452 in gross rent, which is a good deal below the mean income from rent worked out by the historian of the Elizabethan and early Stuart peerage for seventy-three new nobles for the year 1641. If Cottington did not rank among the wealthier landowners, neither was he one of the poorer ones; his income was probably in excess of £3,000 annually by the late 1630s, before he disposed of several properties.[12]

Cottington leased or purchased property avidly for the remainder of the decade. The lease of Kennington Manor in Surrey for eighteen years which the Crown had granted him in 1616 was reassigned to him in 1637. Kennington evidently remained in his hands during the troubles of the 1640s, towards the end of which it passed by conveyance to one Thomas Caldwell. He in turn granted the lease back to its true owner, Cottington's nephew and heir, Francis, for a term of three years beginning in Michaelmas 1655.[13] Lord Cottington took out another lease, some time shortly after the death of his wife in February 1634, of a house in Broad Street, London, for twenty-one years at an annual rent of £84. He lived there intermittently (when not at Hanworth) until the autumn of 1641, when Parliament seized the house for the use of the royal princes, and later turned it into Government offices. Prior to February 1639 he bought the two small manors of Tymberwood and Rainhurst in Kent. To these holdings of only a few hundred acres each Cottington added others, including Filborow and Clamelane. Property formerly held jointly by Sir Paul and Sir Richard Fleetwood came into his hands after 1635, as did some woods in Scotland, and the lordship of Bromfield and Yale in Denbighshire. He is said as well to have acquired land in Ulster by royal grant during the 1630s, but details of these transactions are no less obscure now than certain others which he concealed so well that not even the Parliamentarian sequestrators could discover them.[14]

Cottington was wealthy enough to afford the finest luxuries, which surrounded him at his country houses, but his taste in clothes was surprisingly simple for a man of his means. The two surviving portraits of him, one painted prior to 1616 and attributed to van Somer, the other by an unknown artist executed in Spain when the ambassador was fifty-two, tell a good deal about his appearance. Cottington obviously inclined to portliness. He appears to have been a tall man with heavy bones and large hands, yet with a softness of face and limb that betray his gentlemanly upbringing and lack of adequate exercise. The grave, almost inscrutable expression so often ascribed to him by contemporaries shows in his portraits. He wore a goatee and a moustache, both brown with tinges of red and grey, and combed his hair straight back from his high, furrowed brow. His nose, ridged and with curiously turned nostrils, was less conspicuous than his pursed, thin lips and small eyes that bespeak a certain tensity. He wore clothes starkly plain for a man of his rank and not at all typical of the fashions of many early Stuart personalities, who bedecked themselves in jewels, silks and brocades. He spent a great deal of money on paintings and sculpture, crimson velvet hangings and rugs, silver and gold plate, and ornate furniture, most of which the Parliamentarians confiscated during the Civil War. His expensive taste in household amenities and elegant style of life at his country houses contrasted sharply with his daily routine in London, which was neither ostentatious nor pleasurable. On one hand he was rather typical of his class in purchasing estates and enjoying luxuries; on the other he had little of the personal aristocratic manner or aversion to a steady diet of hard work that has sometimes been associated with the English nobility of his day. The austere simplicity of his appearance and dress reflected that of the Spanish Court and the formative years he had spent in Spain.[15]

CHAPTER 10

The Lord Treasurer's Man

RICHARD WESTON, Earl of Portland, became Lord High Treasurer in July 1628, replacing the Earl of Marlborough, who was made Lord President of the Council. A few weeks later John Felton murdered Buckingham. These two events had a decisive effect on Cottington's career. He went on within a short time to become a Privy Councillor and Chancellor of the Exchequer. He owed both positions primarily to Portland. From this time until the Lord Treasurer's death in March 1635, Cottington was his man, a staunch supporter of peace abroad and of a fiscal policy dedicated to reducing expenditure and raising revenue. Having already followed the events which led to peace with Spain, and what it meant to Cottington personally and professionally, we must return to 1629 to examine his work as an administrator and courtier during the early years of the King's personal government.

Portland and Laud were in the strongest position in 1628-9 to capitalise on the uncertainty that followed Buckingham's death to their own and the Crown's advantage. A contest for control of the administration gradually developed between them. Portland quickly enlisted the support of Cottington, but Laud had not yet joined forces with Sir Thomas Wentworth, Lord President of the Council of the North since December 1628, to combat what in their view was a corrupt and inefficient administration not likely to be altered by Portland and Cottington. Laud at first felt more distrustful of Portland than of Cottington. Such differences as developed later between the archbishop and Cottington came to the surface only gradually. Their rivalry, as much the result of their conflicting personalities as of their divergent views on Government problems, formed later, in the middle 1630s. As for Wentworth, he could not be counted firmly in the camp of either Portland

E

or Laud until at least 1633, although he generally leaned towards Laud's views. Still, Wentworth shared with Portland and Cottington a bias towards friendship with Spain, and like them believed in effective government that should resist encroachment upon the royal prerogative and be financially sound. Wentworth was also indebted to Portland for having urged his appointment to the Privy Council in November 1629, and to Cottington for helping to persuade the King in July 1631 to make him Lord Deputy of Ireland. Although he and Portland were never close, Cottington and Wentworth maintained their friendship throughout the 1630s, except for one or two short periods of misunderstanding.

Portland was an irascible and selfish man; he was also an able and dedicated bureaucrat who understood politics and the needs of the King. He realised that whatever chance he had of translating his aims into firm policies – ending the Spanish war and achieving a better balance between the revenue and expenditure of the Crown – would be enhanced with help from trusted lieutenants in high places. That was the way the Stuart administrative system worked, the way such men as Salisbury, Northampton and Buckingham had been able to dominate the system. It was also through this system that Cottington had managed to rise so high. In fact, the only time he violated the rules of the system by contradicting Buckingham, he nearly lost everything that he had achieved since 1605 by conforming to it.

Cottington and Portland had known each other since at least 1622. They had a good deal in common, not in personal tastes or temperament, but in their overall views of the issues and policies of their day. Both wished to preserve the Stuart central administration intact, because it was dangerous to their own interests to tamper with a system through which they had come to enjoy their honours. Both were anxious to make and keep Spain a friend of England, and not meddle in the continental problems which had burdened western Europe since 1618 and before. Neither man wasted much affection on Parliament or supported its pretensions to the peril of the royal prerogative, but neither were they enemies of Parliament, in which each had sat. Theirs was a natural, convenient and mutually advantageous political alliance that was not fundamentally dependent, as some have suggested, merely on their alleged sympathy for the Roman Church. If they were crypto-Catholics or church papists, which in any case cannot be proven, they did not show it or let their private feelings dictate their public reaction to recusancy. Their friendship benefited both men. Cottington alone had almost no chance of organising a faction strong enough to counterbalance the increasing influence of the Laudians (as was proven after Portland's death). Portland recognised Cottington as a level-headed administrator willing to work hard and take orders.[1]

Portland and Cottington assumed primary responsibility for the management of royal finance at a critical time. It might well be argued justifiably that every Lord Treasurer and Chancellor of the Exchequer since the middle of Elizabeth's reign had faced a financial crisis of one sort or another, but the Crown's financial situation had steadily deteriorated since Salisbury's death. The extravagance of King James, the inflationary spiral that eroded the purchasing power of the Government and drove up wages and prices, the unwillingness of administrators to reduce costs by making reforms in the Household departments, the depression of the 1620s, the heavy cost of the French and Spanish wars and other circumstances had combined to drive the Crown even deeper into debt. If the income of the Crown had not actually fallen every year, it had not kept up with expenditure either, so that the Government took to borrowing heavily in a constricted money market. The Crown borrowed less in the 1620s from institutions than it had previously, but at the same time it borrowed considerably more from individuals or syndicates. This borrowing, the slimness of parliamentary subsidies in the 1620s, and deficits in many years combined to drive the royal debt to well over a million pounds by 1629.[2]

Portland and Cottington had no choice but to follow a hard line in finance. It was not only that the Crown was in debt; they had to proceed on the assumption that the King, who had fallen out with Parliament, would not summon it again except for grave reason and probably not for several years. Without being able to count on at least some extraordinary income authorised by Parliament, Portland and Cottington had somehow to find the additional revenue needed to finance government on one hand, and strive to keep expenditure down to a bare minimum on the other. They

encountered opposition and criticism from all quarters. All sorts
of people, from colleagues on the Privy Council to tradesmen
employed by the Court, clamoured for their money. Being the
tough-minded man that he was, and having endured pressure before
as Chancellor of the Exchequer, Portland disregarded such demands,
except when it suited his and the Crown's purposes to satisfy its
creditors. If they did not press too hard when money was short,
he ignored them; otherwise he paid enough to satisfy them for the
moment. Portland took liberties to make ends meet and avoid
complications. He habitually authorised expenditure on his own
authority directly from the resources of various revenue officers,
especially in the North, by-passing normal channels of Exchequer
business in recording receipts and payments. He also approved payment of debts from anticipated revenue, encumbering future income
and frustrating the purposes of the officers of the Receipt. Such
personal management of royal moneys inevitably aroused suspicion
that he and his associates were profiting illicitly at the public's
expense.[3]

In view of these practices, one cannot expect to prove or dis-
prove categorically whether or not there were legitimate grounds
for complaint. Portland and Cottington certainly made a great deal
of money from or through their offices, but not at the expense of
the Crown. We shall see later that Laud conducted an investigation
shortly after Portland's death into the administration of royal
finance in the hope of discrediting him and embarrassing Cottington.
Instead, he found by and large that debits and credits very nearly
balanced – that expenditure was only slightly higher than receipts
in the seven years of Portland's stewardship. In any case, Cottington
served as Chancellor of the Exchequer initially for only a few months
before leaving on his lengthy Spanish mission. He regretted leaving,
because it was no simple matter to master the intricacies of administrative offices employing nearly four hundred persons and to relate
Exchequer business to the other revenue and legal agencies of
the Government. Those who watched him toil from morning till
night rightly sensed his weariness under the constant pressure of
responsibility.[4]

Cottington plunged into his duties with characteristic energy.
Between 9 May and 11 October 1629 he attended seventeen of the

twenty-eight meetings of the Privy Council. In the same months he served on the Council Committees of Trade and for Ireland, which met regularly on Tuesdays and Fridays respectively, as well as on the Council of War, which sat at least weekly and frequently more often. It is odd, in view of his familiarity with continental affairs, that he did not join the Committee on Foreign Affairs until 1634, although his exclusion from it after Portland's death is easily explained by his rift with Laud over the Lord Treasurership and other matters. In June 1634, to choose one date during his association with Portland, Cottington sat on five permanent committees of the Privy Council – Trade, Foreign Plantations, Ordnance, Ireland and Foreign Affairs – and on various royal commissions. By comparison Laud worked on five, the Earl Marshal on four and the Earl of Dorset on three. Except for Secretary Windebank, Cottington probably served on more committees and commissions during the decade than any of his colleagues. He devoted Thursday mornings to cases in the Court of Exchequer, attended to the Crown lands on Thursday afternoons, and spent Saturdays with Portland (later Juxon) working on the weekly accounts of receipts and issues. He sat also on the Admiralty Board; on the commissions for the repair of St Paul's Cathedral, for compounding with recusants and for establishing or amending contracts on the soap, starch, saltpetre and gunpowder monopolies; to deal with piracy, distraint of knighthood fines, the Poor Law, Crown jewels, royal parks and the schedule of fees paid to officers of the Great Wardrobe.[5]

Even a partial list of his duties suggests something of the scope of his administrative responsibilities, and of the confidence of the King and others in his ability. He was constantly about the business of the Crown, so much so that his all too infrequent visits to his country estates were not only a relief from the pressures of office, but an urgent requirement of health. Of his sense of duty there can be no doubt. The amount of work that he handled is astounding. One need only peruse the Bankes Papers for the years 1634-40, for instance, to realise how much attention he gave to detail; his annotations are on thousands of petitions, requests, warrants, commissions and the like. Even more impressive is the speed with which he executed his duties: he forwarded most papers either on the day that they came to his attention or within two or three days. Rarely did he delay decisions for more than a week or two. Whatever else he had to do or was on his mind, he fulfilled his obligations. On the day before his wife died (21 February 1634), while she lay gravely ill at their house near Charing Cross, he attended a routine meeting of the Admiralty Board at Whitehall; having buried her, he was back at his desk in early March.[6]

Cottington did his duty to the Crown and to Portland by trying hard to reduce expenditure. There are nearly five hundred Exchequer order warrants bearing Cottington's signature and instructions for the period April 1629 to July 1632, some twenty-two months of service (not counting the seventeen months he spent abroad) as Chancellor of the Exchequer. Some of these warrants are straightforward authorisations to pay Government officers their fees or to purchase office supplies and the like. But a large number authorised payment to various creditors of the Crown – persons to whom the Exchequer paid interest on loans, part of the principal, or charges for services rendered. These warrants show that Cottington tried to dole out small amounts of interest (not always all that was due) rather than large sums of principal. On the other hand, the royal family paid little attention to his efforts to discourage frivolous purchases and services. Neither Charles nor Henrietta Maria was frugal. He thought nothing of spending £10,000 on paintings, and the cost of running her Court at Somerset House over a two-year period in the late 1620s exceeded the £18,166 she got from her revenues by £89,378. In June 1629 Cottington grudgingly paid a bill for £2,800 for refurbishing the Queen's bedroom, and fussed over Charles's insistence on buying a diamond ring for £600. In these instances there was nothing Cottington could do but pay the charges.[7]

Cottington tried to reduce costs in other ways, sometimes at the expense of royal officers who deserved better. He felt more keenly the urgency to economise at the outset of his administration in 1629 than two or three years later, when the Crown was not in quite as serious financial straits. He consistently refused to reimburse certain county officials for claims of allowable expenditure in office. Take the case of the much-abused sheriffs, who in most cases preferred not to serve at all, because of the money it cost them. To all intents and purposes they were unpaid, yet they often expended considerable sums of their own money in fees paid to Exchequer officers and other officials on entering service and upon turning in their final accounts. They spent much on hospitality, tax collection, empanelling juries, and housing and transporting prisoners, not to mention subsidising the work of the under-sheriffs. They were even asked to pay out of their pockets uncollected fines and taxes, and were sometimes fined for failing to perform their duties satisfactorily. The sheriffs were expected as gentlemen of means to serve the Crown out of loyalty, not for personal gain, but some of them had been known to inflate their expenses in the knowledge that they would probably never get the full amount. Cottington reduced the amounts payable for such claims as a matter of course, generally crossing out the sum and writing in a lower figure, lower by as much as a third or a half. Most often he secured the opinion of the legal officers as to the legitimacy of the claims for reimbursement, so that his decisions were not capricious. It was an effective way of reducing expenditure, to the loss of those who could afford to subsidise the Crown indirectly.[8]

Ways and means of collecting more in fines and rents owed to the Crown attracted Cottington's attention. He instructed such officers as the remembrancers of the Exchequer, the receivers-general, the sheriffs, the justices of the peace, the magistrates and the messengers to investigate arrears in rents due from Crown lands; the level of fines levied upon licensed exploiters of royal forests; whether improvements made to Crown property justified raising rents; arrears or delinquency in customs duties; enterprises in which the Crown had an interest but which no longer gave 'profit to the King', and so forth. Cottington likewise pursued the clergy who had either evaded or fallen behind in payment of subsidies, first fruits and tenths. On occasion Cottington found an opportunity to tighten finances in certain spendthrift departments, such as the Office of Ordnance.[9]

In 1629 Cottington arranged the sale of certain Crown jewels in order to help meet debts arising from the Spanish war. About the same time Cottington and Portland made an audit of money owed by King Charles to several principal creditors. Sir James Bagg, Vice-Admiral of South Cornwall, claimed that the Crown had repaid him about £25,000 of the £51,600 owing him, including interest at 8 per cent. Since Bagg had loaned different sums 'on the verbal instructions of the late Duke [of Buckingham] in extremity of haste', Portland and Cottington had auditors check the figures. They reported back that Bagg had already been returned £16,500 more than he claimed to have received. In other cases Cottington compensated creditors of the Crown without expending cash. Income from certain Crown property in and about London had been assigned to the Corporation of London in 1627 in partial repayment of 'debts due them from the late and present King'. When the City argued later that the lands had been conveyed absolutely in discharge of these debts, and that it actually owned the property, Cottington, Portland and Attorney-General Heath answered unequivocally that the City was merely the custodian of the property, which still belonged to the Crown. In 1631, when Lord Falkland demanded money owed to him by the Crown and said that it could be raised from the Irish Farm, Portland and Cottington refused, arguing that the Government could not afford to pay him anything until France sent another instalment on Henrietta Maria's dowry, long overdue.[10]

The Exchequer had been concerned about rising costs in the King's Household since Elizabethan times. Portland and Cottington wanted to reduce expenditure here too, but they did not succeed in cutting costs by much. The Chamber (the Household above stairs) had ceased to rival the Exchequer as a national treasury since the days of Thomas Cromwell in the 1530s. But it still had its own financial administration (the Treasurer, Comptroller, Cofferer and four clerks) headed by the Board of the Greencloth, employed more than eighteen hundred persons, and annually spent about 40 per cent of all peace-time royal expenditure. The Household was among the most powerful and unassailable branches of the central administration. Its chief officers were leading figures, many of whom sat on the Privy Council. Since the exercise of patronage in the Household helped the Crown secure the support of the aristocracy and greater gentry, both the King and the Household officials had a vested interest in perpetuating the administration of the Household undisturbed, notwithstanding the urgency of reducing costs. Yet the Household was fraught with problems which erstwhile reformers had itched to remedy, such as too many officials without enough to do; exorbitant costs of food, drink, fuel and lighting for the whole Court; waste and dishonesty among provisioners and managers. The trouble was that not even the Lord Treasurer or the Chancellor of the Exchequer dared attack the Household with impunity.[11]

Still, they tried in 1629-32, even though unsuccessful efforts had been made by a commission beginning in 1626 to see how much costs in the Household had risen since the accession of King James, and to effect reductions. This work brought some results in 1629-1630; the diets were reduced by £12,500 to about £47,200, where the figure remained until 1637. This was accomplished by decreasing the quantity of food enjoyed by officials below the highest levels of authority. It was recommended in addition that board wages be substituted in some cases for diet privileges, and that certain officers be bought out or their offices left unfilled whenever they were vacated. Neither of these expedients appreciably reduced Household expenditure, but larger savings were realised by curtailing extraordinary expenditure at the Queen's Court and, by 1634, in the Great Wardrobe.[12]

Cottington's hand is more clearly apparent in the increase of revenue from Roman Catholic recusants, especially in 1631-4, during part of Wentworth's Lord Presidency of the North. Catholic dissent was of several kinds, and the Government and society responded in different ways. Skill or chance in avoiding discovery, inconsistency in Government policy, the attitudes of local enforcement agencies, loopholes in the penal laws, the difficulty of enforcing the law in remote districts, the social connections of recusant families, the laxity or industry of churchwardens and constables, the sense of community spirit touching Catholics and Protestants living together in the same locality – all these and other factors must be taken into account in considering the position of the Catholic recusants. This involves the question of how much the Crown profited from recusancy because of Cottington's and others' work, and whether his alleged sympathy for the Roman Church affected his treatment of recusants.[13]

Let it be admitted that Cottington seemed sympathetic to Rome at several points in his life; we saw earlier that he may have been temporarily converted to Catholicism in 1623, and practised it for a few years before his death in Spain. Nevertheless, there is no unassailable evidence to support the assumption made by his critics that he was a convert Catholic in the 1630s. He occasionally visited Catholic priests in London, but he had done so in Madrid as well. He was involved in discussions over whether or not the wording of the Oath of Allegiance (1606), offensive to Catholics because it obliged them to deny papal supremacy and transubstantiation, should be altered to win their firmer support of King Charles. Yet Cottington appears not to have favoured any alteration of the oath. He spoke on the side of moderating the heavier penalties prescribed against certain kinds of lay recusants and priests. He had cordial relationships with papal emissaries to the English Court – Leander Jones, Gregory Panzani and George Conn – but so too did other Protestant Councillors and the King himself. What do these oblique connections with Catholics or Catholic questions really prove, after all? They could just as well have been, and there is strong evidence that they were, fostered by the Government and undertaken by Cottington in the line of duty. If he had in fact been a Catholic, surely the Catholic hierarch in England, Bishop Richard Smith of Chalcedon, would have known it. But Smith said in 1631 that the Catholics could not trust Cottington.[14]

With this understanding of Cottington's relations with Catholics and the Roman Church in the 1630s, it must also be asked: what was the attitude of the Government towards them? Again, the answer cannot easily be given, for much depends on whether one is speaking of the Government in terms of the never concrete policies of the administration, or of its local representatives who dealt with recusants throughout the country – the churchwardens, constables, J.P.s, pursuivants, receivers-general, commissioners for compounding and others. While the enforcement of the penal laws was not as rigorous under Charles as under Elizabeth or James, nor as widespread in the numbers of persons affected, the proscription of Catholic recusants did continue, and to a greater degree than has been supposed. The upper classes suffered least and the commonalty most, especially in urban areas where Catholics could not so easily conceal their religion, and particularly in the province of York. Wentworth and his subordinates farmed revenue from recusants north of the Trent with greater diligence than officials elsewhere in the country.

This is where Cottington fitted into the picture. The figures tell part of the tale. The annual income from Catholic recusants in 1625-30 did not exceed £5,300 of the gross royal revenue of some £640,000 in 1625 and £500,000 in 1630. Recusant revenue rose steadily in the next four years, from £6,396 in 1631 to £26,866 in 1634, exactly during the years when Cottington and Portland strove to increase revenue from all sources. Following Portland's death in 1635, and during the hegemony of Laud and Lord Treasurer Juxon until 1641, when Cottington worked with less enthusiasm than he had with Portland, recusant revenue declined, except in 1640 in which the Catholics yielded a record £32,000.[15]

For all his efforts to eradicate Roman Catholicism, Laud considered the Puritans a greater menace to his church than the Catholics. Even so, Laud blamed Portland for being lax with Catholics, saying that 'the wisest physicians [Portland and Cottington] do not always hit upon the malady and malignancy of the disease, for now [the recusants] . . . think themselves freed from all command . . .'.[16] Yet what evidence there is suggests that Cottington did not share Portland's apparent concern about exploiting recusants. On the contrary, he encouraged the strict enforcement of the penal laws in the North and efforts to force the Catholics to compound for their lands. As early as 1629, when Wentworth was just undertaking his work as the Receiver-General of Recusant Revenue in the North, Cottington assured him that the King, Portland and himself agreed entirely with his plans for raising receipts. Cottington made a practice of perusing the returns from officials who collected this money against the possibility that they were cheating the Government, or not collecting as much from recusants as they might have done by being more assiduous.[17]

While Cottington had served the Crown well, he had done so at the cost of temporarily alienating Wentworth in the North by secretly negotiating a contract with Sir Arthur Ingram which permitted him to collect recusant revenue at a handsome commission, thus depriving Wentworth of income.[18] No matter what the obligations of office, it was unlike Cottington to make enemies of important people who might one day reciprocate favours or wrongs done to them. About this time Lady Cottington, who was five months pregnant with her fifth child, asked Wentworth to be the godfather.[19] It would not have been unusual for Cottington to have exploited his wife's condition as a way of placating Wentworth. In any event, this pregnancy brought tragedy for the Cottingtons. Two daughters, Elizabeth and Frances, had died of plague in March 1630, while Sir Francis was abroad. His third daughter, Anne, had died in infancy in November 1632. Afterwards Lady Cottington was never well; she could not overcome the melancholy induced by the deaths of three of her four children. The winter of 1633-4 was a trying period of ill-health for her. She took a turn for the worse in December and the doctors feared the worst. Her son, Charles, had also been sick all winter. She suffered a relapse a few days before giving birth to a daughter, also named Anne, on 20 February, and died two days later, aged thirty-three. She was buried on the 23rd in St Paul's Chapel, Westminster Abbey, where her husband commissioned the King's Sculptor, Hubert le Sueur, to make a monument with a bust of her at a cost of £400. Now a widower with an infant daughter and a sickly son of six, Cottington sold his town house and moved to Hanworth. As if he had not been through enough that winter, he lost thirteen cottages and sixteen barns in the village in a fire that cost him £5,000. He saw to it that the sixty displaced tenants had shelter and food and began to rebuild. Meanwhile, still needing a base in London, he resided briefly in an apartment in old Salisbury House in the Strand, and then leased a house in Broad Street.[20]

Cottington returned to work soon after his wife's funeral. Death was no stranger to a man who had lost four members of his family in as many years, but he recovered rapidly from such personal tragedies, so that his wife's passing does not appear, at least outwardly, to have demoralised him for long. If her occasional references to Francis and his consistently high praise of her to friends may be taken at face value, they apparently had a happy marriage. Towards the end of her life, however, he had been seeing another woman named Mrs Crofts. It does not take much imagination to interpret a remark of Wentworth's to his friend of fifty-five – that he was indeed bold to 'set up a new mill for your little grist'.[21]

Notwithstanding the charms of Mrs Crofts, the anxieties and

burdens of high office had borne down heavily on Lord Cottington since his return from Spain in 1631. Even a man of his stamina and sense of duty needed more relaxation than he was able to enjoy, but business and the demands of a sickly family tied him down. Scarcely any significant matter, especially relating to finance, escaped his attention; the amount of work he handled on relatively minor problems was staggering. It says something of his strength of character that he never lost his wry sense of humour or showed any sign of breaking under the strain. He was apparently good company, yet he had few friends outside his immediate circle of Government officials. Like Portland, he was something of a solitary figure. Although they were never close personal friends, they trusted each other and worked well together. They made a good team, and it was inevitable that they should have been identified inseparably with the fiscal and foreign policies that Portland had shaped since 1628 and that his principal lieutenant had helped to implement. In every sense Cottington's influence and security in the Government was dependent upon Portland. It was not the best position to be in, but one to which Cottington had grown accustomed through a number of such relationships over a period of thirty years in royal service. In early 1634 the coalition of Portland and Cottington appeared lasting, but appearances were deceiving. By the time Lady Cottington died, the Lord Treasurer, then about fifty-seven, showed clearer signs of a disease that was to take his life, imperilling the continued pre-eminence of the man whose fortunes were intimately connected with his own.

CHAPTER 11

Cottington and Laud

THE policy of 'thorough', Miss Wedgwood informs us, was enunciated and worked out in 1633 in the personal correspondence between Wentworth and Laud, and was aimed at breaking through the opposition to administrative reform needed to achieve more efficient and honest government. In the rigid, unimaginative view of Laud, who rarely understood why anyone disagreed with him, the major obstacle to reform was the combination of Portland and Cottington – the Lady Mora and her waiting-maid he named them, the models of corruption and indifference to everything but their own profit through the exploitation of office. Laud had probably felt this way for almost as long as he had served on the Privy Council (since 1627), during which time his grasp on the reins of power over ecclesiastical and political affairs became even firmer. If he had exchanged hard words with Portland and Cottington before his translation to the See of Canterbury, concealing his strongest invective against them in letters to Wentworth, afterwards their rivalry gradually became more intense and apparent. Laud and Cottington reached their highest pitch of disagreement in 1635-6, in the year from the death of Portland to the appointment of William Juxon, Bishop of London, as Lord Treasurer. Commentators from that day to this have usually interpreted their rivalry as a clash of different philosophies of government and of conflicting temperaments. An examination of their relationship during 1633-6 should explain why Cottington lost the contest for the greatest prize in his career.[1]

Cottington and Laud worked amicably together during the early years of Portland's administration. Their duty as Privy Councillors required them to share the burden of many committee assignments that resolved a variety of questions ranging from poor relief to the regulation of tobacco sales. As managers of the royal forests and lands, Cottington and Portland had helped the archbishop to obtain two hundred tons of timber from the Forest of Shotover and Stow Wood towards his building at St John's College, Oxford. Cottington also served Laud's interest on a commission to raise money for the restoration of St Paul's Cathedral, at the cost of severe criticism by Puritan residents of that district of London who suffered financial loss because of this work.[2] Laud resisted on principle the suppression of the Somerset Church-ales, the parochial feasts held in honour of the saint to whom the parish church was dedicated. Sometimes these occasions degenerated into raucous or licentious behaviour, which set the Puritans of the region against them and worried Lord Chief Justice Richardson, then on the Western Circuit, who wanted them stopped to reduce lawlessness. Laud saw to it that Richardson was removed from the circuit on the recommendation of a Privy Council committee, which investigated his charges that the judge had violated the jurisdiction of the Church by instructing the local clergy to discontinue the wakes in defiance of his countermanding order. Richardson asked Cottington to intercede with the Council on his behalf, but he had more sense than to meddle in a matter so close to Laud's personal interest.[3]

Laud also attacked the feoffees for impropriations. Cottington's support of Laud in this threat to the Church affords an opportunity to see him at work with the Barons of the Court of Exchequer. In 1625 four clergymen, four lawyers and four merchants – all London Puritans – constituted themselves feoffees (trustees) of an unincorporated organisation to raise money with which to purchase impropriations (tithes in lay hands) towards the support of Puritan lecturers. What began in London as an apparently innocent venture by one group of feoffees to support lecturers at St Antholin's Church could be copied elsewhere. Laud realised that such control of impropriations was prejudicial to the financial interests of the Church and encouraged the spread of Puritanism. The investigation led to a lawsuit brought by the Crown in the Easter term of 1633 before the equity side of the Court of Exchequer against the London feoffees for impropriations. Attorney-General Noy based his case for the Crown on the fact that the feoffees had illegally constituted themselves a corporation without the permission of the Crown and that they had by gaining control of Church livings meant to by-pass Church authority. The court ordered the organisation dissolved, confiscated its resources amounting to about £7,000, and recommended that the Crown nominate trusted (conformist) vicars to the livings. All was done as Cottington had proposed. So it was that the alleged crypto-Catholic and supposed antagonist of Laud rose to the defence of the Anglican Church and its primate.[4]

Beginning in April 1634 Cottington, Laud, Archbishop Neile of York, Portland, Lord Keeper Coventry and Secretaries Coke and Windebank served on the Council Committee for Foreign Plantations. Its work was closest to Laud's heart, as it afforded him another opportunity to restrict Puritanism in England and in the American colonies. While his theoretical powers were considerable, in actuality he could do very little to control the course of affairs religious or political in areas so far from the homeland. He could do even less to stem the tide of Puritan emigration to America, in spite of Government decrees against it and the co-operation of Cottington on the committee and through his subordinates at the ports.[5]

Cottington took greater interest in the work of the Admiralty Board, to which he was appointed in November 1632. He had much to do here, because of the close relationship between naval affairs and the commerce that provided revenue from customs, and between his jurisdiction over the royal forests and the navy's need for timber. Cottington had handled business relating to the Admiralty since his appointment as Chancellor of the Exchequer and to the Committees for Trade and Ireland. In May 1631 his kinsman, George Cottington, who had served in the Buckingham expedition to La Rochelle during the French war, petitioned the Lords of the Admiralty for a grant of the office of Registrar of the Admiralty that had formerly been held by three others and since voided. Lord Cottington tried to help his cousin, but Katherine, Duchess of Buckingham, interceded directly with Secretary Dorchester in support of her candidate, Sir George Fielding, to whom she insisted her husband had actually promised the place. Not long afterwards an altercation developed between Lord Cottington and Sir Francis Godolphin, captain of the fort in the Scilly Isles, over his seizure of a merchantman mastered by Richard Bramfield. Then in the service of Spain, his ship had been taken for pirating the *Fortune*, owned by a firm of London fishmongers, who pressed charges. When Godolphin refused to surrender his prize, Cottington ordered him brought to London for interrogation, and scolded him for allowing the ship to rot at anchor rather than selling it to the profit of the Crown.

Cottington had concentrated on mercantile affairs while in Spain and knew full well how much could be realised from prizes. Furthermore, any cut in foreign trade reduced that portion of the royal revenue derived from it. Since piracy hurt English trade more than any other factor, he was anxious to suppress it, especially in home waters, where the Turkish and Dunkirk pirates patrolled the sea lanes and took many a merchantman. This helps to explain why he deplored the incompetence of those commanding castles and forts guarding the English coast, and why he strove to have them strengthened or reconstructed. In August 1635 he drew up plans for this work and persuaded King Charles to employ Captain Mason as an inspector. It also explains why Cottington seconded the abortive suggestion of West of England merchants that the principal merchant companies help to finance a naval expedition to Algiers to attack the corsairs in their home port.[6]

Cottington did yeoman service in the summer of 1633, when Laud, Portland and other Councillors accompanied the King to Edinburgh for his long-delayed coronation in Scotland on 18 June at St Giles'. From mid-May to late July Cottington headed a commission which oversaw the government of England. He assumed most of the duties of the Lord Treasurer and, on behalf of the Privy Council, authorised matters requiring speedy action. While he dispatched his duties flawlessly, he groaned under the added pressures of office, complaining to Secretary Coke that he customarily worked past midnight to get everything done. Even on Sundays in June and July he was obliged as a matter of courtesy to visit the Queen at Greenwich; she had been ill from a pregnancy and nearly lost her second son, James. When the royal train returned from Scotland, earlier than expected because of her health, Cottington gladly surrendered the authority that he had exercised for three months.[7]

Late that autumn Portland's health began to break down, and

his debilitating disease continued to weaken him throughout the following year, preventing him from attending to his normal duties. This increased Cottington's responsibilities at the same time that his wife and son were also ill. Portland grew much worse over the winter of 1634-5, and it became apparent by March that he could not live much longer. Cottington visited him frequently at Wallingford House during the last few weeks of his life. On 8 March, while Cottington was on his way to attend the consecration of Dr Wren as Bishop of Hereford, he was called to Portland's bedside. He conferred with the doctors and told his friend that he was dying and should prepare himself. He and Sir John Bankes returned to Wallingford House the next morning to help Portland draw up his will, which took hours because he was nearly delirious and could scarcely speak. That afternoon the King visited Portland but left after a few moments, as squeamish as his father had been at the sight of a suffering man. At about three in the morning of 13 March, the Lord Treasurer died in agony. For two days and two nights Cottington had stayed with him, to the end.[8]

Days before his death the newsmongers began speculating about who might succeed the Lord Treasurer. The number of possible candidates was many, but the actual choices open to the King were few. The odds were that Wentworth, Laud or Cottington would most likely succeed Portland. Since these powerful men knew the stakes involved, Laud and Wentworth worked against Cottington, and he promoted his own candidacy while conniving against them. Each of them had administrative ability, both Wentworth and Cottington understood high finance, and the King had confidence in them all. But Charles wanted Wentworth to remain in Dublin, where he had done a masterful job as Lord Deputy, even though Laud promoted his friend's candidacy, and Cottington wrote sympathetically about their respective chances of succeeding Portland. As Laud now had more influence with the King than anyone else in the Government, he probably could have been Lord Treasurer if he had wished, despite the fact that a bishop had not held that office since 1470. He had been translated to Canterbury only two years earlier, however, and had his hands full reforming the Church and suppressing dissent.

As for Lord Cottington, his training, experience and long

connection with finance made him the logical choice. He wanted to become the Lord Treasurer and made no secret of it. But impediments stood in his way, as always. He became Master of the Court of Wards and Liveries about the time that Portland died, and it was questionable whether the same man should shoulder the burdens of two such important offices, in addition to his other responsibilities. His health had not been of the best lately, and he was nearing sixty – nearly old by seventeenth-century standards. Moreover, his close association with Portland, with an administration that had been widely criticised even by some of his colleagues on the Council, did his candidacy no good. Laud and Wentworth had seen in the Portland–Cottington partnership a pernicious threat to their own and the Crown's interests, to the policy of 'thorough' which had made little headway so long as Portland lived. They had no reason to believe that Cottington alone would act any differently. Besides, Laud distrusted Cottington, and Wentworth shared his feelings to some extent. Then again, the Protestant interests at home and abroad (led by the Palatine Princess Elizabeth) could not tolerate a pro-Spanish and supposedly also pro-Catholic Councillor being in a position as Lord Treasurer to dictate the course of foreign affairs.[9]

Since the King could not make up his mind for the present, he put the Treasurership into commission and named Laud, Cottington, Windebank, Coke and Manchester to administer the office. Laud became chairman of the commission not long after he also assumed the leadership of the Council Committee on Foreign Affairs. These two appointments, and the removal of Cottington from the latter, boded ill for him, giving fair warning that Portland's death posed a greater threat to his security in the Government than he might have supposed at the time.[10] At least he could face the situation somewhat more confidently by reason of his having become Master of the Court of Wards in March, following the forced retirement of Sir Robert Naunton, who had been unable to carry out his duties satisfactorily because of age and illness.[11] This was the last great office that Cottington garnered during his long career.[12]

The chaplain and panegyrist of Laud, Peter Heylin, reported that 'the year 1635 was but new begun, when clashing began to

grow between him [Laud] and Cottington about executing the
Commission of the Treasury'.[13] Laud at once launched an investigation of royal finance during Portland's administration. Whether
or not he did so primarily to discredit Portland and embarrass
Cottington, as some have supposed, is not as important as that
he discovered so little to complain about on completing this work.
The commissioners instructed the Auditor of Receipt of the Exchequer to surrender a batch of financial records going back five
years, and to prepare a balance sheet. From these papers the commissioners were able to verify that, reckoning on an annual basis,
the expenditure of the Crown had exceeded the revenue since 1629
by only about £18,000. Thus the overall picture revealed nothing
like the corruption and extravagance in the Portland–Cottington
administration that Laud had expected to find.[14]

Nevertheless, the study had the effect of sharpening the differences between Cottington and Laud. Both men carried on an
extensive correspondence with Wentworth in 1635, and their
letters provide ample evidence of how they felt towards each other.
What is most interesting about Cottington's evaluation of the work
of the Treasury Commission is his tacit admission that he was
losing the contest over the white staff. 'In our Committee . . . we
manage our business extreme ill, and so, if it continue, we shall
soon spoil all; I am very old and must be gone; therefore if I can
do you any more service speak quickly.' Cottington told Wentworth this in June 1635. He wrote to him again in October: 'My
Lord of Canterbury is angry with me, because he cannot make me
be with him, and truly that is the case between us. His Grace is
very great, and I am very little; his power with the King is much,
and mine none at all; I go seldom to the Court, (yet oftener than I
would) & his Grace [is] seldom from thence. . . .' To this Wentworth replied, knowingly: 'there were hope of reconciliation, if
both [you and Laud] were moved, than where your tempers are
so unequal and differing'. By the end of the month Cottington was
convinced that Laud would become Lord Treasurer, and with his
appointment his own influence at Court would be ended, because
of the hatred between them.[15]

One gets the impression from the Laud–Wentworth correspondence that year that Laud's feelings towards Cottington began as

disapproval, turned into dislike following Portland's death, and ended as outright disdain. While Laud admitted in March that Cottington was talented and industrious, a person fit to be Lord Treasurer, a few months later he was telling Wentworth that Cottington seemed to have changed, to have become more like Portland in the way in which he was trying to manipulate the other commissioners to his own advantage. Laud had obviously been speaking to the King against Cottington. 'I do not purpose to speak any more to . . . [the King] about . . . [Cottington] . . . being [made Lord Treasurer],' he wrote to Wentworth, for 'I have done my duty, and the rest I shall leave to God, and will not give . . . [Charles] cause to think my spleen is fuller than my judgment'. In fact, the archbishop had already quite emptied his spleen and had not chosen to trust such a crucial matter to Providence.[16]

In addition to the inquiry into royal finance, Laud and Cottington had clashed in the Court of Star Chamber and in the Privy Council over issues that are well known to students of this period.[17] It is hard to get at the root of their antipathy. They had known one another for years and worked together amicably during most of Portland's administration. There is no evidence that they were openly hostile before 1634, even though Laud's correspondence confirms that Cottington's supposed crypto-Catholicism and Spanish bias had made him suspect in his eyes at least a year earlier. Before Portland's death they had moved in different circles and in different worlds – Laud in the Church, Cottington in finance and diplomacy – although their paths had crossed frequently at the Privy Council.

Their animosity is the more difficult to fathom because, despite their bickering, they shared fundamental convictions. They believed in authoritarian government, in the subservience of Parliament to the royal interest, in efficient administration, in sound fiscal practices, in the suppression of religious and political dissent, and they believed in hard work, fulfilment of duty and loyalty to friends. Strangely, they failed to recognise the mutuality of their attitudes and traits. Instead, they let their emotions get the better of them, Laud more openly and passionately than Cottington, undoubtedly because there was so much at stake. It is hard to credit the standard view that Laud was motivated by scruples, by a desire only to

reform the Government. His differences with Cottington over
solutions to governmental problems appears to have been not so
much a question of principle as a clash of personalities and a contest
for power with the Lord Treasurership the ultimate prize. The
modern biographer of Laud hit closest to the mark in explaining
the reason for this rivalry: 'the breach which separated . . . the two
was made irreparable by the utter incompatibility of their temperaments. Laud's rigid mind was apt to interpret every difference of
opinion as inspired by deliberate malice, and he was perpetually
accusing Cottington of inspired motives.'[18]

Most commentators on the race for the white staff, including
Wentworth, still believed as late as November 1635 that Cottington
would win. They read a great deal into events that summer and
autumn which seemed to corroborate current speculation on the
appointment. Cottington was known to have spent many hours
conferring with the King, and to have entertained the Queen at
Hanworth. Meanwhile he denigrated his own chances of becoming
Lord Treasurer, confessing to Wentworth in August that 'there is
no more intention in the king to make me his Treasurer than to
make you Archbishop of Canterbury: I go sliding back very
visibly [and] I go so seldom to the Court, as I am scarce a courtier'.
He was quite right. By the turn of the year the talk of his preferment ceased. Something had happened to change the picture.[19]

What had almost certainly happened is that Laud took advantage
of Cottington's absence from Court in December and early January
because of the gout and pneumonia to persuade the King not to
appoint him. He first ventured out again from Hanworth on 19
January to attend the christening of Princess Elizabeth and pay his
respects to the King, who left for Newmarket the next day. It is
likely that Charles had decided by this time to make William Juxon
his Lord Treasurer, although the idea had probably been in his
mind since October.[20]

The official announcement of Juxon's appointment was made on
6 March. It came as an almost complete surprise to everyone but
Laud, who had been instrumental in secretly promoting the candidacy of the singularly honest and basically apolitical Bishop of
London, the last ecclesiastical Lord Treasurer of England. Cottington took the setback in his stride; he put on a good face at Court

but must have been bitterly disappointed. For a month or so he 'disburdened himself of the business of the Exchequer . . .', and spent most of his time hawking and chasing foxes at Hanworth between hurried trips to Westminster. As late as July he was still spending more time away from the capital than he had for years. He visited Lord Salisbury at Hatfield House, and at the end of August went with the other Councillors to Woodstock to greet the royal family on their return from a progress, after which he accompanied them to Oxford. In the interval between these two trips his only son and heir, Charles, sickly for most of his eight years, died at Hanworth and was buried on 27 July. It had been a terrible year, one of the worst for the widower left with only a small daughter (who would also die about 1641) and grieved by the loss of the greatest prize in his life.[21]

CHAPTER 12

Councillor in Crisis

THE appointment of his protégé, William Juxon, as Lord Treasurer in March 1636 was a personal triumph for Laud over Cottington. Notwithstanding the bitterness between them generated by the contest over the white staff, it might have been supposed afterwards that they could have patched up their differences. They were not reconciled, however. If they perforce worked together, they kept their distance. Six months after Juxon's appointment Laud was still impugning Cottington's character and questioning his motives. Cottington soon despaired of efforts to placate Laud. In February 1637 he acknowledged to Wentworth his weakened position at Court and admitted that the Laudians dominated the counsels of the King: 'I am no more a leader, but do meddle with my own particular duties only, in which I find great ease though it doth not altogether extinguish the high malice that was against me. . . .'1 Yet Cottington was still a man of considerable influence in the Government as an administrator and adviser in financial and foreign affairs. In the next few years he necessarily bowed to Laud's wishes on matters of policy, demonstrating time and again that he could be relied upon in a crisis. The Government faced a succession of crises in 1637-41, and Cottington kept his head throughout. No matter what Laud and Wentworth had against him personally, they learned that it was to their and the Crown's advantage to have a man of his experience and nerve at their side.

Cottington continued to serve the King as an adviser on western Europe even though he was not reappointed to the Committee for Foreign Affairs until 1640. It will be recalled that he had negotiated treaties with Spain in 1630-1, one arranging peace and restoring diplomatic and commercial relations, the other providing for an Anglo-Spanish alliance against the United Provinces and for the transportation of Spanish treasure to the Netherlands via England. Spain gained most by this relationship in the sense that she kept England from developing closer ties with France and the United Provinces. The implementation of the anti-Dutch league depended upon Spain's withdrawal of garrisons from the Palatinate and success in persuading her allies to do the same, while the transfer of bullion was meant to be a more or less permanent arrangement. The proposed war on the Dutch was repeatedly delayed (as Cottington had suspected in 1631) by Spain's unwillingness to honour her promises; by complications arising from France's entry into the Thirty Years War in 1635; and by England's inability to engage in a continental war. England played a double and inherently self-contradictory role in western Europe. On one hand she tried to retain the friendship of Spain, hoping that Philip IV might yet be persuaded to evacuate the Palatinate; on the other she gravitated towards closer relations with his enemies. In 1631 King Charles permitted the Marquis of Hamilton to raise seven thousand English and Scots mercenaries for use by King Gustavus Adolphus of Sweden in northern Germany against the Habsburgs. Two years later Charles was nearly drawn into supporting a Protestant conspiracy in the Spanish Netherlands to overthrow its Government with English aid. By 1636 both England and Spain realised that the alliance and the Palatinate were virtually dead letters, though the Spaniards never quite gave up trying to promote a joint invasion of the United Provinces.[2]

The gradual weakening of ties with Spain did not affect the transportation of Spanish bullion to the Netherlands via England. The agreement allowed England to keep approximately one-third of each consignment of silver transported, which was to be paid for through bills of exchange drawn on Antwerp. In July 1636, however, this profitable arrangement was nearly ended by King Charles, who instructed Cottington and Juxon to keep two-thirds of the silver that had been recently brought to England aboard the *Victory*. They apparently misunderstood Charles's orders and permitted the captain to sail with all the silver after the duty on it had been collected, thereby narrowly averting a quarrel with Spain.[3]

Lord Cottington's aggressive administration of the Court of Wards and Liveries, beginning in 1635, was of greater consequence to the Crown than his work in diplomacy. By how much he raised the revenue of the Court of Wards during his Mastership to 1641, and what overall effect his tightening of its operations had on the performance of its officers throughout the country, are questions that can be resolved confidently. It is another matter, however, to ascertain why he earned such an unsavoury reputation in the eyes of the Crown's critics, and to determine how much he profited personally from his office.

It was often deleterious and occasionally disastrous to an estate for a gentleman to die while his heir was a minor, because the administration of such an estate became the privilege of the Crown, which profited from the sale of wardships and the lease of wards' lands. The Court of Wards was a large revenue-collecting Government agency that brought the King more money in the 1630s than he received from all the Crown lands. Although rents were still rising steadily, whenever possible the Master of the Court of Wards preferred to sell wardships that fell into the hands of the Crown rather than retain them for income. That way the King received more money more quickly than he would have had in the long term by renting the lands to tenants, which was an important consideration at a time when the Government needed money badly.[4]

The authority of the Master of Wards and Liveries was on the whole greater than many of the high officials in the Government. He controlled the administrative personnel of the Court throughout the country. The Master or his subordinates assessed the value of, and disposed of the property and persons of, the wards to buyers generally at whatever price the market would bear. When sitting in his capacity as judge, the Master ruled on petitions for redress of grievances and for alterations in the terms of composition. Notwithstanding this authority, the effectiveness of the Master depended ultimately on his aggressiveness in forwarding the business of the Court, especially in uncovering concealments of wards. Such Masters as Lord Burghley, his son Salisbury and Cranfield were energetic bureaucrats who saw to it that concealed wardships, which were accomplished by the intricate legal manoeuvrings of lawyers who created conveyances of land to confound the Court's investigators, were discovered.[5]

One of the first things that Cottington did upon assuming office was to begin to reassert the authority of the Master by closer personal supervision of the Court's operations and officers, especially in the North and in Wales. Except for Cranfield, none of the Masters following Salisbury had been important persons or effective administrators. Consequently their authority had decayed in practice while their underlings made higher profits at their and the Crown's expense. Cottington, however, was a man with a reputation among underlings for efficiency, had had wide experience in fiscal matters, and had learned a good deal about land law as Chancellor of the Exchequer. These advantages, together with his firmness and aggressiveness as an administrator, enabled him to reverse this trend. While he brought the officials and functionaries of the Court into line, he also improved its operations by increasing the number of clerks in the auditor's office as well as of the feodaries and informers employed in the counties. The business of the Court grew under his administration, as did the profits of the Crown.[6]

How much Cottington profited personally from the Mastership only he knew, although some idea of his income can be gained by comparing the gains of earlier, active Masters. Cottington's basic fee from the office was only £133 6s. 8d., to which was added about £250 for diet, livery and casual fees. Of course, these fees bore no relation to the amount of money he actually made as Master. Burghley had a basic fee that was no higher than Cottington's, yet he collected more than £3,000 in 1596-8 alone from private suitors for wardships. Salisbury received at least that much, and probably more, every year during 1608-12. Since inflation tended to increase the face value of profits, and since more wardships were sold under Cottington than under any of his predecessors after the turn of the century, quite probably he had perhaps as much as twice what Salisbury had realised from the office annually. Like other Masters, he made part of the money by purchasing wardships himself. It is not altogether fair to accept uncritically his enemies' charges that he was a ruthless Master: most wardships were sold during his administration at reasonable prices, and he often showed compassion towards persons whom he could easily have victimised.[7]

The stricter operations of the Court of Wards under Cottington is pointed up in the overall increase of net income accruing to the Crown.[8] This increase may be studied in a number of ways. One way is to compare the total annual revenue for the years 1635-41 with certain preceding years. The annual revenue from Wards under Lord Burghley fluctuated between roughly £15,000 and £20,000; while Salisbury increased it from about £17,300 in 1608 to about £23,000 in 1613, the year following his death. There was a spectacular rise in the Court's income under Cottington. The annual net figures for 1637-41 were as follows: 1637, £61,900; 1638, £66,700; 1639, £83,100; 1640, £76,200; and 1641, £69,300. Another way is to compare the prices paid for wardships: of the average of 172 wardships that were purchased annually in 1635-8, about thirty went for between £2,000 and £10,000, while only twenty had sold for £2,000 or more in 1612-34. Finally, if the prices paid for wardships in Somerset are representative of the rest of the country, wardships went for an average of about £400 more under Cottington than during 1612-24.[9]

From the Crown's standpoint, which has sometimes been forgotten by those who have assessed the Court's operations harshly in sympathy with the oppositionists, Cottington's Mastership was extremely successful. It is well that it was: the Government faced a crisis in the late 1630s more serious than any since the Stuarts acceded to the throne. By 1640 the Crown could meet its financial obligations resulting from the Scottish rebellion, which began three years earlier, only with the greatest difficulty. The decision taken by the King and Laud to enforce Anglicanism in Scotland after years of virtual indifference to the growth of Presbyterianism culminated in the collapse of Charles's personal government. With Laud, the King had visited Edinburgh in 1633 to be crowned belatedly. In the following year, without sufficient consultation with the Scottish ecclesiastical and secular leaders, Charles instructed the Scottish bishops to prepare an Anglican prayer-book. Its introduction at St Giles' in July 1637 touched off riots, led to the subscription to the Covenant by Presbyterians, who swore to resist the new liturgy to the death, and eventually brought war.

The Scottish and English Privy Councillors underestimated the seriousness of opposition in Scotland to the liturgical reforms. Even after the Covenant was signed, making the Scots Presbyterians rebels in the King's eyes, he and his advisers took almost no steps to thwart them. It was a month after the riot in Edinburgh before the Scottish Councillors warned the King of the imminence of general rebellion. They had the authority to act at once, but they hesitated, reporting to Charles: 'not knowing what effect this may have & where it may lead to, we will not meddle . . . until we hear of your judgment.' They so misunderstood the gravity of the situation that they recessed until 20 September; thus two months passed without any official response to the challenge to royal authority. The Councillors at Westminster did as little, although Charles sent the Marquis of Hamilton to Edinburgh in June 1638 to try to arrange a settlement. This could never be achieved, however, so long as Charles and his advisers believed as they did that the Crown should not compromise unless the Scots repudiated the Covenant.

Notwithstanding this crisis, it was to be expected that the English Privy Councillors should have attended to their normal duties, which was the case with Cottington and Juxon. Over the winter of 1637-8 they renegotiated the leases of the Great and Petty Farms of the customs, on which they increased the rents. The syndicate administering the Great Farm, composed of Sir Paul Pindar, Sir John Jacob and John Wolstenholme, was dissolved after they and the Crown disagreed on the amount they should pay and on the admission into the syndicate of partners favoured by Juxon. The new lease went to another syndicate that included Lord Goring, Sir Abraham Dawes, Jacob, Sir Job Harby, John Nulls and Nicholas Crispe for a term of three years at an annual rent of £172,500. The lease of the Petty Farm (for wines and currants) was given to six partners for a rent of £72,000.

These contracts, by which Cottington and Juxon raised the annual revenue of the Crown by several thousand pounds, were of substantial financial assistance to the King. The Great Farmers advanced Charles £70,000 and loaned him a great deal more money before the Farms were again renegotiated in 1640. But the expenditure of the Crown was so heavy in these years that, even with the additional money from the Farmers and the increased revenue from the Court of Wards and other sources, there was scarcely any ready cash in the Exchequer. Neither from a financial nor a military standpoint was the Government in a position to suppress rebellion in Scotland and prevent its spread into northern England.[10]

Hamilton concluded after reaching Edinburgh that war with the rebels was virtually inevitable, even if Charles granted their demand for a General Assembly and a Parliament. On hearing this, Charles let it be known that he was already strengthening his defences at Carlisle and Berwick and would make war unless the Scots came to terms. In July 1638 he appointed a Scottish Committee that included Arundel, Coke, Juxon, Cottington, Hamilton, Vane, Lennox and Morton. Henceforth they, in consultation with Charles, handled all matters relating to the government of Scotland and preparations for war. Cottington also sat on three other Privy Council committees whose work was related to national defence: the Irish Committee, which co-ordinated efforts by Wentworth to enlarge the Irish army with military preparations in England; the Admiralty Board, which strove against all kinds of impediments to make the fleet an effective fighting force; and the Ordnance Committee, which oversaw the purchase, manufacture and supply of arms and ammunition.

It did not help the Government to forge a solid front against the Scots that the Scottish Committee and other Privy Councillors divided over whether to go to war or try to pacify the rebels another way. Basically, Arundel, Cottington and Windebank favoured war, while Vane and Northumberland advocated compromise with the Scots. Coke was at first undecided, but he finally came out on the side of peace. Although Laud had had a hand in provoking the Scots' rebellion, he initially refused to commit himself, being 'less able to advise than you', he told Wentworth, 'what is fit to be done'. In November, however, when the Scottish General Assembly in Glasgow abolished the episcopacy, the canons, the liturgy, the Court of High Commission and other mainstays of Anglicanism, Laud could no longer hold his tongue or ignore the necessity of teaching those who had attacked the form and fabric of his Church a lesson. The views of the Lord Deputy were never in doubt. While he cautioned Charles not to go to war rashly, he was unwilling that the Government should make concessions that jeopardized the King's authority in Scotland. If he could subdue the independent spirit of Irishmen, he advised, why should not the

King do the same in Scotland? As the situation there deteriorated, and then developed into war, Wentworth came out ever more strongly in favour of punishing the Scots, so that at the last he was the fiercest hawk among the King's advisers.[11]

If the agonising decision over war or peace divided the Councillors, it also brought Cottington and Laud a little closer together for the first time since the contest over the Treasurership in 1635-6. Neither man had forgotten the bitterness of those days, and they had kept their distance, but at least now, in the face of common peril, they became somewhat friendlier towards each other. It is true that Laud still saw Cottington as a wily conspirator – accusing him to Wentworth of trying to persuade Charles to summon Parliament, hoping thereby that it would force Juxon from office and make it possible for Cottington to become Lord Treasurer after all – but at the same time he enjoyed his old rival's company at dinner, accepted his gift of a doe at Christmas, and was merry over rumours of his plans to marry one of Lord Coventry's daughters. Whether Cottington seriously contemplated marrying again at the age of nearly sixty is difficult to say.

There was much speculation about Cottington's motives in allying with the Lord Keeper's family. Some said that he wanted to make money in the bargain, which was a plausible explanation for a man who liked money and had spent much of what he got maintaining several households. Lord Percy believed that Cottington was simply mending his fences in the event that the impending war with the Scots might lead to the loss of his offices. Laud as usual saw a sinister motive, which was that Cottington hoped to improve his standing at Court through Coventry. Such insinuations suggest that the marriage would have been made but for differences that developed between Cottington and Coventry that autumn over the dowry. Cottington wrote to Wentworth that he would tell him everything eventually, but for the present said only that he had finally decided not to marry.[12]

The Scottish Committee and royal officials throughout the country worked furiously during the winter of 1638-9 preparing for war. Aroused to firm action at last, the Committee instructed Wentworth, still President of the Council of the North in spite of his long absence in Ireland, to have his deputies in Yorkshire muster and exercise the trained bands. At such northern centres as Newcastle, Hull, Berwick and Carlisle, peers and gentry assumed command of their own companies of infantry and cavalry. By November the Scottish Committee had had large stores of ammunition, weapons and supplies deposited in the principal royal magazine in the North at Hull. The Committee also ordered the Lord Lieutenants in the northern counties to alert the trained bands to be ready to march at short notice; selected the higher officers for the army; asked the aristocracy and gentry to donate money in support of the war effort; and saw to the preparedness of the fleet. Moreover, the Committee appointed Sir Jacob Astley the commissary in the North, and instructed him to co-ordinate defence plans with Wentworth and determine how much support might be expected from Scots loyal to the Crown.

The task of finding the money for the army and its supply fell to Juxon and Cottington, who, sitting as a rule three days a week with the Scottish Committee, scratched their heads at the huge sums which they were expected to snatch out of thin air. Cottington was perplexed: 'How we shall defend ourselves without money is not under my cap.' Before long Juxon resorted to a practice for which Portland, during another fiscal crisis ten years earlier, had been criticised: he authorised payment of bills on his own authority directly out of funds held temporarily by receivers of revenue, so that again the tellers of the Receipt of the Exchequer were bypassed, cheating them of fees and circumventing normal accounting procedures. The lack of funds forced the Scottish Committee to ask the aristocracy and gentry in command of troops to underwrite the costs of maintaining them at least until the full army mustered at York with the King about 1 April. It would be a long time before these creditors of the Crown saw any of the money that they laid out.[13]

Some noblemen doubtless believed that they were throwing good money after bad, since many of them were already substantial creditors of the Crown. On the whole, however, the aristocracy responded generously to the King's letter of January 1639, asking them to indicate how much they intended to contribute in support of the war, and whether they and their followers would meet him at York. Seventy-seven nobles responded, only a few of whom said that they could not attend the King personally. Virtually all the peers contributed upwards of £500 or £1,000, or sent fully equipped troops whose support they guaranteed. Cottington did not accompany Charles north in April; in addition to being ill much of February and March from the gout, he was 'gathering money for his Majesty's supplies' and serving on a board of fourteen (later twelve) men who governed the country in the absence of the King and most of the Councillors. Like the others, Cottington paid his share of war costs by purchasing two barrels of gunpowder and outfitting twenty horsemen for £300. It was at this time as well that he and Juxon failed in the first of several attempts to secure a loan from the Corporation of London. Soon after these negotiations collapsed, Cottington learned with relief that Charles, confronted by a much stronger Scottish army commanded by Alexander Leslie, had come to terms at Berwick in June. The first phase of the Bishops' War had ended without so much as a skirmish being fought.[14]

The pacification of Berwick settled more than meets the eye. The Scots' victory by default confirmed the Presbyterian settlement that had been adopted by the General Assembly at Glasgow, and proved that the royal Government could not cope with rebellion. The Privy Councillors do not appear to have understood what was happening. The most striking proof of this is the way that they responded to the pacification – trying to carry on with their ordinary tasks as if nothing had really happened. Charles himself was astonished when the Scots did precisely what they had threatened to do unless he satisfied their grievances – overthrow royal authority in Scotland and sweep away the form and fabric of the Established Church. What is hardest to understand about the attitude of the Government in the summer of 1639 is why the King and his advisers did not realise long before the Short Parliament met that the Scots could not be suppressed without much broader support from the country as a whole.

The King summoned Wentworth to London in August 1639. The Scottish policy of the Government thereafter was virtually synonymous with the wishes of Wentworth, now Earl of Strafford, who had shown in the North and in Ireland that he could enforce law and order and was expected to do the same in Scotland. In

F

October, Charles reorganised the Scottish Committee into a Junto of nine men including Strafford, Cottington, Laud, Juxon, Northumberland, Coke, Windebank, Hamilton and Vane the Elder. They oversaw the final, futile negotiations with the Scots in the following months and, when the talks broke down, undertook to strengthen the northern defences against the probability of another war. On 30 December, Charles once more reconstituted the membership of the old Scottish Committee, which became the Council of War, to include Strafford, Juxon, Hamilton, Cottington, five other Privy Councillors and the three commissary officers in the North – Astley, Sir John Conyers and Sir Nicholas Byron.[15]

The minutes of the Council of War in the three months preceding the Short Parliament in April 1640 show that the Government had finally awakened to the grave situation posed by the Covenanters, the lukewarm support or indifference of many Englishmen, and the lack of money with which to wage war effectively. It was one thing to strengthen fortifications in the North, at Dover and at the Tower, or to appoint officers and garner war material; it was another to rouse the country's martial spirit or to finance war. Not only Juxon and Cottington, but Strafford, Windebank and others worked hard to raise money any way that they could. The Council of War estimated that the projected army of 35,000 foot and 3,000 horse would need a minimum of £300,000, which was about a third of what it had cost annually in the later 1630s to run the Government, and a huge sum in view of the fiscal crisis.

Cottington was terribly worried. In the preceding July, soon after the pacification of Berwick, he had been unable to raise the money to pay the garrisons there and at Carlisle, and this sum was as nothing compared with what the King needed now. Cottington needled the sheriffs and others to collect ship-money, but this source yielded less than he expected because of the history of firm resistance to it and the notoriety of the Hampden trial. He wrote to the aristocracy and gentry in Charles's name, asking that they contribute as much as they could possibly afford. He sold wardships and leased wards' lands as vigorously as the market would bear. He began the renegotiation of the Great and Petty Farms of the customs with an eye towards raising the rents yet again. Although it cost the King £92,000 to redeem the Crown jewels that had been pawned in the United Provinces, he got them back in case he needed to raise money quickly. The financier Philip Burlamachi was persuaded to loan the Government £30,000 more. Cottington also pressed the salt monopolists to pay arrears in rents. In spite of Cottington's industry in gathering money in these and other ways, it was not enough. The King spent it faster than he could raise it, sometimes frivolously: over his protest Charles commanded him to arrange the purchase of Wimbledon Manor (for £14,770) simply because the Queen took a fancy to the property.[16]

When it became apparent that the Government could not meet its obligations, the King and the Council of War began to consider the possibility of summoning Parliament to secure the extraordinary revenue that he had done without since 1629. Strafford supported the idea in the conviction that he could manage an English Parliament as handily as Irish Parliaments. Cottington and Hamilton had recommended earlier that Parliament should be convened as a political and financial expedient, and agreed with Strafford. All the other Privy Councillors concurred with them except Laud, who wrote a paper to prove what in his view was the unconstitutionality of Parliaments, and how rebellion had in the past sometimes resulted from its meetings. The King decided to call Parliament in the end because he really had no other choice except bankruptcy, and because, as Windebank put it in summation of the Council's feelings, doing so would prove to his critics that Charles was anxious to follow the traditional way of answering their complaints and of winning their support against the Scots.

Thus the King took a step which might well have saved the Stuart political system several years earlier, but which now set the wheels of his ruination and that of many of his advisers in motion. After the writs went out for the election of Parliament that should convene at Westminster on 13 April, both the Court and the Country strove to secure the election of members sympathetic to their goals. Along with the other Councillors, Cottington used what political influence he possessed, especially in Wiltshire. Hindon, near Fonthill Gifford, placed its two seats at his disposal, and he nominated Miles Fleetwood and George Garrett to fill them. The fact that most of the other seats in Wiltshire went to persons on whom the Crown could not rely for support was rather typical of the elections throughout the country. The hopeful signs which Charles and his advisers saw in March, such as Strafford's success in raising troops and money during a short trip to Ireland, and the willingness of the Corporation of London to loan the Crown money (an arrangement which soon fell through), disappeared on the eve of the Short Parliament, when disorder in London and elsewhere increased tension and augured ill for the welfare of the King.[17]

The Short Parliament, which sat for only three weeks, showed that oppositionists to Stuart policies had long memories. John Pym responded to Lord Keeper Finch's opening remarks, stressing the urgency for subsidies and the willingness of the King to hear petitions, by enumerating the grievances of his countrymen in a memorable speech which left little doubt that the King would not have his way without making major concessions. On the one hand, Charles would not answer grievances favourably until Parliament granted him subsidies, and on the other, Parliament refused to give him anything unless he first made amends. As the King and the Commons moved farther apart, Cottington watched events with increasing concern, convinced that the Scottish crisis would end in war unless the country showed unity in the face of it.

Charles soon concluded that Parliament had failed him. At a meeting of the Council of War on the morning of 5 May, he said that he was considering dissolving Parliament. Vane, who had replaced the aged Coke as Principal Secretary, and most of the other Councillors advised Charles to do so. Strafford arrived half an hour late and cautioned against making rash decisions. Laud came even later, as Cottington was weighing the pros and cons of dissolution, and saying that there was danger of intervention by France or Sweden in support of the Covenanters. In the end all the Councillors except Northumberland and Holland agreed with the King that Parliament should be dissolved, and it was done that same morning. The Council met again in the afternoon in the knowledge that the Scots were probably even then marching south. Strafford led the solemn debate while Secretary Vane scratched out the words, barely able to keep up with exactly what he was saying. Since the Scots meant war, Strafford advised, honour demanded that Charles should wage a vigorous offensive that would bring him victory in a few months. To this purpose, Strafford assured the King, 'You have an army in Ireland you may employ here to reduce this Kingdom . . .', which was an apparent reference to Scotland ('this Kingdom') in the context of his remarks. Before another year had passed Strafford would hear his words ringing in his ears time and again.[18]

Notwithstanding his assurances, Strafford knew that the security of the nation depended on money. The failure of Cottington to wring a loan of £100,000 from the London Common Council is well known, as are his efforts to borrow from the City merchants and the Customs Farmers, who together raised £290,000. The Government even made overtures in a fit of irrationality for loans from Spain, France and the Pope, all of whom refused. By July the situation was grave: there was rioting in London; the navy was unable to stop the Dunkirker and Turkish piratical raids along the coasts of Cornwall, Kent and Sussex; lethargy and insubordination among the trained bands weakened the royal army. With all these problems on his mind, on 20 August, the same day on which the Covenanters crossed at Coldstream into England unopposed, Charles left for York to take command of his troops. Strafford and Northumberland accompanied him, while Cottington and most of the Councillors remained behind in charge of the caretaker Government.[19]

From May to November, Cottington also immersed himself in work of an unusual sort for him. Disorder in the City, such as the riot outside Lambeth Palace in May, persuaded Charles to appoint Cottington the Constable of the Tower. He began at once to garrison and provision it, and to use it as a base for keeping order, but in this respect, as Miss Wedgwood put it, there was little that he could do 'to attack . . . an atmosphere of hostility and suspicion'. The defences of the Tower were his major concern, and to be sure that things were done right, he moved into the citadel for about three months beginning in August. He brought in two hundred soldiers and stocked large quantities of ammunition, food and supplies against a possible siege. He also had the heavy cannon moved to the highest ramparts and pointed them westwards towards the City. In July, on order from Charles, he seized the bullion in the Tower that had been deposited by English and Spanish merchants, on the pretext that the King was borrowing it and would pay 8 per cent interest. Charles announced shortly afterwards that he would debase £300,000 of the coinage to be minted from this silver, so that shillings would contain only one part silver and three parts copper. But he thought again, and finally decided to keep only a third of the bullion, on which he agreed to pay interest, and not to debase the coinage for fear that doing so would raise prices and reduce the purchasing power of the Crown. Charles had been the author of these works, but both the Common Council and Parliament subsequently held Cottington to blame for them, as well as for menacing the City by strengthening the Tower.[20]

Cottington also became Lord Lieutenant of Dorset on 13 June, succeeding the lately deceased Earl of Suffolk, and held this office until 15 May 1641. Although far from the county, he nevertheless took pains to enlist capable officers to lead its trained bands; by September the Dorset contingent numbered fourteen companies of foot and 1,500 cavalrymen. When officers could not secure sufficient arms, when wagons and drivers were too few to move provisions, and when the port towns refused to co-operate in enlisting soldiers and paying taxes, Cottington expedited these problems through his deputies in Dorset. But there was little that he could do from a distance to quell riots among the Dorset troops, such as one in which a Roman Catholic lieutenant was murdered near Faringdon in Berkshire.[21]

Perhaps the greatest achievement of Cottington in the second half of 1640 was his purchase for the Crown of 2,310 bags of pepper (607,522 lb.) on credit from the East India Company for £63,283 11s. 1d., at some jeopardy to his own financial welfare. The Governor and Court of the Committees were anxious to sell the pepper, because the Company was heavily in debt and needed capital. Their asking price was 2s. 1d. if the pepper were exported, and 2s. 2d. if it was to be sold at home. It took tortuous negotiations as well as pressure and cajolery by Cottington before the Company agreed to sell the pepper to the Crown at the lower price. The contract of purchase obliged the Crown to pay for it in semi-annual instalments until December 1642. What sweetened the transaction for the Company and persuaded it to sell at that price was Cottington's intimation that the Crown might give the Company financial advantage later, as well as the fact that he and several Customs Farmers pledged certain royal revenue and their own estates as security against the debt. Cottington sold the pepper for £50,626 17s. 1d., a seeming loss to the Crown of about £12,657. On the other hand, the arrangement was basically of much greater advantage to the Crown than meets the eye. First, it acquired more than £50,000 when it badly needed ready cash to finance the war. Second, the Crown expected that much of the debt could be paid off through the future customs duties charged to the Company. Third, if the Crown had borrowed £50,000 at the going rate of 8 per cent instead of getting that amount by selling the pepper, the interest on the loan would have been nearly £6,100 for the contractual period ending in 1642. For these reasons the actual loss to the Crown was reckoned at the Exchequer as being only about £6,600, which was not much considering the advantages of having the money at once.

Nor is there any indication that in 1640 either the King or his backers – Cottington and eleven others – meant to cheat the Company of its money. No one could foresee that the Crown would be unable to repay the debt on time because of circumstances beyond its control. It is a near-certainty that neither Cottington nor the Customs Farmers would have pledged their own estates as security had they believed that the Crown would default on the debt, leaving them liable. In the next few years virtually all the backers, including Cottington, did become liable under law for the unpaid balance of the debt, although, because of his being first in Royalist Oxford and afterwards on the Continent in exile, the Company never collected his share of the debt through the suits which it brought against him.[22]

In the North, meanwhile, the situation had gone from bad to worse for the King. 'I have nothing to say to you,' he wrote curtly to Windebank on 23 August 1640, 'but to conjure my Lord Treasurer & Cottington in my name to hasten monies to me. . . .' The Covenanters marched unopposed over the Northumbrian hills towards the Tyne even as Charles wrote. They entered Newcastle on the 30th and were in occupation of a large region of north-eastern England. Without money, an effective army or navy, or broad national support, Charles had to reconsider summoning

Parliament again. Then he devised a plan with which the Privy Council concurred to try to avoid having to call it. He would summon the peers of the realm in late September to a Great Council at York and ask for financial support to carry on the war. From every county the nobles converged on the northern capital, while Cottington, Laud and Windebank, the Earl Marshal and the Lord Privy Seal remained in London in charge of the administration. Their duties were light; all they could do was to authorise payment of as many bills as the Crown could afford. Otherwise they awaited word of the decision reached at York. Secretary Vane predicted that the Great Council would disband quickly, and he was right. On its first day of meeting Charles took its advice to summon Parliament and to hold the army together until a firm decision on the war could be made after consultation with both Houses. Towards the support of the army Cottington and Juxon were instructed to ask the London Common Council again for a loan of £200,000. When the Council refused, Charles had no choice but to make a truce with the Scots at Ripon, recognising their occupation of six counties and agreeing to pay them £850 a day so long as they remained in England.[23]

In the same month of October the draper, Sir William Calley the Elder, Cottington's old friend from the early days in Spain, died and left him a gold ring bearing the image of a skull and crossbones. Whether Calley's bequest had any symbolical meaning for Cottington is anyone's guess, but he needed no mystical sign to tell him that Parliament would severely test the endurance of the Stuart ecclesiastical and political policies. If no one could foretell what might transpire in the next few months, it was clear that any changes which Parliament forced the Government to make would be to the disadvantage of those who had shaped policy in the previous decade.

Northumberland had the courage to face the danger to the principal advisers of the King posed by the leadership of the House of Commons. He sensed as early as 26 November that all the Privy Councillors were in peril, especially Strafford, Laud, Windebank and Cottington, whom he believed in imminent danger of ruin. The first sign of retribution in the Commons against Cottington came only a few days after the opening of Parliament. A parishioner of St Gregory's Church, which Cottington had had a hand in having demolished during the reconstruction of St Paul's, denounced him before the Committee for Religion. On 16 November an M.P. reminded the Commons that Cottington had menaced the City by turning the cannon on the Tower towards it, but the House dropped the matter when one of the Privy Councillors answered that Cottington had surrendered the office of Constable a week earlier. From December to June he stood in danger of losing Fonthill Gifford, which he had acquired in 1632 from the estate of the 2nd Earl of Castlehaven. His heir, James, Baron Audley, demanded recovery of this property on the grounds that Cottington had got it illegally at his expense. After lengthy proceedings in both Houses, the Lords confirmed Cottington's rightful ownership of Fonthill Gifford. Except for Audley's suit, neither the Commons nor the Lords troubled Cottington until May 1641. He sat in the Lords from time to time, but he said nothing except in defence of his own interests. To have said more would have been dangerous: Strafford was impeached, Windebank was called to account for countenancing papists and escaped to the Continent, and Laud was charged with high treason and later imprisoned in the Tower.[24]

One of the Scottish commissioners in London, Robert Baillie, expected the Commons to turn on Cottington in January 1641, but the examination of his administration in the 1630s was delayed until the early spring. Meanwhile, so far as a man in his vulnerable position could follow a normal schedule of work, he tried to carry on as usual. It does not appear that he was intimidated by the charges brought against Strafford and Laud into altering his administration of either the Court of Wards or the Exchequer. Petitions on wardships crossed his desk almost daily in early 1641, when he completed transactions on at least twenty-five cases to the profit of the King. He did so in spite of the fact that the Commons had appointed a committee in February to study suspected irregularities in the Court of Wards and corruption among its officials, which resulted the following November in charges (articles 43-6) being brought against this Court in the Grand Remonstrance.[25]

Apart from Juxon, who escaped all harm at the hands of Parliament, Cottington was the only major adviser of the King to steer clear of serious trouble during early 1641. If Cottington could not help Windebank, who wrote to him from Calais asking for money, he took a firm position in defence of Strafford. They had been friends for a long time despite the bitterness over the Treasurership six years earlier, and the Scottish troubles strengthened their friendship. That spring Strafford needed friends as never before. But the Commons, assisted by the Scottish commissioners and agents brought from Ireland to testify against his administration as Lord Deputy, prepared its case so thoroughly that Cottington could do nothing to change its mind by the time the trial opened on 22 March. Vane testified that Strafford had advised the King in the Council of War on 5 May 1640 to use an Irish army to subdue 'this Kingdom', which the leadership in the Commons took to mean England, and not Scotland, as he had probably intended. Cottington and two other Councillors (neither of whom had been present at this meeting) categorically denied that Strafford had meant any such thing. Cottington also took exception to the sixteen charges of the indictment accusing Strafford of having abused his authority in the Irish prerogative courts to increase the King's authority, and of having interfered with Irish manufacture and trade to his own profit. His defence of his old friend did no good, particularly as, after Strafford had been sentenced to be executed, the King abandoned him in spite of the exhortations of Cottington and Juxon to stand up to Parliament. Shortly before his death, on 12 May, Strafford asked Archbishop Ussher of Armagh to convey his thanks to Cottington for his help. It was ironic that the axe with which Strafford was decapitated was the very one that Cottington had had fashioned while Constable of the Tower.[26]

Cottington spent most of March and April at Hanworth recuperating from an attack of the gout, going into London occasionally to attend to urgent business at Court and in Parliament. It was during this period that he decided to surrender his offices. Historians have made much of a plan supposedly conceived by the Earl of Bedford to reshuffle the major offices of the Privy Council in order to include moderates acceptable to both the King and Parliament. Bedford should become Lord Treasurer in place of Juxon, Pym was to replace Cottington as Chancellor of the Exchequer and Lord Saye and Sele was to be Master of the Court of Wards. Bedford's death in May is said to have frustrated this plan. While changes in the Privy Council were certainly in the offing in April and May, it cannot be established that Cottington resigned his offices to accommodate the plan. A more plausible explanation is that he resigned out of fear for his life and estates. Whatever his actual reasons, he surrendered the Mastership shortly before 17 May to Saye and Sele, and the Chancellorship, which was put into commission, about the end of the month. His only other office, the Lord Lieutenancy of Dorset, went to the Earl of Salisbury.[27]

The surrender of his offices dispersed the 'black cloud' that the younger Calley saw overhanging Cottington. He secured the King's permission to absent himself from Court and the House of Lords, retreated to Hanworth, and in July moved to Fonthill Gifford, out of harm's way as he thought. He had spent thirty-five years in the service of the Crown and now, at the age of sixty-two, looked forward to the ease of retirement at his favourite estate. But events in the following year denied him the leisure and peace of mind that he craved at what he mistakenly believed to be the end of his career.[28]

CHAPTER 13

Councillor in War

WHETHER with their offices, their lands or their lives, the major advisers of the King paid the price which Parliament exacted of those who had furthered prerogative monarchy. Cottington's resignation from office in 1641 and retreat to Fonthill Gifford has traditionally been seen as a desertion of his political principles for the sake of wealth and ease. But in fairness to him, his difficulties and sacrifices on behalf of the Royalist cause during the last decade of his life should be considered before reaching a final judgement of his character and motives.[1]

His long association with the King's rule and his substantial wealth left Cottington vulnerable to punishment and exploitation even before the country fought the Civil War. There is no evidence that he lost any income from estates before August 1642, or that he had not put away enough money and plate to tide him over in the event of hostilities. Nor does it appear that he suffered from want at any time before the end of the war. Nevertheless, his financial situation began to deteriorate as early as June 1641. Cottington's sudden and disadvantageous sale of Thistleworth Park is proof of his concern about personal finances. Sir William Russell had obtained Thistleworth from the Crown for twenty-five years' purchase, and in turn had sold it to Cottington for £300. He disposed of it in mid-1641, perforce under a new title, which cost him additional money and cut into the amount realised from the sale. The fact that Cottington initially paid more for Thistleworth than it was worth at current prices, and then sold it at a loss, suggests that he was beginning to convert some of his investments into cash against a rainy day.[2]

In August 1642, a week before the Civil War began and while Cottington was living nearly a hundred miles away at Fonthill

Gifford, a company of Parliamentarian soldiers damaged his property at Hanworth. According to his servant there, Henry Cowes, who unsuccessfully petitioned Parliament to punish the troops for trespass and to make them pay for the damage, they 'attempted to pull down the pales [fences] . . . and endeavoured to ransack and pillage the [manor] house . . .'. Cowes and Cottington again petitioned Parliament in January 1643, shortly after Hanworth had been looted by soldiers. Entering the house forcibly, they seized a cache of small arms and ammunition, two pieces of ordnance and a chest containing plate and money, which they deposited in the Guildhall in London. Parliament knew better than to return weapons to the servant of an arch-Royalist and, at the request of the parishioners of St George's Church, Hanworth, who were Cottington's tenants, gave them the money and plate.[3]

Over the winter of 1642-3 Cottington was deprived of more property and menaced by Parliamentarians. Parliament appropriated the Broad Street house early in 1643 for the use of the Duke of Gloucester and Princess Elizabeth, and in September converted the residence into offices for the Commissioners for Excise. In December 1642 Sir Edward Hungerford, a cavalry officer then skirmishing in Somerset and Wiltshire, threatened to sack and burn Fonthill Gifford unless Cottington contributed £1,000 to the use of Parliament. On Christmas Eve, with the troops camped near by, Cottington dashed off a letter to the Earl of Pembroke and Montgomery, begging him to intercede with Parliament to restrain Hungerford. Not because the Parliamentarians took compassion on a sick old man, but rather because they decided to assess his worth systematically before demanding payment, Hungerford was instructed to spare the estate.[4]

The efforts by the Court of the Committees of the East India Company to recover the delinquent debt owed to the Company by the Crown were of grave concern to Cottington. Instalments on the debt, which he and the Customs Farmers had guaranteed in 1640 by pledging their estates as collateral, fell due semi-annually, beginning on Lady Day 1641. By the following January, when King Charles left London for the North, the Crown had fallen behind in the payments by about £22,000. Since the Company needed the money to satisfy its shareholders and questioned the intention of the Government to meet its debt, pressure was brought on the guarantors for payment.

Word of the Company's claim against him reached Cottington in January 1642. He wrote to King Charles on the 24th, asking that the Treasury Commissioners take steps either to meet the debt or to satisfy the Company that it would be paid in short order, so that 'imminent ruin fall not upon me . . .'. When Charles had done nothing by April, Cottington contacted Secretary Nicholas to make certain that the Commissioners delayed no longer in extricating him from his predicament. Finally, in midsummer, they proposed to the Company that the money for the debt might be raised by selling certain royal parks, and that assignments should be given to the Company on soil and timber rights in the Forest of Dean. The Company accepted this arrangement, but the war began before a settlement was reached, with the result that all was left in suspense indefinitely.[5]

Nevertheless, his partial responsibility for the pepper debt continued to vex Cottington until virtually all his property had either been sold or sequestered by Parliament. Since the Crown could not pay the debt, and Parliament refused to allow the Court of the Committees to recover the money by applying current customs duties owed as credit, the Company pressed the available bondsmen. But efforts to secure the money from Cottington, who had by then become Lord Treasurer at Oxford, proved fruitless, since the Royalists needed all they had to prosecute the war. The Court of the Committees subsequently brought suit in succession in the Court of Exchequer and in the Court of Common Pleas for the recovery of the debt. Cottington was named a defendant, but he was beyond harm, primarily because the Parliamentarians had disposed of nearly all his estates and houses. As late as September 1649 the Company was still striving to secure those of his lands, reputedly worth £600 p.a., which had not yet been alienated. It was not until 1662, ten years after Cottington's death, that the Commissioners of Customs settled with the Company for the Crown for £10,500.[6]

Cottington evidently remained at Fonthill Gifford during the first eight months of the war, until April or May 1641. If he kept close counsel with the King and his fellow Councillors or materially assisted the Royalist cause, there is nothing to support this assumption. It is not particularly convincing to argue that he absented himself from Oxford, where Charles set up headquarters in October 1642, only for reasons of health and age. Cottington was indeed elderly and ill, and there was danger in travelling approximately sixty miles from Fonthill to Oxford through country controlled by the Parliamentarians. But a determined man might have willingly endured danger for the sake of a cause. There must have been other reasons for his seeming indifference. The early months of the war were a time of decision for Englishmen – whether to support the King, join the Parliamentarians or try to avoid involvement altogether. The thought of remaining neutral, so far as a man of his background would allow, surely crossed Cottington's mind. Persons around the country faced the same agonising decision, and reached it as often on the basis of self-interest as of principle. At least one of Cottington's relatives, James (possibly his brother, but more likely his first cousin), was a Parliamentarian from the first and served as a Commissioner for Assessment in Somerset.[7]

The Parliamentarian operations in Wiltshire in the spring of 1643 dashed any hope that Cottington may have entertained about remaining at Fonthill Gifford. By April, Parliament controlled practically all the West of England, except Cornwall and an enclave around Wardour Castle in Wiltshire, near which Cottington resided. These operations, which endangered his person and estate anew, may have persuaded him a week or two earlier to leave the area for Oxford, for the outcome of Ludlow's Wiltshire campaign was never in doubt. Ludlow related how, upon entering the county, Hungerford and Colonel William Strode were besieging Wardour Castle in which Royalists from the district had taken refuge. Even before the defenders had surrendered the stronghold, however, the Royalist Earl of Marlborough had occupied Fonthill Gifford, but he evacuated it shortly before Parliamentarian cavalry captured the house. Presumably Cottington had left the estate with his valuables before the situation became desperate, otherwise he would surely have been taken prisoner.[8]

A veil of anonymity shrouds Cottington during his residence in Oxford in 1643-6. He comes down to us as a man standing in the wings while the main protagonists played their roles as decision-makers in the Royalist camp. He served as counsellor and elder statesman, advising the King on financial, diplomatic and political problems, sitting irregularly on the Council of War, chairing sub-committees and serving rather lamely as Lord Treasurer. Cottington was the only one of the King's old guard of major advisers besides Juxon to have survived the purge of 1640-1, the only one on hand in Oxford with first-hand knowledge of the administration during the King's personal government. It is curious in view of this that Charles did not make greater use of him, or that contemporaries said so little about his activities.[9]

Much of what we know about the Royalists' activities in Oxford during 1643-6 is derived from the cryptic minutes of the Council of War, an *ad hoc* advisory and administrative body appointed by the King. Although its personnel varied from meeting to meeting, depending on the business being discussed, it generally included higher army officers, Privy Councillors and heads of Government agencies. The war council handled finances connected with the prosecution of the war by the Royalist army headquartered in Oxford; saw that the troops had arms and supplies; governed the permanent garrison protecting the city; and co-ordinated military affairs with the civic and university officials. In some ways the war council resembled the Privy Council in its operations, which were adapted to fit the exigencies of war-time, although a junto of Privy Councillors continued to sit apart from the war council. Lord Cottington served on both the Council of War (attending less than half its recorded meetings) and the Privy Council, and chaired subcommittees on finance and diplomacy of both councils.

The Council of War concentrated on immediate but not crucially important questions, and rarely discussed long-term or overall strategy. The King preferred working with small groups, discouraging the war council from assuming too much independence. After May 1643 Charles usually took the advice of an informal junto of Privy Councillors, who gradually superseded the Council of War as policy-makers. In September the King created a new and even smaller junto of advisers, including Culpeper, Hyde, Nicholas, Richmond and Cottington, who chaired its meetings at Oriel College and headed the Royalist civil administration whenever Charles was away.[10]

Cottington was made Lord Treasurer on 3 October 1643, upon

the dissolution of the Treasury Commission. He technically held this office for the rest of his life, although it carried little dignity under the circumstances and ceased to be of any importance after his flight to the Continent (in 1646). The following January the King reinstated Cottington as Master of the Court of Wards and Liveries, by then a largely honorific position which he made something of to the benefit of the Crown, despite the existence in London of a Parliamentarian Court of Wards headed by Lord Saye and Sele. In fact, Cottington collected about £26,000 in 1643-5; he himself received an annual fee of 200 marks, a living allowance of £100 and the customary fees and gratuities. Prestige and ample income were his so long as the Royalist Government at Oxford survived.[11]

Most of Cottington's days were taken up with detailed administrative duties. He handled the personal finances of the King's and Queen's Households at Christ Church and Merton Colleges as well as most of the diplomatic correspondence. He authorised the issuance of warrants to Court officials, for expenditure connected with the visit of the French ambassador and for the repayment of loans. He also executed warrants by the King to empower finance officers to perform tasks in the Exchequer and to dismiss other officials. The Lord Treasurer saw that the commissioners for assessment of taxes in the counties surrounding Oxford and controlled by the Royalists collected enough to support the city and garrison, and intervened personally whenever tax delinquency became chronic in particular areas. He gave an inordinate amount of time to keeping track of those who paid their weekly assessments regularly and those who did not, and to the punishment of obdurate delinquents.[12]

Cottington had his hands full trying to raise money to meet the Crown's heavy financial obligations, the more so because the Parliamentarians controlled London and most of the richer regions of the country. By December 1643 the Royalists needed money so desperately that Cottington and Hyde (Chancellor of the Exchequer) began the practice of rewarding informers with a quarter of the money recovered from debtors of the Crown. But money trickled in slowly: the Crown could not even afford to repay Privy Councillors who had made small loans 'for supply of our urgent

occasions', including one of £50 by Cottington. He left no stone
unturned in search of money, as can be seen in an agreement that
Cottington made with France through Henrietta Maria in May 1645
to supply tin from the Cornish mines, which yielded a great deal
of money from the trade and the customs collected on it. He can
also be observed at work that year when he arranged the purchase
of war material. The safe delivery of one thousand barrels of gunpowder, thirty tons of brimstone and three hundred tons of saltpetre from Antwerp for £11,850 proved to be a complicated
operation which Cottington managed with skill.[13]

While such purchases helped to strengthen the Royalists in the
field in the weeks preceding the Battle of Naseby (June 1645), their
situation became ever more desperate. The Parliamentarians began
the first siege of Oxford about a fortnight before the King left the
city with an army destined to be defeated by Fairfax and Cromwell.
A large garrison remained in Oxford, but it was in critically short
supply of provisions and might have had to surrender had not
Fairfax been called away north. His troops had surrounded Oxford
on 22 May, and skirmished and burned on the outskirts for two
weeks. On the 27th, while the city was under heavy attack, Cottington himself led a company of soldiers to the southern bulwarks,
where, incidentally, there was little action. They were men whom
he knew personally, eighteen of them being cripples who 'had been
fed by his . . . bounty and would by no means stop behind . . .',
in spite of their wounds and broken limbs.[14]

Parliament had confiscated much of Cottington's property by
that time. On the authority of the Commons, which ordered on 9
February 1644 that the goods of militant Royalists should be
seized and sold, some belonging to Cottington were disposed of
and the money used in support of Fairfax's army. In August 1645,
when the Committee for Advance of Money was told that Cottington's servants had hidden valuables in his Broad Street house and
at Hanworth, the properties were searched and valued for sale at
£10,000. The Committee ordered that all Cottington's lands and
goods should be sequestered and that a thorough search be undertaken throughout the country to uncover what he or his agents
may have concealed. The investigators followed every lead. In
April 1646 the Committee sent men to collect £300 in arrears of

rent owed by five Cottington tenants at Blueberry Manor (Berkshire) and took possession of the estate on 13 May. Everyone concerned with the Cottington lands seems to have wanted a share of the spoils.[15]

The war had for all practical purposes been lost two months earlier, when Sir Jacob Astley surrendered the last Royalist army. The King admitted defeat in May by riding to the Scots camp outside Newark to give himself up, and it was only a matter of time before the Royalist stronghold at Oxford would have to capitulate. While its commandant, Sir Thomas Glemham, hoped to hold out in spite of a critical food shortage, plague, and the encirclement of the city by the enemy, the Privy Councillors refused to prolong the suffering that would have resulted from resistance to a siege, especially as the outcome was never in question.[16]

The Royalist delegation led by Cottington surrendered the city and garrison of Oxford on 20 June after five weeks of negotiation with Fairfax. Most of the articles of capitulation defined the general conditions of surrender, such as the withdrawal of the garrison and officials, and the disposition of their weapons, stores and personal effects. Several articles related directly to Cottington and his colleagues, who, faced with defeat, now had to consider what the Parliamentarians meant to do with them. On the whole the settlement was generous and lenient. The commonalty could remain in Oxford or leave with their belongings. This applied as well to most gentlemen and their families, who were permitted to take their personal weapons and whatever else they wished to their homes or to those of friends. All the Royalists in the city, except those specifically excluded by Parliamentary ordinance, having lands and goods subject to sequestration could compound for them at reasonable rates any time within the next six months. Thereafter they would be free from financial penalty or taint of delinquency. Even those excluded from composition were permitted a period of grace of six months, or until such time as they were either allowed to compound or to emigrate.[17]

Cottington was one of those excluded from composition. He presumably left Oxford on 23 June with the rest of the leaders, the newly struck seal of the Master of the Court of Wards and

Liveries lying in a chest in the city library, a symbol of his own and the Royalists' fallen fortunes. One of his last official acts had been to countersign a paper conveying custody of the King's Garter jewels to Lieutenant-General Hammond for a consideration of £500. With half this money in his purse to tide him over the next few months – the probable reason for the exchange – Cottington departed from the city.[18]

He remained somewhere in England until that autumn, trying repeatedly to persuade Parliament to permit him to compound and, when it refused, seeking its permission to emigrate. On 2 September he petitioned the Lords for a licence to go abroad with his servants and goods, promising that Parliament's base opinion of him would be reversed by his exemplary conduct in retirement. He also asked that he be allowed to 'sell such of his poor goods as are yet left him (scarce worth the mentioning), towards the buying of bread'. Finally, he begged for 'competent means out of his estate for his future subsistence, lest he perish for want of maintenance' during his exile 'in his old decrepit age . . .'. The Lords denied the petition. However uncharitable this might seem, it is improbable that Cottington was as badly off as he tried to make out.[19]

He left England without licence some time between 2 September and 26 November 1646, crossing the Channel to France on the same vessel with Hyde and two of Strafford's former lieutenants, his lawyer, Sir George Radcliffe, and Christopher Wandesford, Master of the Rolls in Ireland. Many Royalist émigrés went to Caen or Paris, but Cottington chose to live at Rouen, where he received some help from Henrietta Maria. He enjoyed a peaceful life, virtually uninterrupted by official duties. He was still Lord Treasurer, but apart from his occasional and mostly futile efforts to raise money for the King in England, he had little opportunity to exercise his authority. From time to time he wrote to friends at foreign capitals in search of funds, and was involved in trying to promote Royalist commerce with the Spanish dominions in Latin Europe. Sometimes he helped a friend, such as Giacomo Anfossi, a Genoese living at Rouen, whom Cottington recommended to King Charles as English consul at Leghorn.[20]

Otherwise Cottington had little to do but nurse his ailments and enjoy the company of old friends at Saint-Germain, a major émigré centre that he visited periodically. Hyde wrote to Cottington from Jersey in August 1647 about one of these trips, assuming that his days at Henrietta's Court must have been 'proportionable to the leisure and vacancy . . . [that you would enjoy] if you were at your country house at Rouen and had nothing to do, but see my Lord Hopton play at bowls'. Hyde went on to say that by the time Cottington returned to Rouen there would be a messenger awaiting his instructions on what should be done in support of the Royalists in England. Indeed, what could be done? This question troubled the ageing Lord Treasurer for the rest of his life, during which he would have nothing to do with English domestic affairs, for it was his misfortune never to set foot in his homeland again.[21]

CHAPTER 14

Exile

THE victory of the Parliamentarians left them the lords of the hour, but they did not relentlessly press their advantage against their vanquished countrymen. In England there was nothing like the savage retribution which Continentals often inflicted upon their enemies in the early seventeenth century. Rank-and-file Royalists returned home unharmed to pick up the pieces of their shattered lives; while the Parliamentarians made something of their superiority by divesting the Royalist aristocracy of their land, goods and income. This was to be expected, yet even here the penalties might have been harsher. Relatively few Royalists were specifically excluded from pardon and composition. Most of them were allowed to compound for delinquency at moderate rates, often with the advantage of mitigating circumstances which persuaded the Government to reduce their fines still further.[1]

Would that King Charles had shown as much of a spirit of reconciliation during 1646-8. Some Parliamentarians did more harm to their own interests than to the Royalists' by quarrelling over politics and religion, and over social and economic reform. The struggle between Parliament and the army for control of the Government unfortunately created in the mind of the King a false impression of their irreconcilable divisiveness and decided him against making compromise. His escape from Hampton Court, his negotiations with the Presbyterian M.P.s and the Scots in a futile attempt to turn the clock back to 1641, and his rejection of the Propositions of Newcastle and of the Heads of the Proposals brought on the brief, decisive second civil war in 1648.

All this while many Royalist leaders were living in exile in the Channel Islands, France, the Low Countries and Ireland. They reviled their fortunes, endured years of dependence on foreigners and plotted the overthrow of the Parliamentarians.[2] Many émigrés were still young men or middle-aged in 1647 and could look forward to better days. By contrast, what could Lord Cottington have had to anticipate? How much could continued personal sacrifice for principles – a cause – have meant to a man nearly seventy who had been stripped by his enemies of honour, dignity, comfort – the advantages which a person of his long service to the Crown might have enjoyed in normal times? But the times were out of joint. The principles by which he had helped to govern England had been challenged and besmirched. His master, the King, had been hunted down and confined, while he himself had been driven from his homeland, deprived of nearly everything. Cottington lived simply at his house near Rouen and corresponded intermittently with Hyde. The trivial things which they discussed are reminders of how far they had fallen from Olympus. In an exchange of letters in 1648 they spoke of how their lettuce and onions grew; whether Cottington could spare some vegetable seeds; and what a difficult time Hyde had had getting Cottington's Spanish clock repaired. Since he was poorly off himself, it can be imagined how cynically the old Lord Treasurer answered a request by Prince Charles for money for an expedition to Scotland.[3]

So long as Cottington lived, and even afterwards, the Parliamentarians searched for, seized and sold or leased his property. The trustees whom Parliament empowered by ordinance (5 June 1648) to lease the lands of contumacious Royalists towards raising £50,000 for an Irish campaign, felt cheated when their operatives could not locate Royalists' land in several counties. Robert Smyth, of Monmouthshire, was perplexed by requests that he specify Cottington's property in that county when there was none. Most agents discovered that his lands had already been exploited by the Government for other purposes, such as those which went in October 1646 to Sir Francis Knollys, and the lease of the demesne of Kennington Manor in Surrey, which had been assigned to the support of the Elector Palatine. Not satisfied with the income from the Cottington estates, the Parliamentarians began to lease or sell his houses and, in one case at least, considered demolishing it for scrap. Much of the rest of his holdings in Kent, Middlesex,

Berkshire, Hampshire and Wiltshire was given to John Bradshaw, Lord President of the Council of State.[4]

The records of the Committee for Advance of Money show that the Government left no stone unturned in search of Cottington's personal property. A coronet found in an iron chest, formerly in his custody, was appraised for sale at £73 6s. 8d. The cottage of one Frisher, a Cottington tenant at Knoyle Manor in Wiltshire, was turned upside down on the strength of a rumour that he had £200 belonging to his landlord. From May to July 1652 the Committee hounded Thomas Smithsby, formerly the King's saddler, who was said to have hangings and carpets belonging to Cottington. Smithsby and his wife were interrogated, confessed that they had kept these items as collateral for a debt which Cottington owed them, and implicated his agent, Lawrence Squibb. The investigators then required Smithsby and Squibb to make separate inventories of all the personal property of Cottington which they knew about. When Squibb tried to conceal items and was found out, the Committee pressed him until he admitted that the Smithsbys had taken the goods in pawn for £200, which was sent to Cottington at Rouen. Still not satisfied, the Committee discovered that others had purchased things from Squibb and Smithsby. The buyers were allowed to keep their purchases provided they paid the Committee whatever the items had cost them, as follows: Captain Thomas Burgess, a bed, bedding, crimson velvet hangings and three velvet carpets, £206; John Powell, tapestries, £528; Joseph Collett, unspecified items, £47 15s.; and Thomas Browne, 'a crimson plush bed with a French fringe of gold and silk valence, a sarcenet quilt with gold fringe, and a plush carpet', £68. The Committee took its pound of flesh, but not before Squibb had spirited the £849 15s. to Cottington, and presumably more from earlier sales, which helps to explain how he managed to support himself abroad.[5]

The second civil war, which began in April 1648 with Royalist uprisings in Wales and south-eastern England and ended at Preston four months later, initially heartened the émigrés. They believed at the outset that the alliance between King Charles and the Scots and the differences between Parliament and the Cromwellians would bring a Royalist victory. In May, Henrietta Maria summoned Hyde, Cottington and other important Royalists to Paris for con-

sultation with Prince Charles, who was planning to join the Royalist
fleet off Helvoesluys. Hyde left Jersey and joined Cottington at
Rouen, where they heard that the Prince had gone to Calais. From
July to September they travelled up and down the coast of the Low
Countries in pursuit of him, going initially by ship from Calais
to Dunkirk. Another week was lost there before they found a
French officer willing to take them directly to Flushing, or so they
thought. Privateers overtook their vessel on 12 July, robbed them,
stripped the clothing off their servants and carried them to Ostend.
Cottington lost everything – trunks, clothes, jewels, money. He
complained to the Governor of Ostend of their indignities, had the
satisfaction of an official apology, and eventually recovered some
of his valuables after a great deal of trouble.[6]

Further complications delayed them. When Prince Charles failed
to answer a letter by Cottington asking for a ship, he and his friends
moved on to Middelburg on Walcheren Island, where they stayed
with English merchants for two weeks before setting out for
Rotterdam. Storms at sea prevented them from reaching Flushing
until 20 August and nearly swamped their ship. Hyde marvelled
at Cottington's stamina throughout their ordeal. Although some
thirty years his senior, Cottington bore his 'ill accommodation'
aboard the frigate 'with the same . . . cheerfulness as he received
the fairest lodgings'. Even so, Hyde could see how hard the voyage
had been on the old man, who 'stoops under a vile cough he hath
taken by the cold nights, and sitting long above the hatches, there
being indeed no other place in which he can sit, and is not without
an alarm in his feet and knees of the gout . . .'. It was Hyde who
found the courage to persevere at the sight of Cottington 'leaping
nimbly' out of bed on the morning that they had news of a fair
wind.[7]

When Cottington and Hyde left Rouen, the outcome of the war
in England hung in the balance. By the time they reached the Prince
at The Hague in mid-September he no longer urgently needed their
advice. A month earlier Cromwell had cut Sir Marmaduke Langdale's
Royalist army to pieces at Preston and captured the remnants of
the Scottish forces. The King's cause had been hopeless long before
the end, but he refused to face the fact. Parliamentarian commissioners bargained with him at Newport on the Isle of Wight,

trying in vain to persuade him to accept terms before the army officers took matters into their own hands. Regardless what might be said about Charles – his courage, indomitable spirit or downright stupidity – he ignored the seriousness of his predicament in the mistaken belief that he still had a chance of being his own kind of King in defiance of circumstances which he could no longer control. He refused the Commons' last offer on 1 December. On the 5th, Colonel Pride purged the Lower House of all but a rump of army supporters. Just before Christmas began the drama that ended on a scaffold outside the Banqueting Hall in Whitehall.

The 'groan' uttered by thousands of spectators at the stroke of the executioner's axe reverberated in all the capitals of Europe – in Paris and Madrid, in Augsburg and Venice, and in The Hague too. The dreadful news paralysed the émigrés. In their eyes there was now a new King of England and a new Government in exile. Expressions of grief by the States General and the crowned heads of Europe poured into Charles II's Court. His dejection at his father's death and his own wretched situation, in which he could not even afford to buy mourning clothes without money from the Prince of Orange, much less take vengeance on his enemies, was shared by his advisers.[8]

The rehabilitation of the Royalists began with their resolution to destroy the Cromwellians. Charles II acted swiftly; steps needed to be taken to organise Royalist ranks for the struggle ahead. Clarendon said that the new Privy Councillors were sworn in soon after news of the regicide reached The Hague. In fact, Cottington and the others took their oaths on 3 May, some three months later. It cannot be said that Cottington felt as eager for action as did the King: he realised the difficulties ahead and had almost given up hope of returning to England. The likelihood was that Charles would leave The Hague and expect his Councillors to accompany him. Cottington dreaded the thought. All he could think of was to find a place in which to spend the rest of his life peacefully.[9]

Cottington had more in common with those Royalists in England who resigned themselves to accept what they were unable or unwilling to change than with his colleagues at The Hague. If he gladly wrote letters on behalf of Charles II to the Emperor, Philip IV and other princes to try to raise money, how could he fit into the strenuous plans to overthrow the English Republic? There were basically three alternatives open to Charles – conquest of England with foreign aid, through an Irish alliance or with the help of the Scots Presbyterians – and each was hotly debated by the Privy Councillors, who could not make up their minds which course was best.[10]

In the end it was Cromwell, because of the speed and effective-ness of his invasion of Ireland in the second half of 1649, who set the course that the Royalists would follow. Charles allied with the Scots, invaded England and was defeated at Worcester two years later. Before the Irish invasion forced Charles to change his plans, however, he had decided in May to move his Court to Ireland, instructing his servants and lesser officials to leave at the earliest moment aboard ships lent by the Prince of Orange. The Councillors were to send their trunks ahead on the same ships and be ready to sail at short notice. This forced Cottington to a decision. Should he accompany the King or stay behind? The damp climate in Holland aggravated his gout, and he disliked the Dutch way of life. If he returned to France, where his pro-Spanish views were as well known as his squabbles with Henrietta Maria, the French Court would probably deny him aid. While Cottington considered these possibilities, another presented itself. Clarendon relates how there came to The Hague at this time from Madrid an Englishman bearing news of Philip IV's passionate reaction to the execution of Charles I, and how Philip hoped to exchange ambassadors with Charles II as an initial step towards helping him recover the throne. The report misrepresented the Spaniard's true feelings, as events subsequently proved, but it afforded Cottington an opportunity to settle his future without humiliating himself.[11]

The idea of a Spanish embassy to solicit money probably origin-ated with the Prince of Orange in April 1649, but Cottington made the most of it. He dared not promote it too vigorously, lest his own enthusiasm were interpreted as an evasion of responsibility. Should Charles approve the embassy, Cottington reasoned that he would surely be chosen to lead it, since no one at The Hague could match his knowledge of Spain or diplomatic experience. But Cottington knew that he would need help. As he told Hyde, he was 'not fit to be relied upon alone in an affair of that weight . . .

[and] might probably die upon the way, or shortly after his coming thither, and then the whole affair . . . must miscarry . . .' without another to carry on. This was a sound argument, but there were others which convinced Hyde that he should accompany Cottington to Spain. He trusted Cottington: they were old friends and had been through a great deal together since 1641. The King's primary need was for money to support an English invasion, and the Spanish embassy might well result in procuring what he required. There were also personal considerations. Hyde disapproved of an alliance with the Presbyterians and shared the King's impatience with the overbearing Queen Mother, who insisted that Charles should ally with the Irish Catholics. What Hyde failed to realise is that he had fallen in completely with Cottington's secret plans. He wanted Hyde's assistance because he expected, even before departing from The Hague, never to leave Spain.[12]

King Charles had no more idea than Hyde what Cottington had in mind, but the prospect of financing the Irish expedition with Spanish gold was reason enough to approve the embassy. On 24 March, Cottington and Hyde were appointed ambassadors extraordinary, and two weeks later completed their plans. Charles instructed them to call on Archduke Leopold in Brussels first, to seek funds, clear diplomatic channels for their mission, and obtain his assurance that Prince Rupert's Royalist fleet might have access to ports in the Netherlands. The King also specified their goals in Spain. Money should be their primary concern, and they should solicit it from anyone 'well-affected and willing to assist' the Royalists, whether Catholic or Protestant, Spanish or English. The ambassadors should also make any treaty offered by Spain which would provide men, ships or funds for an Anglo-Spanish invasion of England, assuring King Philip that he would be repaid upon the restoration of Charles.[13]

Cottington and Hyde left The Hague on 27 May, reaching Antwerp in three days. There Hyde joined his wife and children and made arrangements for their security during his absence before the ambassadors took advantage of the opportunity to enjoy themselves for a change. They also called on Governor Don Juan de Borgia, who conducted them through the castle that guarded the harbour on the eve of their departure for Brussels, where they lodged with the English resident, Henry de Vic. They had busy weeks conferring with Archduke Leopold and the Duke of Lorraine which resulted in the promise of 20,000 crowns for King Charles and 2,000 pistoles for themselves. Together with their own savings, the ambassadors now had the money which the King required them to raise for the trip to Spain.[14]

In Brussels the ambassadors sensed something of the coolness with which the Spaniards would receive them in Madrid. Spain had to be cautious; she had no way of knowing how long the new English Republic might survive or how it would conduct foreign affairs. Since the Rump appeared to be anti-Dutch and anti-French, however, at least Spain saw the possibility that an arrangement might be worked out with Cromwell. Besides, the Republic's navy was so strong that it could be a serious threat to Spanish commerce and the New World colonies.[15]

On 22 July the ambassadors followed the King to Paris (via Ghent, Mons and Péronne on the river Somme), which they entered on 2 August. They lodged at the Grand Moyes Inn in the Faubourg Saint-Germain and dined that evening with Sir George Carteret, John Evelyn the diarist and others, pleased that they could spend several days with friends. In fact, they stayed much longer. King Charles wanted them at hand while he organised the Irish expedition, and they also tried to further his interests in conferences with Cardinal Mazarin. He gave Cottington and Hyde the impression that he welcomed their offer to use their good offices with Don Luis de Haro, the principal adviser of Philip IV, in resolving the Franco-Spanish war, when all along the Cardinal wanted to be rid of the Royalists so that he could concentrate on suppressing the Frondeurs. The envoys were also drawn indirectly into the quarrels which divided the exiles, partly as a result of the tension between Charles and Henrietta Maria, who insisted on meddling in his affairs.[16]

Cottington, Hyde and fifteen aides and servants set out at long last for the Spanish frontier on Michaelmas (29 September) or the next day. Their journey of four hundred miles over rough roads to San Sebastian in three weeks that wet autumn was an ordeal. Yet Cottington was 'as lusty as ever' and took the discomfort in his stride. It was another eighteen days before King Philip permitted them to leave for Madrid. They rode mules through the mountains as far as Vitoria and went the rest of the way in litters to Alcobendas, north of Madrid, only to learn that the Council of State still had not assigned them a house befitting their station. It was apparent that Haro wished to discourage them from staying too long; he had hinted repeatedly in correspondence that they were not really welcome. By this time (December 1649) the Spanish Government was already moving diplomatically in the direction of recognising the English revolutionary regime, and the Royalist envoys could prove to be an embarrassment. They lodged with the English resident, Sir Benjamin Wright, and had their first audience with the King on 10 December.[17]

The ambassadors faced a more difficult task than they at first imagined, even though the Spanish Court and the foreign diplomatic corps appeared sympathetic to the aims of the Royalists. Notwithstanding their gracious words and courtesies towards the English envoys (including, finally, a house), the King and his advisers scrupulously evaded talk of money, although they granted other requests which were made on the basis of new instructions sent by Charles II. The ambassadors initiated negotiations towards the restoration of Frankenthal to the Elector Palatine, which was handily arranged the following month, and persuaded King Philip to open his ports to Prince Rupert's Royalist fleet, then cruising off Cadiz, provided he gave prior notice of entry and neither smuggled in contraband nor violated Spanish neutrality. This agreement lasted only until November 1650, however, because Rupert attacked Republican merchantmen off Málaga in Spanish waters and was defeated by Blake's superior fleet.[18]

Meanwhile Cottington and Hyde failed to achieve two other goals of their mission, one of which involved mediation of the Franco-Spanish war, which Charles II believed would dispose these powers to help him financially. Both belligerents evidently wanted peace, and Mazarin admitted that Cottington had an outside chance of arranging a cease-fire prefatory to peace negotiations. But the ambassadors failed by March 1650 to move the talks off dead centre because the war was going well for Spain on the Netherlands border and Philip IV rejected France's demand that she be given his provinces along the Pyrenees.[19]

The envoys also tried to obtain a loan for Charles II from the Holy See. Robert Meynell had gone to Rome in the summer of 1649 to negotiate with Innocent X, while Cottington was to confer with the papal nuncio in Madrid and persuade King Philip to intercede with the Pope. Although it is unlikely that the Pope would have given the Royalists anything, Charles undercut Cottington's efforts by allying with the Scots Presbyterians in the Treaty of Breda. In July 1650 Meynell wrote Cottington 'In plain English', that 'nothing can be expected hence in favour of . . . [the King] in these circumstances; for I have had a flat answer . . .'. Cottington received the same answer in Madrid.[20]

The arrival of an English Republican agent sent to establish diplomatic relations with Spain put Cottington and Hyde on the defensive in the early months of 1650. The English Council of State chose a capable man from its small stable of experienced diplomats in Anthony Ascham, who had worked with Dr Isaac Dorislaus at The Hague. Ascham disembarked at Santa Maria, near Cadiz, and was immediately taken ill. While he recuperated, troubled by thoughts of his difficult mission and the shocking news of Dorislaus's murder, which made him fear for his own life, Cottington remonstrated with Haro against Philip's receiving an agent of the Government that had executed Charles I. On 5 June, Ascham and his companions reached Madrid (coincidentally passing Cottington and Hyde outside the city) and took rooms in an inn which had neither locks nor bolts on its doors and windows. Some time the next morning, probably about noon, six young Royalists[21] burst into Ascham's room, mortally wounded his interpreter, Juan de Riva, and stabbed the agent to death.[22]

Cottington and Hyde learned of the assassinations almost immediately, because of the noisy crowd that surrounded the inn. Instead of fleeing the city, the murderers panicked and sought asylum at the Venetian embassy, but the ambassador admitted only Henry Proger, who was entitled to it by reason of his being on Hyde's staff. The others took refuge in the Church of San Andrés, where, in violation of sanctuary, constables arrested them and took them to prison. Their deeds had created a potentially explosive international incident involving the Royalists, the English Commonwealth and the Church, which promptly excommunicated the chief constable responsible for arresting them. The English Council of State wrote to King Philip immediately after the news reached them, demanding that the Royalists be executed; that Ascham's remains, which had been buried upright in the inn grounds because he was a Protestant, be returned to England; and that his secretary, George Fisher, now agent, be protected. This letter increased Philip's anxiety that the Commonwealth might take military or commercial reprisals unless he complied with the demands. He also had to consider how the Royalists might react, since his Government, although reluctant to assist Charles II, had not yet decided firmly whether or not to recognise the Republican regime.[23]

The furore over the case blew over in a few weeks. Spanish opinion was dead set against the Protestant agent sent by the heretical Government of England. The Church had acted firmly in defence of sanctuary to the embarrassment of the Government. The diplomatic corps in Madrid, annoyed that the authorities had forced the Venetian ambassador to surrender Proger, stood without exception behind Cottington, Hyde and the assassins in order to protect the right of political asylum. For these reasons the Government merely kept the murderers imprisoned until 1653, when all of them made their escape except William Spark, the only Protestant among the six, who was recaptured and executed the following January. Ascham's murder had no adverse effect on the embassy of Cottington and Hyde; it was apparent before it happened that they could not achieve their major goals. Thereafter they strove to obtain money from the Council of State in reimbursement of their expenses before terminating their mission. It was not until the middle of 1651, three months after Cottington and Hyde left Madrid, that King Philip authorised payment of 50,000 pieces of eight to the use of Charles II, from which they deducted their costs.[24]

Their eagerness to settle their debts confirms their expectation that their embassy would shortly be ended. Philip IV put off recognition of the Commonwealth so long as Charles had a chance of recovering his throne on the battlefield. But Cromwell's victory over the Scots at Dunbar in September 1650 proved the strength of the Republic and the hopelessness of the Royalist counter-revolution. About the same time that Philip instructed Cardeñas in

London to establish formal relations with the Republic, he let Cottington and Hyde know that they were no longer welcome. Hyde could not leave soon enough; he had disliked Spain from the first and was anxious to rejoin his family and the Royalist Court. Cottington had other plans.

Hyde first learned of them to his astonishment shortly before 29 December 1650. 'Whatever you expected and believed if you were here,' he wrote to Nicholas, 'you would not think Lord Cottington would be so mad as to stay in Spain. . . .' Cottington had asked Haro the previous day for permission to live in Valladolid. He spoke of his advanced age, his infirmities and the impossibility of his travelling any distance in the dead of winter. Haro agreed on condition that Cottington did so quietly as a private person, not as a representative of the Royalists. Haro also told him that Philip had granted him an annual pension of 1,500 ducats – a gracious gesture to an old and respected adversary whose identification with Spanish culture was well known.[25]

On the morning of 6 March 1651 the ambassadors rode together to the outskirts of Madrid and parted for ever. Hyde was bound for Antwerp, where he began that phase of his career that culminated in the Lord Chancellorship during the early years of the Restoration. Cottington went to Valladolid, stayed a week at the Jesuit English College founded by Robert Parsons in 1589, and moved into a house of his own. He spent the last fifteen months of his life in the city where he had launched his career as a royal servant in comparable obscurity more than forty-five years earlier.[26]

G

CHAPTER 15

Epilogue

LORD COTTINGTON lived in virtual seclusion in Valladolid for the rest of his life under the care of the Jesuits and three English servants. The vicissitudes of international politics and the administrative problems to which he had devoted his life no longer concerned him. Not that he had lost interest in the Royalist counter-revolution or the activities of his former colleagues. He still felt a part of the movement, but no one took seriously his offer to help forward it in Spain. His surviving letters for this period are terse and personal, written in a crabbed hand typical of the old and infirm. His mind was as sharp as ever, and he had not lost his sense of humour. Most of his friends had forgotten him; only Hyde and Edward Proger, Groom of the Bedchamber to Charles II, wrote with any regularity. Cottington learned of the Battle of Worcester (3 September 1651) more than two months after the fact, and was disappointed that the King had not written to wish him well in retirement.[1]

Cottington had never found the climate or the living conditions in Castile congenial. He had survived serious illnesses there three times and endured epidemics of measles, smallpox and plague. The gout had tormented him for years and he suffered from attacks of gallstones. Now, at the age of seventy-two, his strength waned. In the middle of May 1652 he told Proger that he was ill. Cottington died on the night of 18-19 June, two days after making his will, after a last illness of three weeks.[2]

The alienation of virtually all his property in England and the expense of supporting himself abroad for seven years left Cottington little to bequeath to his heirs. He had no immediate relatives left except his older brother, Maurice, who survived him by three years, and who had two sons, Francis and Charles, and two daughters, Jane and Dorothy.[3] Since they all lived in England and the will could not for the present be probated there, he named two Jesuits, Joseph de Aquila and John Freeman, and a merchant, Peter Aquado, executors of his estate in Spain. They were obliged to bury his remains decently and simply; to have masses said at his funeral in the chapel of St Andrews and simultaneously in every other church and chapel in Valladolid; to observe the anniversary of his death with masses; and to see that two thousand masses were recited in the next few years for the repose of his soul, one-fourth of them in the College chapel and the remainder in the city's convents. Cottington was generous to the religious communities of Valladolid. He bequeathed 100 reals to each of the four convents; the same amount to St Andrews; jewels and household effects to the Jesuits of the English College, who later sold them and used the proceeds to help build their new church. Cottington also asked his friend in England, Sir Francis Seymour, to pay the servants who had attended him to the end 1,200 ducats each plus an annuity of £20. To John Wardour, a novice at the English College, he left a silver bowl. Finally, whatever remained of his property in England, or that might be recovered later, Cottington left to his nephews, Francis and Charles.[4]

In accordance with Cottington's wishes, his body was interred in the old chapel of St Andrews in the English College, where it should remain until 'the Almighty God settle the differences of the Kingdom of England . . .', and his nephews could remove it thence. But the Jesuit executors construed his intent to be 'till such time as God restored to his church the kingdom of England', and had these words inscribed on his tomb, which was destroyed, after the remains had been removed, when the chapel was demolished. Some time before 1660 one of Cottington's servants brought his will to England and presumably gave it to his older nephew, Sir Francis, who occupied Fonthill Gifford after Bradshaw's death in 1659 and confirmed his ownership of it by law. His estate and that of his uncle then passed to Charles, the older of his two sons. Twelve years later, in 1678, Lord Cottington's remains were exhumed, transported to England by his grand-nephew, Charles, and re-interred beside those of Lady Cottington in St Paul's Chapel, Westminster Abbey.[5]

In a little over a hundred years following the death of Lord
Cottington, the male line of the Cottingtons of Somerset and
Wiltshire apparently became extinct, and their considerable holdings
had passed out of the hands of the family. Cottington's nephew,
Sir Francis, died in 1666 in possession of Fonthill Gifford, Free-
mantle Park and other lands which he had recovered with great
difficulty after the Restoration. He bequeathed the farm of Upper
Howtgill in Wiltshire to his brother, Charles, money to his sister,
Jane, who was then about sixty years old and lived at Godminster
Manor, and Fonthill Gifford to his wife, Elizabeth. Fonthill
evidently passed at her death to her heir, Charles (d. 1697). His
brother, Francis (born in 1666), married and eventually settled at
Fonthill. He in turn left a son, also named Francis. This last Francis,
the great-grand-nephew of Lord Cottington, was probably still
alive in 1755. All these Cottingtons of Wiltshire were Roman
Catholics, kept priests in their households and were occasionally
penalised for recusancy. They were quite well off financially until
the second quarter of the eighteenth century, when the survivors of
the family had lost most of their property. In 1744 Francis sold
Fonthill, which had been the basis of the family's wealth for three
generations after Lord Cottington's death, to Alderman William
Beckford of London and moved to Freemantle Park, Hampshire.
Ten years later, he sold Blueberry Manor in Berkshire. The
Godminster Cottingtons disposed of small parcels of land in the
vicinity of Pitcombe in 1736-43; most of the old manor remained
in their hands until *c.* 1749, when the heirs of John Cottington
(d. 1724), who cannot be positively identified, sold it to one
Charles Berkeley. Thereafter the Cottingtons in Somerset and
Wiltshire drop out of sight.[6]

So it was in the two centuries since the marriage of Philip
Cottington and Margery Middlecote that the family had risen from
merchant clothiers operating in eastern Somerset to wealth and
power in the person of its only illustrious member, and thereafter
gradually retreated into the comparative obscurity from which he
had temporarily brought it. After all this time Lord Cottington of
Hanworth still remains something of an enigmatic figure, not easy
to know or capable of being neatly characterised. Those of his
contemporaries who freely criticised him barely knew him, did not

know him except in his official capacity as a diplomat or an administrator, or bore him a grudge for some reason. To most of his acquaintances he seemed a cold and phlegmatic man, quiet and reserved. He made few close friendships and fewer lasting ones. He generally shut the world out and kept his counsel to himself.

Clarendon has left the soundest evaluation of Cottington, and spoke from intimate knowledge. Of Cottington's reputation, he wrote:

> The lord Cottington, though he was a very wise man, yet having spent the greatest part of his life in Spain, and so having been always subject to the unpopular imputation of being of the Spanish faction, indeed was better skilled to make his Master great abroad than gracious at home; and, being Chancellor of the Exchequer . . . had his hand in many hard shifts for money; and had the disadvantage of being suspected at least a favorer of the Papists, . . . by which he was in great umbrage with the people: and then, though he were much less hated than either of the other two [Laud and Strafford], . . . yet there were two objections against him which rendered him as odious as any to the great reformers; the one, that he was not to be reconciled to, or made use of in any of their designs; the other, that he had two good offices [Exchequer and Wards], without the having of which their reformation could not be perfect.[7]

Clarendon also cast a critical eye on the personality of Cottington:

> He was a very wise man . . . and by his natural temper, which was not liable to any transport of anger or any other passion, but could bear contradiction, and even reproach, without being moved . . . : for he was very steady in pursuing what he proposed to himself, and had a courage not to be frighted or amazed with any opposition. . . . He was of an excellent humour, and very easy to live with; and under a grave countenance covered the most of mirth, and caused more, than any man of the most pleasant disposition. He never used any body ill, but used many very well for whom he had no regard: and his greatest fault was, that he could dissemble, and make men believe that he loved them very well when he cared not for them. He had not very

tender affections, nor bowels apt to yearn at all objects which deserved compassion. [He] . . . left behind him a greater esteem of his parts [talents] than love of his person.[8]

Cottington did assume into his personality and style of life a good deal that was characteristically Spanish. His thought and behaviour were deeply influenced by his long association with Spanish culture. His clothes, his manner, even his use of certain kinds of phrases in his correspondence, bespoke his intimacy with Spain. There was something about his personality and demeanour that annoyed some of his associates. Moreover, Cottington was closely associated with royal policies (few of which he originated) that offended critics of the Crown and their apologists down to our times.

Far from being indifferent to his responsibilities or entirely self-interested, as his critics have charged then and since, Cottington was dutiful and industrious to a fault as a diplomat and administrator. In one sense he was his own worst enemy. He sprang from a family of merely local importance and lacked both a higher education and the kind of social connections that helped others to move ahead rapidly. He entered diplomacy at the lowest level at the then comparatively late age of twenty-five, by which time others had already secured places in the Government, the Church or the professions. The letters which he wrote during his early years in Spain, and some when he was in his thirties and forties, reveal his almost compulsive drive for personal recognition and success – wealth and power.

Cottington's associates and acquaintances, with remarkably few exceptions, did not think him obnoxious or unpleasant. On the contrary, they enjoyed his company, especially his sense of humour, and admired his stamina, even temperament and abilities. He rarely lost his temper, mistreated subordinates or became vindictive. He could be relied upon in a crisis. The pressures of office obliged him to follow a rigorous schedule of work that might have made him irascible or bitter, yet there was no trace of these traits in his personality. He maintained a balanced attitude towards life in spite of personal tragedies and professional setbacks that would have soured a man of less fortitude and tough resilience.

A tarnished reputation has dogged Francis Cottington down through the centuries to our own time. His critics accused him of being sly, a dissimulator and 'Spaniolised', to use their own term. This was a damning epithet for a Government official in the early seventeenth century, when many Englishmen, particularly those who had good reason to find fault with the domestic and foreign policies of the Stuarts, harboured an almost inbred distrust of Spaniards, who were their traditional enemies. Religion coloured the views of many Englishmen, of course. Since they believed (on hearsay) that Cottington was either a crypto-Catholic or sympathetic to Catholicism, an opinion which seemed to be corroborated by his apparently uniform pro-Spanish attitudes and his Spanish ways, this was even more reason to distrust him. Moreover, he served the Stuarts well, sometimes at the expense of the same persons who attacked the policies and practices of the Government in Parliament, in the press and in the pulpit. Since Cottington was clearly a supporter of the Crown and was putatively Roman Catholic and pro-Spanish for the better part of his life at a time when being any one of those things could bring the wrath of the Stuart system's critics on his head, it is small wonder that his reputation suffered heavy damage. He undoubtedly earned by some of his actions the reprobation of his contemporaries. Historians have by and large echoed those charges, more often than not without testing them against the evidence. A careful examination of his whole life as a diplomat and courtier suggests that it bears reassessment.

Notes

1. Clarendon, *History*, v 156. All references to the *History* are given by volume (not section number) and page. On the West Country woollen industry, see Kate E. Barford, 'The West of England Cloth Industry', *Wiltshire Archaeological and Natural History Magazine*, XLII 531-42; P. J. Bowden, 'Wool Supply and the Woollen Industry', *EcHR*, 2nd ser., IX 44-58.

2. P.R.O., Chancery, Inquisitions *post mortem*, C.142/133/94; P.R.O., Chancery Proceedings, Series I, C.2/118/7; H. W. F. Harwood, 'Philip Cottington's Will', *The Genealogist*, XIII 203; F. A. Crisp (ed.), *Abstracts of Somersetshire Wills*, 6 vols. (London, 1887-9) VI 72; T. E. Rogers, *Records of Yarlington, being the History of a Country Village*, 2nd ed. (Wincanton, 1902) p. 39.

3. MS. Pitcombe Transcribed Register, n.p.; P.R.O., Chancery Proceedings, C.2/89/58; B.M., Harley MS. 1445, f. 56; *Somersetshire Wills*, VI 72; J. Foster (ed.), *Alumni Oxonienses*, early ser., 4 vols. (Oxford, 1891-2) I 133; J. Le Neve and T. D. Hardy (eds.), *Fasti Ecclesiae Anglicanae*, 3 vols. (Oxford, 1854) III 30; H.M.C., *Tenth Report*, Appendix, III 246-7; *Notes and Queries for Somerset and Dorset*, XVII 197-8; Alan G. R. Smith, 'The Secretaries of the Cecils, circa 1580-1612', *EHR*, LXXXIII 493, 500, 503.

4. P.R.O., Chancery Proceedings, C.2/89/58 and C.2/118/7; *Notes and Queries for Somerset and Dorset*, IV 1-2, XVI 245, XXII 59-60; Kenneth Ashcroft, 'Godminster', *Pitcombe and Shepton Montague Parish Magazine* (Sep 1965) pp. 2-3; William Phelps, *History and Antiquities of Somersetshire*, 4 vols. (London, 1836-9) I 256-7.

5. MS. Pitcombe Transcribed Register; P.R.O., Inquisitions *post mortem*, C.142/361/104; Clarendon, *History*, v 156; *Somersetshire Wills*, VI 60; V.C.H., *Hampshire and the Isle of Wight*, IV 121; W. J. Jones, *The Elizabethan Court of Chancery* (Oxford, 1967) pp. 160, 370, 468, 483.

6. Practically all sources say that Francis was the fourth and last son, the last-born of the Cottington children. But the MS. Pitcombe Transcribed Register shows that Maurice, James, Francis and Edward were

born in that order. Elizabeth, baptised in November 1575, may have been born before or after Maurice, but certainly before her other brothers. No baptismal record for Francis Cottington exists in any of the surviving parish registers of his district.

7. MS. Pitcombe Transcribed Register; B.M., Harley MS. 1105, f. 7; P.R.O., Inquisitions *post mortem*, C.142/361/104; John Collinson, *History and Antiquities of the County of Somerset*, 3 vols. (Bath, 1791) II 270-1; *Notes and Queries for Somerset and Dorset*, XII 56-7; *Alumni Oxonienses*, I 333; Henry Foley (ed.), *Records of the English Province of the Society of Jesus*, 6 vols. (London, 1877-80) IV 408-10; *The Responsa Scholarum of the English College, Rome: Part One, 1598-1621*, Catholic Record Society, LIV (London, 1962) pp. 65-6.

8. Conyers Read, 'The Fame of Edward Stafford', *AHR*, XX 292-313; J. E. Neale, 'The Fame of Sir Edward Stafford', *EHR*, XLIV 203-20; Clarendon, *History*, V 156.

9. On the importance of the household in education, see Kenneth Charlton, *Education in Renaissance England* (London, 1965) esp. chap. vii; Lawrence Stone, *The Crisis of the Aristocracy, 1558-1641* (Oxford, 1965) chap. i and *passim*; Ruth Kelso, *The Doctrine of the English Gentleman in the Sixteenth Century* (Urbana, Ill., 1929) *passim*; Patricia-Ann Lee, 'Play and the English Gentleman in the Early Seventeenth Century', *The Historian*, XXXI 364-80. The educational role of guardians of wards, such as the relationship between Stafford and Cottington, is exemplified in a similar case in B. W. Beckingsale, *Burghley: Tudor Statesman* (London, 1967) chap. xvii.

10. *DNB*, XVIII 855-6; Clarendon, *History*, V 155-6; B.M., Stowe MS. 4225, ff. 43-6; David Mathew, *The Social Structure in Caroline England* (London, 1948) p. 44, n. 2. Information on Cottington's knowledge of languages and science is based on my reading of his correspondence, particularly in P.R.O., S.P.S.

11. See Maurice Lee, Jr, 'The Jacobean Diplomatic Service', *AHR*, LXXXII 1264-6; Stoye, p. 26; Garrett Mattingly, *Renaissance Diplomacy* (Boston, 1955) chaps. xxii-xxv.

12. Clarendon, *History*, V 156. See also Robert W. Kenny, *Elizabeth's Admiral: The Political Career of Charles Howard Earl of Nottingham, 1536-1624* (Baltimore and London, 1970) pp. 284-5, and his 'The Earl of Nottingham's Embassy to Spain in 1605', *History Today* (Mar 1970).

Chapter 2: Secretary in Spain

1. D. H. Willson, *King James VI and I* (London, 1959) pp. 271-6; L. B. Wright, 'Propaganda against James I's "Appeasement" of Spain', *Huntington Library Quarterly*, VI 149-72.

2. B.L., Add. MS. C.28, 'Burghley Papers', ff. 582, 586-90; Henry Ellis (ed.), *Original Letters Illustrative of English History*, 2nd ser., 4 vols. (London, 1827) III 201-2, 205-15.

3. H.M.C., *Downshire MSS.*, III 96; Stoye, pp. 325, 330-1; G. B. Harrison (ed.), *A Jacobean Journal, being a Record of Those Things most Talked of during the Years 1603-1606* (New York, 1941) pp. 191-2. In a letter to William Trumbull from Madrid on 23 June 1611, Cottington said that he had been in Spain for six years and four months. This fixes his arrival there in April 1605, the same month in which Nottingham reached Corunna. Moreover, Cornwallis's letters from that time are in Cottington's hand.

4. B.M., Add. MS. 35,837, ff. 56-9, Cornwallis to Lord Cranborne, the Groyne, 16 and 27 Apr 1605; ibid., ff. 61-3, Cornwallis to Northampton, the Groyne, 29 May 1605; Stoye, pp. 329-33; P.R.O., S.P.S., 94/11/18, Sir George Buck to Cranborne, the Groyne, 30 Apr 1605; S.P.S., 94/11/71, Sir Robert Meynell to ?, Valladolid, 2 May 1605.

5. Harrison, *A Jacobean Journal*, pp. 213-16; Stoye, pp. 333-5; Kenny, 'The Earl of Nottingham's Embassy to Spain in 1605', *History Today* (Mar 1970); J. Alban Fraser, *Spain and the West Country* (London, 1935) pp. 197-8.

6. Stoye, pp. 336, 338-41; P.R.O., S.P.S., 46/61/153; Fraser, *Spain and the West Country*, pp. 177-8; N. E. McClure (ed.), *The Letters of John Chamberlain*, 2 vols. (Philadelphia, 1939) I 211-12.

7. Stoye, pp. 336-8.

8. H.M.C., *Downshire MSS.*, II 17, Cottington to Trumbull, 6 Nov 1606; S.P.S., 94/13/52, Cornwallis to Cranborne, Valladolid, 6 Mar 1606. All letters cited hereafter in the notes, up to note 8 of Chapter 6, were written in Madrid unless specified otherwise.

9. Berkshire R.O. (Reading), Trumbull MSS., XXI, no. 1, Cottington to Trumbull, 4 Jan 1607; H.M.C., *Salisbury MSS.*, XVIII 265, Cranborne to Thomas Edmondes, London, 27 Aug 1606; H.M.C., *Downshire MSS.*, II 17, 19, 51-2, 62, Cottington letters to Trumbull and Beaulieu, 1608; Stoye, pp. 340-2.

10. S.P.S., 94/15/131, Resoute to Salisbury, 20 Sep 1608.

11. See A. J. Loomie, *The Spanish Elizabethans* (New York, 1963), his *Toleration and Diplomacy: The Religious Issue in Anglo-Spanish Diplomacy, 1603-1605* (Philadelphia, 1963), and Stoye, pp. 325-9, for background. Kenny, *Elizabeth's Admiral*, and Fraser, *Spain and the West Country*, deal with the military and commercial (Irish) relations between England and Spain in the late sixteenth century.

12. See Harold Livermore, *A History of Spain* (London, 1966) chap. ix, and R. Trevor Davies, *The Golden Century of Spain, 1501-1621* (London, 1954) chaps. v, ix, esp. pp. 229-33.

13. S.P.S., 94/14/65-6, Cornwallis to Privy Council, 27 June 1607.

14. S.P.S., 94/14/69, Cornwallis to Salisbury, 27 June 1607; Sir Ralph Winwood, *Memorials of Affairs of State in the Reigns of Queen Elizabeth and King James I*, 3 vols. (London, 1725) II 321-2; *DNB*, V 73-4; Loomie, *Spanish Elizabethans*, chap. vi *passim*.

15. S.P.S., 94/14/140, Cornwallis to Privy Council, 18 Sep 1607.

16. S.P.S., 94/15/102-3, same to same, 20 Aug 1609; Trumbull MSS., XXI, no. 24, Cottington to Beaulieu, 27 Aug 1609.

17. Charles H. Carter, *The Secret Diplomacy of the Hapsburgs, 1598-1625* (New York, 1964) pp. 31-3, suggests some of the duties of English diplomats.

18. See Willson, *King James VI and I*, pp. 276-80; Carter, *Secret Diplomacy of the Hapsburgs*, pp. 17-20, 33-4; Philip Caraman, *Henry Garnet 1555-1606 and the Gunpowder Plot* (New York, 1964) *passim*; and Martin J. Havran, *The Catholics in Caroline England* (Stanford, 1962) chaps. i-ii.

19. Winwood, *Memorials*, II 217; H.M.C., *Downshire MSS.*, II xx-xxi, 17, 27; Trumbull MSS., XXI, no. 2, Cottington to Trumbull, 17 Jan 1607; Gardiner, *History*, II 134-5.

20. S.P.S., 94/16/299, 'Memorial of cargoes laded in Spain', 1609; Trumbull MSS., XXI, no. 25, Cottington to Trumbull, 16 Sep 1609; B.L., North MS. b. 1, f. 36, Feb 1605, and a. 2, ff. 46-7, 20 May 1605; Gardiner, *History*, II 134-5. Cottington's memorandum contains numerous accounts of cases like the *Trial* involving merchantmen seized during 1605-9 off the coasts of western and south-western Europe.

21. S.P.S., 94/16/290-4, 299-300, 1609.

22. S.P.S., 94/16/290-4, 'Causes of His Majesty's subjects settled by Cornwallis', 1609; S.P.S., 94/15/133, Cornwallis to Privy Council, 30 Sep 1608; S.P.S., 94/15/19, Cornwallis to Duke of Lerma, 6 Feb 1608; S.P.S., 94/16/225, 'Memorial to Philip III on merchants to Andalusia', Oct 1609.

23. S.P.S., 94/15/84, Jude to Salisbury, 16 July 1608; B.M., Stowe MS. 169, f. 301, Cottington to Trumbull, 22 Feb 1607; Trumbull MSS., XXI, nos. 6, 8-11, 22, 27, Cottington letters to Trumbull, 10 Feb 1608–26 Nov 1609.

24. S.P.S., 94/16/270, 'Notes from Cornwallis Letters', 1609.

25. S.P.S., 94/16/180-2, 'Edict for banishing the Moriscos of Valencia', 22 Sep 1609; S.P.S., 94/16/188-90, Cottington to Salisbury, 28 Sep 1609; S.P.S., 94/16/238, same to same, 26 Nov 1609; Trumbull MSS., XXI, no. 17, Cottington to Trumbull, 7 Jan 1610; B.M., Add. MS. 35,847, ff. 105-7, 114-16, 124-7, Cottington to Salisbury, 18 Oct, 10 Dec 1609, 4 Mar 161c

26. H.M.C., *Downshire MSS.*, II 40-1; Winwood, *Memorials*, II 340-2, 348-9.

27. S.P.S., 94/16/210, Jude to Thomas Wilson, Dieppe, 17 Oct 1609; S.P.S., 94/16/187, same to same, Lerma, 24 Sep 1609; S.P.S., 94/16/184, Cornwallis to Salisbury, Aranda de Duero, 23 Sep 1609; Trumbull MSS., XXI, no. 24, Cottington to Beaulieu, 27 Aug 1609; ibid., no. 26, Cottington to Trumbull, 27 Sep 1609; B.M., Stowe MS. 171, ff. 1-2, Cornwallis to Thomas Edmondes, 28 Mar 1609; H.M.C., *Downshire MSS.*, II 116; Winwood, *Memorials*, III 51, 69.

Chapter 3: The Spanish Agent

1. Trumbull MSS., XXI, no. 17, Cottington to Trumbull, 7 Jan 1610; G. E. C[ockayne], *Complete Peerage of England Scotland Ireland Great Britain and the United Kingdom*, rev. The Hon. Vicary Gibbs, H. Arthur Doubleday *et al.*, 13 vols. (London, 1910-59) XI 109-10.

2. S.P.S., 94/17/121, 'Account of the Earl of Rosse's Travels', 27 July 1610; Davies, *Golden Century of Spain*, pp. 270-1.

3. S.P.S., 94/17/17, Cottington to Cornwallis, 19 Jan 1610.

4. H.M.C., *Downshire MSS.*, II 116; S.P.S., 94/16/234, Cornwallis to Salisbury, London, 13 Nov 1609; *Issues of the Exchequer; being Payments Made out of His Majesty's Revenue during the Reign of James I* (London, 1836) pp. 123, 133.

5. S.P.S., 94/16/214, 250, 263, Cottington to Salisbury, 22 Oct, 3 and 17 Dec 1609; S.P.S., 94/17/19, 46, same to same, 20 Jan, 4 Mar 1610; Trumbull MSS., XXI, nos. 35-6, 38, Cottington to Trumbull, 19 Aug, 29 Oct, 9 Dec 1610.

6. B.M., Add. MS. 35,847, ff. 114-16, 130-2, 164-5, Cottington to Salisbury, 10 Dec 1609, 11 and 25 May 1611; S.P.S., 94/17/55-6, 84-6, 213-14, same to same, 24 Mar, 11 May, 16 Oct 1610; S.P.S., 94/18/83, same to same, 12 May 1611.

7. Winwood, *Memorials*, III 264-5, Cottington to Trumbull, 5 Mar 1611; B.M., Add. MS. 35,847, ff. 145-6, 157-8, Cottington to Salisbury, 27 Sep 1610, 9 Jan 1611; Trumbull MSS., XXI, no. 37, Cottington to Trumbull, 10 Nov 1610; S.P.S., 94/17/68, Cottington to Salisbury, 18 Apr 1610; Caraman, *Henry Garnet*, pp. 322-4, 401; Havran, *Catholics*, pp. 77, 131; *DNB*, XIII 63-4.

8. On the Irish with the Armada, see Evelyn Hardy, *Survivors of the Armada* (London, 1966) pp. 4-9, 11 ff., 66, 170.

9. B.M., Stowe MS. 169, f. 143, Salisbury to Edmondes, Hampton Court, 30 Sep 1607; Winwood, *Memorials*, II 386, Cornwallis to Privy Council, 19 Apr 1608; B.M., Add. MS. 35,847, ff. 124-5, Cottington to Salisbury, 4 Mar 1610; Trumbull MSS., XXI, nos. 17, 21, 7 Jan, 7 Mar 1610; S.P.S., 94/16/246-7, Cottington to Salisbury, 6 Dec 1609; S.P.S., 94/17/115, Cottington to Livinus Munck, 6 July 1610.

10. H.M.C., *Downshire MSS.*, II 404, Cottington to Trumbull, 7 Dec 1610; Trumbull MSS., XXI, no. 37, same to same, 10 Nov 1610; S.P.S., 94/16/188-90, Cottington to Cornwallis, 28 Sep 1609; S.P.S., 94/16/239-40, Cottington to Salisbury, 16 Nov 1609; S.P.S., 94/17/37-8, 41, 109, same to same, 9 and 16 Feb, 26 June 1610.

11. There are dozens of letters in S.P.S. for the years 1605-30 which mention the *Vineyard* case, on which this paragraph is based. See also Joseph Jacobs (ed.), *Familiar Letters of James Howell, Historiographer Royal to Charles II*, 2 vols. (London, 1892) I 151-2, 167, 277-8, on Howell's negotiations.

12. S.P.S., 94/17/207-11, Cottington to Salisbury, 14 Oct 1610.

13. S.P.S., 94/17/264, 1610.

14. F. P. Wilson, *The Plague in Shakespeare's London* (Oxford, 1927) pp. 120-2; Charles F. Mullett, *The Bubonic Plague and England* (Lexington, Ky., 1956) chap. 6; Winwood, *Memorials*, III 118, Cottington to Trumbull, 14 Feb 1610; S.P.S., 94/17/1, Cottington to Cornwallis, 1 Jan 1610; S.P.S., 94/17/29-33, 51-2, Cottington to Salisbury, 5 Feb, 21 Mar 1610; B.M., Add. MS. 35,847, f. 127, same to same, 15 Apr 1610.

15. H.M.C., *Downshire MSS.*, II 40-1; S.P.S., 94/14/235, Cornwallis to Salisbury, 2 Dec 1607; S.P.S., 94/16/239-41, Cottington to Cornwallis, 16 Nov 1609; *CSPD 1611-18*, p. 86.

16. H.M.C., *Downshire MSS.*, II v-vii.

17. Trumbull MSS. XXI, nos. 25, 29-30, Cottington to Trumbull, 16 Sep 1610, 10 Jan, 5 Mar 1611; H.M.C., *Downshire MSS.*, II 301, 320, 362, 393, same to same, 27 May, 4 July, 16 Sep, 11 Nov 1610; S.P.S., 94/17/164-5, Salisbury to Cottington, Kensington, 21 Aug 1610; S.P.S., 94/17/249, Cottington to Salisbury, 4 Dec 1610.

18. S.P.S., 94/18/17-19, 35, 59-62, 65-7, Cottington to Salisbury, 22-23 Feb, 2 Mar, 10 and 23 Apr 1611; H.M.C., *Downshire MSS.*, III 60, Beaulieu to Trumbull, Paris, 18 Apr 1611; Trumbull MSS., XXI, nos. 40, 42, Cottington to Trumbull, 30 Mar, 25 May 1611.

19. S.P.S., 94/18/48, Salisbury to Cottington, London, 3 Apr 1611; S.P.S., 94/18/91-2, Digby to Salisbury, Alcobendas, 4 June 1611.

20. S.P.S., 94/18/105, 16 June 1611. Digby's account of his expenses is indicative of travel costs in those days: loading and shipping his belongings to San Sebastian by sea, £12; Channel crossing for his party, £72; hiring horses, mules and carriages, £457; customs duties and travel from San Sebastian to Madrid, £391; fees paid to Spanish officials in Madrid, £38; total cost of the journey, £970. There is no mention of food costs.

21. H.M.C., *Downshire MSS.*, III xiv-xvi, 110-11, 141-2, Sanford to Trumbull, 20 July, 17 Sep 1611; S.P.S., 94/18/184-5, Digby to Sir Dudley Carleton, 14 Sep 1611.

22. Trumbull MSS., XXI, no. 43, Cottington to Trumbull, 23 June

1611; S.P.S., 94/18/92, 123-4, Digby to Salisbury, 4 June, 5 July 1611.

23. H.M.C., *Downshire MSS.*, III 141, Sanford to Trumbull, 17 Sep 1611; S.P.S., 94/18/155-6, Digby to Salisbury, 17 Aug 1611.

24. H.M.C., *Downshire MSS.*, III 124, Beaulieu to Trumbull, Paris, 18 Aug 1611; ibid., 139, John More to Trumbull, London, 10 Sep 1611; S.P.S., 94/18/148, Digby to Salisbury, 9 Aug 1611.

Chapter 4: Clerk of the Council

1. Trumbull MSS., XXI, no. 45, Cottington to Trumbull, London, 17 Oct 1611. On Sherburne, see Smith, 'The Secretaries of the Cecils', *EHR*, LXXXIII 494, 504, and G. E. Aylmer, *The King's Servants: The Civil Service of Charles I, 1625-42* (New York, 1961) pp. 79-80, 156-8.

2. *Chamberlain Letters*, I 326-7, Chamberlain to Carleton, London, 31 Dec 1611; *CSPD 1611-18*, pp. 86, 99.

3. B.M., Cotton MSS., Titus C, IV, ff. 479-80, Cottington to Northampton, London, 12 Sep 1613; Trumbull MSS., XXI, no. 46, Cottington to Trumbull, London, 22 Dec 1611.

4. H.M.C., *Downshire MSS.*, III 211-12, Beaulieu to Trumbull, Paris, 2 Jan 1612; *CSPV 1610-13*, pp. 259-60.

5. H.M.C., *Downshire MSS.*, III 215, Sanford to Trumbull, 5 Jan 1612; S.P.S., 94/19/1, Digby to Salisbury, 4 Jan 1612.

6. S.P.S., 94/19/11-14, Digby to Salisbury, 19 Jan 1612; S.P.S., 94/19/7-9, Digby to Privy Council, 19 Jan 1612; H.M.C., *Eighth Report*, pt 1, p. 216a, Bristol to Cottington, London, 1 June 1624; ibid., p. 216b, Cottington to Bristol, London, 22 July 1624.

7. Lee, 'Jacobean Diplomatic Service', *AHR*, LXXII 1273-4; Smith, 'The Secretaries of the Cecils', *EHR*, LXXXIII 497; S.P.S., 94/19/83-4, 97-8, Digby to Salisbury, 30 May, 15 June 1612; Stoye, p. 345.

8. S.P.S., 94/19/15-16, 26, 30, Digby to Salisbury, 25 Jan, 2 and 6 Feb 1612; H.M.C., *Downshire MSS.*, III 196, John Throckmorton to Trumbull, Flushing, 4 Dec 1611; ibid., 201, John More to Trumbull, London, 13 Dec 1611.

9. Trumbull MSS. XXI, no. 47, Cottington to Trumbull, 8 Apr 1612; H.M.C., *Downshire MSS.*, III 261, 302, Sanford to Trumbull, 27 Mar, 23 May 1612; ibid., 249, Samuel Calvert to Trumbull, London, 26 Feb 1612; S.P.S., 94/19/67, 83-4, Digby to Salisbury, 10 Apr, 30 May 1612. Digby wrote to Salisbury not knowing that he had died on 12 May 1612.

10. S.P.S., 94/19/149-50, Digby to Sir Thomas Lake, 13 Sep 1612; S.P.S., 94/19/170-1, Digby to James I, 12 Nov 1612; H.M.C., *Downshire MSS.*, III 400, Sanford to Trumbull, 7 Nov 1612; H.M.C., *Portland MSS.*, IX 131-2, Cottington to John Holles, 6 Nov 1612; *DNB*, IX 1056-7.

11. *CSPV 1610-13*, p. 557; H.M.C., *Downshire MSS.*, IV xix, 112, Sanford to Trumbull, 22 May 1613; S.P.S., 94/19/372, Digby to James I, 27 May 1613; S.P.S., 94/19/386, Digby to Rochester, 27 May 1613. See C. H. Carter, 'Gondomar: Ambassador to James I', *Historical Journal*, VII, 189-208.

12. H.M.C., *Downshire MSS.*, IV xviii.

13. *APC 1613-14*, p. 147; H.M.C., *Downshire MSS.*, IV xviii-xix, 170, John More to Trumbull, London, 24 July 1613; ibid., 182, Beaulieu to Trumbull, Paris, 17 Aug 1613; S.P.S., 94/20/21, Digby to Rochester, 3 Aug 1613.

14. *Chamberlain Letters*, I 476, Chamberlain to Carleton, London, 9 Sep 1613; H.M.C., *Downshire MSS.*, IV 240, More to Trumbull, London, 29 Oct 1613; ibid., 204, same to same, London, 23 Sep 1613; *CSPD 1611-18*, pp. 198, 200; F. M. G. Evans, *The Principal Secretary of State* (Manchester, 1923) p. 50; Aylmer, *King's Servants*, p. 204.

15. Evans, *Principal Secretary of State*, pp. 49-50.

16. S.P.S., 94/20/81-6, Digby to James I, 22 Sep 1613; Willson, *King James VI and I*, pp. 336-44.

17. *APC 1613-14*, pp. 4-5, 88, 282; S.P.S., 94/20/77, Digby to Rochester, 13 Sep 1613.

18. B.M., Cotton MSS., Titus C, IV, ff. 422-59, 504-10, and esp. ff. 479-80, Cottington to Northampton, London, 12 Sep 1613; Willson, *King James VI and I*, pp. 300-7.

19. John Forster, *Sir John Eliot*, 2 vols. (London, 1864) I 374 n.; *APC 1615-16*, p. 18; Willson, *King James VI and I*, pp. 380-1; C. D. Bowen, *The Lion and the Throne* (Boston, 1956) pp. 350-1, 356, 387; James Spedding, *An Account of the Life and Times of Francis Bacon*, 2 vols. (Boston, 1878) II 50.

20. On the background to the Anglo-Spanish marriage treaty, see S. R. Gardiner, *Prince Charles and the Spanish Marriage, 1617-1623* (London, 1869) I, *passim*. The detailed negotiations by Digby and Cottington are discussed in Chapters 5 and 6 below.

21. 'Correspondencia oficial de Don Diego Sarmiento de Acuña, Conde de Gondomar', in *Documentos Inéditos para la Historia de España*, 4 vols. in 2 (Madrid, 1944-5) III 210-13, Gondomar to Philip III, London, 25 Jan 1614; Gardiner, *Prince Charles and the Spanish Marriage*, I 15; *Narrative of the Spanish Marriage Treaty*, ed. and trans. S. R. Gardiner (London, 1869) Camden Society, 1st ser., CI, pp. 111-12. See also Cottington's extensive correspondence with John Stone in Madrid, Trumbull in Brussels, and Edmondes and Beaulieu in Paris in S.P.S., 94/20-1, in Trumbull MSS., XXI, and in B.M., Stowe MS. 175.

22. *Documentos Inéditos*, III 204, Gondomar to Philip III, London,

6 Dec 1613, and III 262-3, Gondomar to Lerma, 25 Jan 1614; Carter, *Secret Diplomacy of the Hapsburgs*, pp. 3-8.

23. *Documentos Inéditos*, III 132-4, 251-63, 265-6, Gondomar to Lerma, London, 5 Oct 1613, 25 and 28 Jan 1614; Anthony J. Cooper, 'The Political Career of Francis Cottington, 1605-52', Oxford B.Litt. thesis (B.L., MS. B.Litt. d. 1151) pp. 25-6. I am grateful to Mr Cooper for permission to read his thesis.

24. S.P.S., 94/22/50, Winwood to Cottington, London, 12 July 1616; *Letters from George Lord Carew to Sir Thomas Roe* (London, 1860) Camden Society, 1st ser., LXXVI, p. 23.

Chapter 5: Babylon Revisited

1. *APC 1615-16*, p. 359; *CSPV 1615-17*, pp. 134, 160; B.M., Add. MS. 35,847, ff. 215-16, Cottington to Winwood, 22 May 1616; S.P.S., 94/22/7-8, Cottington to ?, 12 Feb 1616; S.P.S., 94/22/16, Cottington to Winwood, 16 Mar 1616; Trumbull MSS., XXI, no. 51, Cottington to Trumbull, 13 Mar 1616.

2. S.P.S., 94/22/102-3, Abstract of Digby's Negotiations, 1611-16.

3. Trumbull MSS. XXI, nos. 51, 55, Cottington to Trumbull, 12 Mar, 12 May 1616; S.P.S., 94/22/19, 26, 36, 84, Cottington to Winwood, 13 and 26 Mar, 12 May, 30 Nov 1616.

4. S.P.S., 94/22/55, 84, Cottington to Winwood, 19 Aug, 30 Nov 1616; S.P.S., 94/22/68, Cottington to Lake, 23 Sep 1616; P.R.O., S.P.Dom., 16/377/177; P.R.O., Close Rolls, 54/2203/30; Bowen, *Lion and the Throne*, pp. 185-6, 220-2.

5. *CSPV 1615-17*, pp. 172, 248, 262, 328, 354, 368-9, 378, 551, 564; B.M., Add. MS. 35,847, f. 211, Cottington to Winwood, 13 Mar 1616; Trumbull MSS. XXI, no. 60, Cottington to Trumbull, 10 Dec 1616; S.P.S., 94/22, various Cottington letters, Mar–Nov 1616.

6. Trumbull MSS. XXI, nos. 49, 56, 6 June 1616, 19 Jan 1617; S.P.S., 94/22/193, 208, 233, 240, and 94/23/20, 82-4, 86, 92, 100, various Cottington letters, Sep 1616–Mar 1618.

7. *Documentos Inéditos*, I 56, 59, Sarmiento to Philip III, 4 and 30 Nov 1616, and II 61, same to same, 15 July 1618; S.P.S., 94/22/126, Cottington to Lake, 26 Apr 1617; S.P.S., 94/23/45-6, Digby to ?, London, 16 June 1618; B.M., Add. MS. 35,847, f. 233, Cottington to Lake, 31 May 1618; *CSPD 1611-18*, pp. 489, 493, 529, 538, 547, 572, 603; Rushworth, I 9-10.

8. H.M.C., *Downshire MSS.*, III xv-xvi; H.M.C., *Tenth Report*, Appendix, I 525, Digby to Edmondes, 9 Aug 1611; Duke of Sully, *Memoirs* (London, 1877) IV 139; S.P.S., 94/18/125-6, Digby to Salisbury, 20 July 1611; B.L., Perrott MS. 4, ff. 56-67, n.d.

9. S.P.S., 94/22/106-7, Cottington to Lake, 10 Jan 1617; H.M.C.,

Tenth Report, I 102-3, Winwood to Buckingham, London, 29 July 1617; H.M.C., *Buccleuch MSS.*, I 192, Cottington to Winwood, 1 Apr 1617.

10. S.P.S., 94/22/160, Digby to Carleton, London, 26 June 1617; S.P.S., 94/22/184, Digby to Lake, Santander, 29 Aug 1617; S.P.S., 94/22/182, 186-9, Cottington to Winwood, 23 Aug, 16 Sep 1617; S.P.S., 94/22/192-3, Cottington to Lake, Burgos, 6 Oct 1617; H.M.C., *Buccleuch MSS.*, I 206-7, Thomas Rossiter to ?, Paris, 29 July 1617.

11. S.P.S., 94/22/197, Digby to Lake, Burgos, 8 Oct 1617.

12. Trumbull MSS., XXI, no. 61, Cottington to Trumbull, 11 Jan 1618; ibid., no. 164, Digby to Trumbull, 9 Nov 1617; S.P.S., 94/22/200, 204, Cottington to Winwood, 21 Oct, 4 Nov 1617; S.P.S., 94/22/212, 237, Cottington to Lake, 19 Nov, 14 Dec 1617; S.P.S., 94/23/22, 31-3, same to same, 24 Mar, 3 May 1618; S.P.S., 94/23/39-40, Cottington to Carleton, 22 May 1618.

13. This phase of the negotiations is summarised in Gardiner, *History*, III 284, 300-7, 361-3, 366, and given much fuller treatment in his *Narrative of the Spanish Marriage Treaty*, pp. 139-62.

14. Berkshire R.O. (Reading), Buckingham MSS., D EHyo1, nos. 9-10, Cottington to Buckingham, 6 and 19 Apr 1619; S.P.S., 94/23/176-7, Cottington to Naunton, 6 Apr 1619; *CSPD 1619-23*, p. 86; Devon, 'Issues of the Exchequer, James I', p. 244; Nehemiah Wallington, *Historical Notices of Events Occurring Chiefly in the Reign of Charles I*, 2 vols. (London, 1869) I 11-12.

15. S.P.S., 94/23/57, 77, Cottington to Lake, 16 July, 8 Oct 1618; S.P.S., 94/23/68-9, Cottington to Naunton, 17 Sep 1618.

16. S.P.S., 94/23/84-5, 145, 149-51, Cottington to Naunton, 3 and 18 Dec 1618, 7 and 28 Jan 1619; S.P.S., 94/23/96-7, Cottington to Buckingham, 18 Dec 1618; Trumbull MSS., XXI, nos. 69-70, Cottington to Trumbull, 7 Jan, 5 Feb 1619; B.M., Add. MS. 35,847, ff. 256-7, Juan de Ciriza to Cottington, 21 Jan 1619.

17. Buckingham MSS. (Reading), no. 47, Cottington to Buckingham, 1 Apr 1619; S.P.S., 94/23/169, Cottington to Carleton, 13 Mar 1619; S.P.S., 94/23/228, Cottington to Naunton, 18 Sep 1619; B.M., Add. MS. 35,847, ff. 258-60, same to same, 19 Apr 1619; Trumbull MSS., XXI, no. 84, Cottington to Trumbull, 17 July 1619.

18. P.R.O., S.P., Flanders, 77/13/455, Cottington to Trumbull, 12 Dec 1619; B.M., Add. MS. 35,847, ff. 245-6, 262-3, Cottington to Naunton, 5 and 30 Oct, 20 Nov 1619; S.P.S., 94/23/254, 266-7, Cottington to Carleton, 20 Nov, 31 Dec 1619; Trumbull MSS., XXI, nos. 84, 87-8, 78 (misnumbered), Cottington to Trumbull, 17 July, 19 Nov, 12 Dec 1619, 2 Jan 1620.

19. This paragraph is based on Cottington letters in S.P.S., 94/21-4, 1616-20, and in the Trumbull MSS., XXI.

20. B.M., Harley MS. 1580, ff. 361-2, Cottington to Buckingham, 13 Mar 1620; B.M., Add. MS. 35,847, f. 258, Cottington to Naunton, 14 Mar 1620; S.P.S., 94/23/323, Aston to Calvert, 28 Mar 1620; S.P.S., 94/23/305, 331, Cottington to Naunton, 13 Feb, 4 Apr 1620.

21. S.P.S., 94/23/279-90, Instructions to Aston, 5 Jan 1620.

22. B.L., Ashmole MS. 829, Cottington to Tomkins, 22 Oct 1620; S.P.S., 94/24/19-20, John Stone to ?, Lisbon, 11 Aug 1620.

23. S.P.S., 94/24/245, Aston to Calvert, 16 July 1621; B.M., Harley MS. 1580, ff. 363-7, Cottington to Buckingham, 5 Mar, 30 Sep, 17 Dec 1621; Trumbull MSS., XXI, no. 98, Cottington to Trumbull, 2 June 1621; *CSPD 1619-23*, p. 502.

24. Trumbull MSS., VII, nos. 28, 30-1, Beaulieu to Trumbull, London, 28 Sep, 11 and 26 Oct 1621; S.P.S., 94/25/217, Digby to Prince Charles, 14 Sep 1622; B.M., Harley MS. 1580, f. 369, Cottington to Buckingham, 25 June 1622; *DNB*, XIII 1301; *CSPD 1619-23*, p. 296; A. Clifford (ed.), *Tixall Letters: or the Correspondence of the Aston Family*, 2 vols. (London, 1815) I 41-2, Beatrice Digby to ?, St Giles, 15 Dec 1621; *Chamberlain Letters*, II 339, 402, Chamberlain to Carleton, London, 3 Feb, 20 Oct 1621.

Chapter 6: Secretary to the Prince

1. On events in Rome and Madrid during Cottington's last few months in Spain and information on Digby's activities in Mar–Sep 1622, see: Trumbull MSS., XXI, nos. 106-8, Cottington to Trumbull, 19 May, 23 July, 18 Aug 1622, and VII, nos. 50-1, 56, Beaulieu to Trumbull, London, 22 and 29 Mar, 10 May 1622; B.M., Egerton MS. 2595, f. 92, Calvert to Doncaster, London, 10 May 1622, and f. 135, Digby to Doncaster, 1 June 1622; B.L., Tanner MS. 73, pt 1, f. 161, Cottington to Calvert, 7 July 1622; S.P.S., 94/25/58, Aston to Calvert, 17 Apr 1622; S.P.S., 94/25/122-3, 141, 166, Digby to Prince Charles, 30 June, 13 July, 9 Aug 1622.

2. Trumbull MSS., VII, no. 80, Beaulieu to Trumbull, London, 4 Oct 1622, and XXII, no. 97, Dickenson to Trumbull, London, 10 Oct 1622; *CSPD 1619-23*, p. 453; *Chamberlain Letters*, II 455, 457, Chamberlain to Carleton, London, 5 and 12 Oct 1622.

3. Trumbull MSS., XXI, no. 109, Cottington to Trumbull, London, 22 Oct 1622; ibid., XXII, no. 98, Dickenson to Trumbull, London, 12 Dec 1622; ibid., VII, nos. 82, 91, Beaulieu to Trumbull, London, 18 Oct, 27 Dec 1622; *Chamberlain Letters*, II 460, 468, Chamberlain to Carleton, London, 26 Oct, 21 Dec 1622; *APC 1621-3*, p. 346; Evans, *Principal Secretary of State*, p. 81; *CSPD 1619-23*, pp. 457-8, 470.

4. Trumbull MSS., VII, no. 82, Beaulieu to Trumbull, London, 18 Oct 1622; ibid., XXII, no. 98, Dickenson to Trumbull, London, 12 Dec 1622; *CSPD 1619-23*, p. 460.

5. Stone, *Crisis of the Aristocracy*, pp. 105, 608, 805.

6. On the early connection between Cottington and Ann Brett, see *Chamberlain Letters*, I 476, II 316. On the Palmers and Merediths, see: Somerset House (London), Prerogative Court of Canterbury, 85 Soame, will of Sir Robert Brett, 1620; *CSPD 1619-23*, p. 492; Cockayne, *Complete Peerage*, III 462-3; Aylmer, *King's Servants*, p. 102; Stone, *Crisis of the Aristocracy*, p. 255; John Nichols (ed.), *Progresses, Processions, and Magnificent Festivities of King James the First*, 4 vols. (London, 1828) IV 305-6; Thomas Birch (ed.), *Court and Times of James the First*, 2 vols. (London, 1848) II 365; Thomas Wotton (ed.), *English Baronetage*, 4 vols. (London, 1741) I 439-40; D. Gardiner (ed.), *The Oxinden Letters, 1607-1642* (London, 1933) Introduction.

7. The house was situated on the old Rounceval property, which extended from Charing Cross to approximately the centre of Northumberland Avenue. Cottington paid rates on the property until 1634, when he appears to have sold it. See G. Gater and W. H. Godfrey (eds.), *Survey of London* XVIII (1937) 4-6.

8. P.C.C., 85 Soame, Brett's will, probated 20 Sep 1620. Trumbull MSS., XXI, no. 89, Cottington to Trumbull, Madrid, 23 Jan 1620.

9. Charles R. Mayes, 'The Early Stuarts and the English Peerage (1603-1649)', Univ. of Minnesota dissertation (1955) pp. 91-2, 101, 106-7, 167-8; Wotton, *English Baronetage*, IV 272; Nichols, *Progresses of James I*, IV 805; B.L., North MS. a. 2, f. 154, 'A Project for erecting a new Dignity between Barons and Knights'.

10. S.P.S., 94/26/40, Bristol to Charles, Madrid, 22 Feb 1623.

11. R. T. Petersson, *Sir Kenelm Digby* (Cambridge, Mass., 1956) p. 57, suggests that the plan was arranged with the knowledge of Gondomar, then in Spain, which seems improbable in view of Olivares's surprise on seeing Buckingham and Charles.

12. Clarendon, *History*, I 21-2; Nichols, *Progresses of James I*, IV 1115; Earl of Birkenhead, *Strafford* (London, 1938) pp. 126-7. No account of this encounter by Cottington, if he made one, has survived.

13. *Chamberlain Letters*, II 480, Chamberlain to Carleton, London, 22 Feb 1623; S.P.S., 94/26/81, Bristol to Carleton, Madrid, 10 Mar 1622; Trumbull MSS., VII, nos. 98, 101, Beaulieu to Trumbull, London, 21 and 28 Feb 1623; B.L., Tanner MS. 73, pt 2, f. 217, Charles to James, Paris, ?21 Feb 1623; *Familiar Letters, Howell*, I 164, Howell to Thomas Savage, Madrid, 27 Mar 1623; *CSPD 1619-23*, pp. 502-3; Rushworth, I 76; Wilson, *History of King James I*, pp. 763-4; George Roberts (ed.), *Diary of Walter Yonge, Esq.* (London, 1848) Camden Society, XLI, p. 67.

14. S.P.S., 94/26/38, Bristol to Charles, Madrid, 22 Feb 1623; S.P.S., 94/26/81, Bristol to Carleton, Madrid, 10 Mar 1623; S.P.S., 94/27/191-200, Bristol to James, Madrid, 18 Aug 1623.

15. On events in these early weeks, see: *Familiar Letters, Howell,* I 164-5, Howell to Savage, Madrid, 27 Mar 1623; Ellis, *Original Letters,* 1st ser., III 134-6, 141-3, Mead to Stuteville, London, 28 Mar, 4 Apr 1623; S.P.S., 94/26/89, Aston to Carleton, Madrid, 27 Mar 1623; S.P.S., 94/26/132, Buckingham to Richard Grimes, Madrid, 8 Apr 1623; Trumbull MSS., VII, nos. 102-5, 107, 109-10, Beaulieu to Trumbull, London, 12, 21 and 28 Mar, 4 and 19 Apr, 9 and 23 May 1623.

16. Gardiner, *Narrative of the Spanish Marriage Treaty,* pp. 198-259; S.P.S., 94/26/181, Conway to Francis Steward, Windsor, 21 Apr 1623; Trumbull MSS., VII, nos. 99, 113, Beaulieu to Trumbull, London, 7 Mar, ? June 1623; Charles Dodd, *Church History of England from the Commencement of the Sixteenth Century to the Revolution of 1688,* 5 vols., ed. M. A. Tierney (London, 1839-43) V cccxxxviii-ix; Gardiner, *History,* V 1-9, 17-19, 27-9; Nichols, *Progresses of James I,* IV 815-16; Philip Gibbs, *The Romance of George Villiers* (London, 1908) pp. 155-6.

17. H.M.C., *Third Report,* p. 284; Gardiner, *History,* V 34-40; Ellis, *Original Letters,* 1st ser., III 141-3; *CSPD 1619-23,* p. 535; S.P.S., 94/26/93-8, Bristol to James, Madrid, 18 Mar 1623.

18. S.P.S., 94/27/20, 24, James to Charles and Buckingham, Greenwich, 14 and 15 June 1623; S.P.S., 94/27/13, Aston to Carleton, Madrid, 10 June 1623; Trumbull MSS., VII, no. 114, Beaulieu to Trumbull, London, 13 June 1623; H.M.C., *Cowper MSS.,* I 142-3; Gardiner, *Prince Charles and the Spanish Marriage,* II 343-7.

19. B.M., Harley MS. 1580, f. 371, Cottington to Buckingham, Greenwich, 26 June 1623; S.P.S., 94/27/42, Conway to Buckingham, Greenwich, 25 June 1623; S.P.S., 94/27/104, Simon Digby to ?, Madrid, 9 July 1623; Gibbs, *Villiers,* pp. 177-8, quoting Katherine Villiers to Buckingham, London, ? June 1623.

20. B.M., Harley MS. 1580, ff. 307-8, Conway to Buckingham, Theobalds, 17 July 1623; Nichols, *Progresses of James I,* IV 886.

21. Cottington and Stafford were not personally relieved of this debt until 1631. In a reckoning made in 1721, the trip cost the Government £50,027, excluding charges for gifts to the Spaniards. See Ellis, *Original Letters,* 1st ser., III 167 n.; H.M.C., *Fourth Report,* pt 1, Appendix, pp. 276-7; Frederick C. Dietz, *English Public Finance, 1485-1641,* 2 vols., 2nd ed. (New York, 1964) II 197.

22. *CSPD 1619-23,* pp. 5, 13-14, 30; Ellis, *Original Letters,* 1st ser., III 148, Buckingham to James, Madrid, 25 Apr 1623; Trumbull MSS., VII, no. 121, Beaulieu to Trumbull, London, 25 July 1623; S.P.S., 94/28/40, note on dispatches, 10 Sep 1623; S.P.S., 94/27/121, Conway to Calvert, Andover, 24 July 1623.

23. S.P.S., 94/27/205, Aston to Carleton, Madrid, 20 Aug 1623; S.P.S., 94/28/35, Bristol to James, Madrid, 9 Sep 1623; Gardiner, *History,* V 101-3.

24. S.P.S., 94/28/16, Bristol to James, Madrid, 24 Sep 1623; Trumbull MSS., VII, nos. 132-4, Beaulieu to Trumbull, London, 17, 24 and 31 Oct 1623; Nichols, *Progresses of James I*, IV 166-7; Birch, *Court and Times of James the First*, II 431-2, Mead to Stuteville, Oxford, 8 Nov 1623; Gardiner, *Narrative of the Spanish Marriage Treaty*, pp. 249-58; Cooper, 'Francis Cottington', p. 47.

25. B.M., Add. MS. 38,446, ff. 220-2, Olivares to Cottington, Madrid, 31 Oct 1623; Trumbull MSS., VII, no. 129, Beaulieu to Trumbull, London, 12 Sep 1623; S.P.S., 94/28/16, Bristol to ?, Madrid, 5 Sep 1623; Gardiner, *History*, V 118-19.

26. S.P.S., 94/28/100, Bristol to James, Madrid, 24 Sep 1623; S.P.S., 94/28/105, 218, Bristol to Calvert, Madrid, 25 Sep, 31 Oct 1623; S.P.S., 94/29/27, Bristol to Conway, Madrid, 13 Nov 1623; H.M.C., *Eighth Report*, I 216, Bristol to Cottington, Madrid, ? Oct 1623; Gervas Huxley, *Endymion Porter: The Life of a Courtier, 1587-1649* (London, 1959) pp. 113-16.

Chapter 7: Eclipse

1. H.M.C., *Eighth Report*, I 216, Bristol to Cottington, Madrid, ? Oct 1623; S.P.S., 94/29, various Bristol letters, Nov–Dec 1623; S.P.S., 94/30/37, Bristol to Calvert, Madrid, 22 Jan 1624; S.P.S., 94/30/40, Bristol to James, Madrid, 22 Jan 1624; S.P.S., 94/30/114, Aston to ?, Madrid, 29 Mar 1624; Gardiner, *History*, V 134-42, 165, and *Narrative of the Spanish Marriage Treaty*, pp. 259-68; *DNB*, V 962-3.

2. *Chamberlain Letters*, II 517, Chamberlain to Carleton, London, 11 Oct 1623; *CSPD 1623-5*, p. 119; Nichols, *Progresses of James I*, IV 951, 957.

3. B.M., Add. MS. 38,446, ff. 220-2, Olivares to Cottington, Madrid, 21 Oct 1623; *CSPD 1623-5*, p. 104; Gardiner, *History* V 16-19, 28-9. Several points raised in this paragraph will be developed below.

4. S.P.S., 94/30/58, Cottington to ?, London, 30 Jan 1624; S.P.S., 94/31/194, Aston to Cottington, Madrid, 2 Sep 1624; B.M., Harley MS. 1580, f. 65, same to same, Madrid, 24 Dec 1624; *CSPD 1623-5*, pp. 159, 246, 320, 489; Evans, *Principal Secretary of State*, pp. 306-7; Nichols, *Progresses of James I*, IV 972-3.

5. Clarendon, *History*, I 40-2; *Chamberlain Letters*, II 611, Chamberlain to Carleton, London, 23 Apr 1625; *CSPD 1625-6*, pp. 2, 12, 537.

6. R. Carew, *Survey of Cornwall*, ed. F. E. Halliday (London, 1953) pp. 160-1; D. H. Willson, *Privy Councillors in the House of Commons, 1604-1629* (Minneapolis, 1940) p. 78; Trumbull MSS., VII, no. 148, Beaulieu to Trumbull, 13 Feb 1624; *Chamberlain Letters*, II 543, Chamberlain to Carleton, London, 31 Jan 1624; Forster, *Sir John Eliot*, I 129;

H.M.C., *Eighth Report*, pt 1, p. 216a; Gardiner, *History*, v 176-80; *CSPD 1623-5*, p. 171.

7. *CJ*, I 725-6, 729, 731, 733-4, 736, 758, 790; Willson, *James VI and I*, pp. 442-3.

8. Trumbull MSS., VII, no. 162, Beaulieu to Trumbull, London, 7 May 1624; H.M.C., *Eighth Report*, pt 1, p. 216a, Bristol to Conway, Sherborne, 21 Sep 1624; *CSPD 1580-1625, Addenda*, p. 669; B.L., Perrott MS. 4, ff. 121-6, 3 Mar 1624; Gardiner, *History*, v 235-7; *DNB*, v 963. A copy of the interrogation – questions and answers – is in Berkshire R.O. (Reading), Trumbull Add. MS. 4, n.f.

9. S.P.S., 94/31/194, Aston to Cottington, Madrid, 2 Sep 1624; H.M.C., *Eighth Report*, pt 1, p. 216a, Bristol to Cottington, London, 1 June 1624; and 216b, Cottington to Bristol, London, 22 July 1624; Trumbull MSS., VII, no. 179, Beaulieu to Trumbull, London, 12 May 1625; Gardiner, *History*, v 317-36 *passim*; J. V. Kitto (ed.), *Registers of St Martin-in-the-Fields, 1619-1636*, Harleian Society Publications, LXVI, pt 2 (London, 1936) pp. 1, 38.

10. W. P. Courtney, *Parliamentary Representation of Cornwall to 1832* (London, 1882) p. 326; Willson, *Privy Councillors in Commons*, p. 78.

11. *APC 1626*, pp. 131-2; H.M.C., *Buccleuch MSS.*, I 265-6, William Montagu to Lord Montagu, London, 16 May 1627; H.M.C., *Cowper MSS.*, I 324, Cottington to Sir John Coke, Hanworth, 25 Sep 1627; *CSPD 1627-8*, pp. 252, 334, 455, 471, 484, 570; *CSPV 1626-8*, p. 545; *DNB*, v 963.

12. *Forty-Third Annual Report of the Deputy Keeper of the Public Records*, Appendix, I (London, 1882) 36, 106; *CSPD 1627-8*, p. 544; *CSPD 1628-9*, pp. 75, 150, 170, 628; Daniel Lysons, *Historical Account of those Parishes in the County of Middlesex which are not described in the Environs of London* (London, 1800) pp. 46, 95-8, 101; V.C.H., *Middlesex*, II 392-5; P.R.O., C.54/3196/8, conveyance of Hanworth to Cottington. He rebuilt part of the manor house following the 1634 fire. In August 1635 he entertained the Queen there during his unsuccessful attempt to become Lord Treasurer. In March 1637 he enclosed another 100 acres. The house was gutted on 26 March 1797 and not rebuilt. The Cottingtons' second child, Elizabeth, was baptised at St Martin's on 12 May 1626. On these last two points, see Kitto, *Registers*, p. 42, and B.L., Bankes MSS., 37/38, 7 Mar 1637.

13. Courtney, *Parliamentary Representation of Cornwall to 1832*, p. 150; Carew, *Survey of Cornwall*, pp. 181-2; *CSPD 1628-9*, pp. 24, 65; Forster, *Sir John Eliot*, II 98-104; Willson, *Privy Councillors in Commons*, pp. 99-101. Cottington was not sworn a Councillor until November 1628.

14. *CJ*, I 873, 877, 890, 903.

15. W.W. MSS., Strafford Papers, 12(a), no. 36, Edward Osborne to Thomas Wentworth, London, 24 Aug 1628; *CSPD, Addenda, 1625-49*, pp. 291-2.

16. The quotation is in *CSPD, Addenda, 1625-49*, p. 293. Aylmer, *King's Servants*, p. 62.

17. Aylmer, *King's Servants*, pp. 88, 111, 113-14, 212, 231; *CSPD 1628-9*, pp. 507, 524.

18. *APC 1628-9*, pp. 227-8, 273-4; B.M., Add. MS. 5873, ff. 113-14, Cambridge University to Cottington, 11 Dec 1628; H.M.C., *Seventh Report*, pt 1, p. 544, Thomas Barrington to Lady Johanna Barrington, 6 Dec 1628.

19. H.M.C., *Thirteenth Report (Lonsdale MSS.)*, Appendix, pt 7, pp. 65-6; W. Notestein and F. H. Relf (eds.), *Commons Debates for 1629* (Minneapolis, 1921) p. 115.

20. *CJ*, I 929; Gardiner, *History*, VII 3-6, 32-5, 59-65; Cooper, 'Francis Cottington', pp. 58-9. Cottington's only other recorded committee work in this Parliament involved reconsideration of the disposition of recusants' lands in connection with the 1606 penal law (*CJ*, I 923, 925).

Chapter 8: Ambassador Extraordinary

1. Aspects of this problem will be ventilated in Chapters 10 and 11 below.

2. On the Spanish peace feelers, see Emile Cammaerts, *Rubens: Painter and Diplomat* (London, 1932) pp. 169-71, 177-8; *CSPV 1629-32*, pp. xxii-xxiii; and *Letters of Peter Paul Rubens*, trans. and ed. Ruth S. Magurn (Cambridge, Mass., 1955) pp. 285, 287-8.

3. *Familiar Letters, Howell*, I 255, Howell to Peter Wyche, London, I Sep 1628; *CSPV 1629-32*, p. xxiii; Gardiner, *History*, VII 97, 100, 102-3; Cooper, 'Francis Cottington', pp. 85-6; Cammaerts, *Rubens*, pp. 179-83; *Rubens Letters*, pp. 283-6.

4. *Rubens Letters*, pp. 312, 492, Rubens to Olivares, London, 22 July, 21 Sep 1629.

5. H.M.C., *Cowper MSS.*, I 386-7, letter endorsed 'à Monsieur Damville à Liège', n.d.; *Rubens Letters*, pp. 299-302, Rubens to Olivares, London, 30 June 1629.

6. *CSPV 1629-32*, pp. 145-6; *Rubens Letters*, pp. 302, 315-16, Rubens to Olivares, London, 30 June, 22 July 1629; Gardiner, *History*, VII 104-5.

7. W.W. MSS., 12(a), nos. 71, 73, Cottington to Wentworth, London, 5 and 20 Aug 1629.

8. *Rubens Letters*, pp. 189, 304, 306-7, 318, 324-6, Rubens to Olivares, London, 30 June, 2, 6 and 22 July, 24 Aug 1629.

9. *APC 1629-30*, pp. 66, 69, 83, 88; Ellis, *Original Letters*, 1st ser., III

283-4, Mead to Stuteville, Cambridge, 7 Nov 1629; W.W. MSS., 12(a), nos. 71, 73, Cottington to Wentworth, London, 5 and 20 Aug 1629; Trumbull Add. MS. 52, William Trumbull to his son William, London, 15 Sep 1629; *Familiar Letters, Howell*, 1 277-8, Howell to Bristol, London, 20 May 1629; H.M.C., *Cowper MSS.*, 1 387; *CSPV 1629-32*, pp. 148-9, 226; *Rubens Letters*, pp. 324-6, 338-9, 346-7, Rubens to Olivares, London, 24 Aug, 21 Sep 1629; Leopold von Ranke, *History of England Principally in the Seventeenth Century*, 6 vols. (Oxford, 1875) II 11-14.

10. P.R.O., C.115/M.31/8119, John Flower to Scudamore, London, 7 Nov 1629; C.115/M.24/7757, G. Moore to Scudamore, London, 14 Nov 1629; H.M.C., *City of Exeter MSS.*, p. 191, Nicholas Spicer to Mayor of Exeter, London, 5 Sep 1629; S.P.S., 94/34/98, Cottington to Endymion Porter, Portsmouth, Falmouth, Lisbon, 2 and 6 Nov, 5 Dec 1629; *CSPD 1629-31*, pp. 66, 69, 72, 83, 126, 133; S.P.S., 94/34/141-3, Gardiner to ?Dorchester, Madrid, 14 Jan 1630.

11. S.P.S., 94/34/120-1, Cottington to Dorchester, Lisbon, 13 Dec 1629; S.P.S., 94/34/118, Cottington to Porter, Lisbon, 13 Dec 1629.

12. S.P.S., 94/34/164, Cottington to Dorchester, Madrid, 29 Jan 1629; *CSPV 1629-32*, pp. 273-4.

13. B.L., Ashmole MS. 829, f. 157, docquet granting the ambassador-ship to Cottington, Oct 1629; S.P.S., 94/34/167, 169-70, Charles I to Cottington, ? Jan, 4 Feb 1630.

14. S.P.S., 94/34/194-5, 214, Charles to Cottington, Feb, 7 Apr 1630.

15. S.P.S., 94/34/198, Cottington to Dorchester, Madrid, 3 Mar 1630; *CSPV 1629-32*, p. 341; Thomas Birch, *Court and Times of Charles the First*, 2 vols., ed. R. F. Williams (London, 1848) II 65, Beaulieu to Sir Thomas Pickering, London, 10 Mar 1630.

16. P.R.O., C.115/M.32/8175, Flower to Scudamore, London, 27 Mar 1630; W.W. MSS., 12(b), no. 97, Anne Cottington to Wentworth, London, 29 Dec 1629; S.P.S., 94/34/200, 240, Dorchester to Cottington, London, 2 Mar, 31 May 1630; S.P.S., 94/34/221, Cottington to Porter, Madrid, 17 Apr 1630; S.P.S., 94/34/232-5, Cottington to Dorchester, Madrid, 14 May 1630; S.P.S., 94/34/240-50, Charles I to Cottington, 29 June 1630; E. W. Brayley, *History and Antiquities of the Abbey Church of St Peter, Westminster*, 2 vols. (London, 1818-23) II 177.

17. S.P.S., 94/34/251, 257, Dorchester to Cottington, London, ? June, 9 July 1630.

18. S.P.S., 94/35/61-70, two letters attached, same to same, Madrid, 24 Aug 1630.

19. W.W. MSS., 12(b), no. 140, Calvert to Wentworth, Greenwich, 27 Sep 1630; ibid., no. 149, Philip Mainwaring to Wentworth, Roehampton, 9 Oct 1630; P.R.O., C.115/M.32/8179, Flower to Scudamore, London, 11 Sep 1630; S.P.S., 94/35/5, Cottington to Carlisle, Madrid,

24 Aug 1630; S.P.S., 94/35/29-30, 71-5, Cottington to Dorchester, Madrid, 5 Sep, 12 Nov 1630.

20. W.W. MSS., 12(b), no. 187, Cottington to Wentworth, Madrid, 5 Jan 1631. The text of the treaty of 1630 is in Rushworth, III 90-9, as well as in B.M., Harley MS. 2554, ff. 16-26.

21. Gardiner, *History*, VII 176-7. Cf. B. E. Supple, *Commercial Crisis and Change in England, 1600-1642* (Cambridge, 1959) p. 104.

22. *CCSP*, I 49; B.L., Clarendon MS. 5, ff. 38-9, 44, copy of the secret treaty.

23. W.W. MSS., 12(b), no. 176, Calvert to Wentworth, London, 1 Dec 1630; S.P.S., 94/35/127, 137, Cottington to Dorchester, Madrid, 5 and 13 Jan 1631; S.P.S., 94/35/171, same to same, Portsmouth Road, 5 Mar 1631; S.P.S., 94/35/129, Cottington to Edward Nicholas, Madrid, 5 Jan 1631; B.M., Egerton MS. 1820, ff. 3-5, Arthur Hopton to Dorchester, 6 Feb 1631; *CSPD 1629-31*, pp. 347, 377, 414, 528; *CSPV 1629-32*, pp. 471, 485; H.M.C., *Cowper MSS.*, II 411, Nicholas to ?, London, 7 Sep 1630.

Chapter 9: Baron Cottington of Hanworth

1. W.W. MSS., 12(b), no. 136, Calvert to Wentworth, Greenwich, 12 Sep 1630; ibid., 12(c), no. 181, Mainwaring to Wentworth, London, 19 Dec 1630. It is difficult to establish exchange rates of money in the early seventeenth century. It may help to say that four ducats equalled approximately £1 sterling. Hence 500,000 ducats was roughly the equivalent of £125,000.

2. P.R.O., C.115/M.30/8068, Flower to Scudamore, London, 28 Mar 1631; C.115/M.30/8077, same to same, London, 12 Mar 1631; Birch, *Court and Times of Charles the First*, II 103, Mead to Stuteville, Oxford, 13 Mar 1631; *CSPV 1629-32*, pp. 458-9, 471, 479-81, 485; C. V. Wedgwood, *Thomas Wentworth First Earl of Strafford, 1593-1641* (London, 1961) p. 117; K. N. Chaudhuri, 'The East India Company and the Export of Treasure in the Early Seventeenth Century', *Economic History Review*, 2nd ser., XVI 37; J. D. Gould, 'The Royal Mint in the Early Seventeenth Century', *EcHR*, 2nd ser., V 243.

3. P.R.O., C.115/M.30/8188, Flower to Scudamore, London, 16 July 1631; *CSPD 1631-3*, p. 59; Stone, *Crisis of the Aristocracy*, p. 2.

4. V.C.H., *Hampshire*, IV 252-3; *Forty-Third Annual Report of the Deputy Keeper of Public Records*, Appendix, I 147, 163; *CSPD 1629-31*, p. 46; *CSPD 1631-3*, pp. 172-3; *CSPV 1629-32*, pp. 471, 490-1; S.P.S., 94/35/117, Cottington's account of extraordinary expenses, Dec 1630; Aylmer, *King's Servants*, pp. 164-5.

5. B.L., Perrott MS. 4, ff. 15-16, 'Officers of the Exchequer', temp. *c.* late James I; Aylmer, *King's Servants*, pp. 164-5, 211, 276, 349, and

his table of incomes of selected offices, pp. 204-10. For an example of how Government officers benefited from opportune investments, see J. P. Cooper, 'The Fortune of Thomas Wentworth, Earl of Strafford', *EcHR*, 2nd ser., XI 231-2.

6. Wiltshire R.O. (Trowbridge), copy of patent, 20 Dec 1631, granting Cottington Brewham Lodge; *Forty-Third Annual Report of the Deputy Keeper of Public Records*, Appendix, 1 163; P.R.O., C.54/2912/1 and 2948/12; P.R.O., S.P. 16/377/177; P.R.O., E.403/2751/149; V.C.H., *Middlesex*, II 314-16; Stone, *Crisis of the Aristocracy*, p. 356; *CSPD 1631-3*, pp. 173, 178, 291; *CSPD 1639-40*, pp. 35-6.

7. P.R.O., S.P. 16/377/177; V.C.H., *Wiltshire*, III 90; William Cobbett, *State Trials* (London, 1809) III, cols. 401-18; Sir Richard Hoare, *History of Modern Wiltshire*, IV (London, 1829) pp. 12-13, 22-3 and Plate III.

8. W.W. MSS., 17(c), no. 209, Garrard to Wentworth, Sion, 9 Oct 1637.

9. W.W. MSS., 12(d), no. 258, Weston to Wentworth, London, 26 Sep 1631; *CSPD 1633-4*, p. 206.

10. B.L., Royal Society MS. 92, f. 32.

11. W.W. MSS., 12(d), Weston to Wentworth, London, 26 Dec 1633; ibid., Letter Book 3, f. 53, Cottington to Wentworth, London, 26 Dec 1633; ibid., f. 36, Wentworth to Cottington, Dublin, 24 Nov 1633; Aylmer, *King's Servants*, p. 30, n. 1; Richard Bagwell, *Ireland under the Stuarts and during the Interregnum*, 3 vols. (London, 1909-16) I 279; David Mathew, *Age of Charles I* (London, 1951) p. 157.

12. Stone, *Crisis of the Aristocracy*, p. 761; *CSPD 1650*, p. 93.

13. P.R.O., C.54/3172/29; P.R.O., S.P. 16/377/177.

14. P.R.O., S.P. 16/377/177; P.R.O., C.54/2912/1 and 3214/7; Stone, *Crisis of the Aristocracy*, p. 415.

15. Wiltshire R.O., Francis Cottington's will, 1652; National Library of Scotland (Edinburgh), MS. 1879, ff. 15-46, Cottington's Account Book for 1623; Clarendon, *History*, I 155-7, 198; Cockayne, *Complete Peerage*, III 463, n. a; B.L., Ashmole MS. 1513, ff. 33-8; M. A. E. Green (ed.), *Calendar of the Proceedings of the Committee for Advance of Money, 1642-1656* (London, 1888) pp. 578-81. The earlier portrait is reproduced in B.L., English MSS., Miscellaneous, b. 4, facing f. 100; in Edmund Lodge, *Portraits of Illustrious Personages of Great Britain*, 4 vols. (London, 1821-34) III, n.p.; and in *Notes and Queries for Somerset and Dorset*, XII, facing p. 57.

Chapter 10: The Lord Treasurer's Man

1. The preceding paragraphs are based on: *APC 1628-9*, pp. 227-8, 273-4; *Familiar Letters, Howell*, I 269-70, Howell to Countess of

Sunderland, Westminster, 5 Aug 1629; *CSPD 1628-9*, pp. 412, 507, 524; Aylmer, *King's Servants*, pp. 88, 113-14, 231, 345-9; Dietz, *English Public Finance*, II 249-51; Wedgwood, *Strafford*, pp. 68, 81, 89, 114; Hugh F. Kearney, *Strafford in Ireland, 1633-41* (Manchester, 1959) pp. 29-31.

2. Robert Ashton, *The Crown and the Money Market, 1603-1640* (Oxford, 1960) pp. 163-73; Dietz, *English Public Finance*, II, chaps. vi-x; Stone, *Crisis of the Aristocracy*, pp. 416-24; Supple, *Commercial Crisis and Change*, chaps. 3-5.

3. Dietz, *English Public Finance*, II 257-9; Aylmer, *King's Servants*, pp. 192-6.

4. *Rubens Letters*, pp. 189, 318, Rubens to Olivares, London, 6 and 22 July 1629; W.W. MSS., 12(a) no. 71, Cottington to Wentworth, London, 5 Aug 1629; Mathew, *Social Structure in Caroline England*, p. 44, n. 2.

5. *APC 1628-9*, pp. 276-7; *APC 1629-30*, pp. v-viii, 91; P.R.O., P.C. 2/44/1, 3; Edward R. Turner, *The Privy Council of England in the Seventeenth and Eighteenth Centuries, 1603-1784*, 2 vols (London, 1927-8) II 221-5; *CSPD 1633-4*, pp. 351-2; Cooper, 'Francis Cottington', Appendix II.

6. B.L., Sir John Bankes MSS. (1634-40); H.M.C., *Cowper MSS.*, II 51, John Broughton to Sir John Coke, London, 11 Apr 1634; W.W. MSS., 13(c), no. 199, Admiralty Board order, 21 Feb 1634; ibid., no. 212, Commissioners of the Admiralty to Wentworth, London, 5 Mar 1634.

7. B.M., Harley MS. 764, 'Register of Exchequer Orders and Warrants', ff. 12, 16, 19, 21, 26, 30, 36, 47-9, 55, 130-1, dated Apr 1629 to May 1632; H.M.C., *Skrine MSS.*, p. 122; *CSPD 1625-6*, pp. 267, 361.

8. On the sheriffs, see: J. T. Cliffe, *The Yorkshire Gentry from the Reformation to the Civil War* (London, 1969) pp. 139, 250-5, 372-3; C. H. Karraker, *The Seventeenth Century Sheriff* (London, 1930) *passim*; Jean S. Wilson, 'The Sheriffs' Rolls of the Sixteenth and Seventeenth Centuries', *EHR*, XLVII 31-45; Aylmer, *King's Servants*, pp. 184 ff.

9. BM., Harley MS. 764, ff. 10-11, 16, 19, 29, 36, 39-42, 45, 53, 56, 122-4, 135. This collection also includes many petitions to Cottington from debtors in prison, mainly in the Fleet, London. *CSPD, Addenda, 1625-49*, pp. 396-7; Aylmer, *King's Servants*, pp. 62, 67; Dietz, *English Public Finance*, II 216-17.

10. B.M., Harley MS. 764, f. 27; *CSPD 1628-9*, pp. 582-3; *CSPD 1629-31*, pp. 53, 216, 305-6; *CSPD 1631-3*, p. 129; *CSPD 1633-4*, p. 297; *CSPD, Addenda, 1625-49*, p. 413.

11. On the Household, see: Dietz, *English Public Finance*, II 412-20; Aylmer, *King's Servants*, pp. 26-32, and his 'Attempts at Administrative Reform, 1625-40', *EHR*, LXXII 246-58.

12. Ibid., 250-3; Ellis, *Original Letters*, 1st ser., III 283-4, Mead to Stuteville, Cambridge, 7 Nov 1629.

13. On recusancy and the penal laws, see: Havran, *Catholics*, chaps. 1, 5-7; Brian Magee, *English Recusants: A Study of the Post-Reformation Catholic Revival and the Operation of the Recusancy Laws* (London, 1938); Gordon Albion, *Charles I and the Court of Rome* (London, 1935) chaps. i-iii *passim*.

14. David Mathew, *Catholicism in England* (London, 1955) p. 83; Albion, *Charles I and the Court of Rome*, pp. 43, 149, 165; Forster, *Sir John Eliot*, II 725-6; Westminster Cathedral Archives, Roman Letters, 1624-36, f. 101, Bishop of Chalcedon to Peter Fitton, 11 July 1631; ibid., A Series, XXVI, f. 162, John Southcot to Bishop of Chalcedon, London, 11 Apr 1632; P.R.O., P.C. 2/42 (1632) and 2/51 (1640), *passim*; P.R.O., C.115/M.35/8400, John Pory to Viscount Slego, London, 21 Apr 1632; ibid., 8091, John Flower to Scudamore, London, 21 Apr 1632; W.W. MSS., 12(d), no. 249, George Calvert to Wentworth, London, 7 Sep 1631.

15. Cliffe, *The Yorkshire Gentry*, p. 202; Dom Hugh Bowler, 'Some Notes on the Recusant Rolls of the Exchequer', *Recusant History*, IV 83; H. R. Trevor-Roper, *Archbishop Laud*, 2nd ed. (London, 1962) pp. 306-12, 332-4, 370-1; Dietz, *English Public Finance*, II 268, 278; Havran, *Catholics*, pp. 91-2.

16. Laud, *Works*, VI 334-5, Laud to Wentworth, 15 Nov 1633.

17. W.W. MSS., Letter Book 1, ff. 76-8, Wentworth to Cottington, York, 1 Oct 1632; ibid., Letter Book 3, f. 7, same to same, Holywell, 24 July 1633; ibid., 12(a), no. 70, Cottington to Wentworth, London, 1 Aug 1629; ibid., 13(b), no. 49, John Coke to Wentworth, London, 20 Sep 1633; ibid., no. 63, Archbishop of York to Wentworth, London, 3 Oct 1633; *Strafforde's Letters*, I 51, Cottington to Wentworth, London, 5 Aug 1629.

18. On the contract, see Anthony F. Upton, *Sir Arthur Ingram, c. 1565-1642* (Oxford, 1961) pp. 155-6, 223-31. A copy of the contract (Jan 1634) is in Leeds City Library, Temple Newsam MSS., TN/LA/8/4. On Wentworth's alienation, see W.W. MSS., Letter Book 3, f. 23, Ingram to Wentworth, York, 2 Sep 1633; ibid., 8, no. 244, Wentworth to Ingram, Dublin, 30 Sep 1633; ibid., 14(b), no. 119, Cottington to Wentworth, London, 2 July 1634.

19. Ibid., 13(b), no. 105, Anne Cottington to Wentworth, London, 23 Nov 1633.

20. *Strafforde's Letters*, I 80, 214, Cottington to Wentworth, London, 30 Nov 1632, 11 Mar 1634; ibid., Garrard to Wentworth, London, 27 Feb, 1 Apr 1634; W.W. MSS., Letter Book 3, ff. 54, 140, Cottington to Wentworth, 1 Jan, 29 Oct 1634; ibid., 14(a), no. 214, Sir Gervase Clifton to Wentworth, Newmarket, 10 Mar 1634; *Registers of St Martin-in-the-Fields*, pp. 101, 283; *CSPD 1634-5*, p. 158; Margaret Whinney and Oliver Millar, *English Art, 1625-1714* (Oxford, 1957) pp. 110-11, 120 n. 1.

21. W.W. MSS., 12(d), no. 264, Cottington to Wentworth, London, 14 Oct 1631; ibid., Letter Book 3, ff. 83-5, 157, Wentworth to Cottington, Dublin, 14 May, 22 Dec 1634.

Chapter 11: Cottington and Laud

1. Peter Heylin, *Cyprianus Anglicus: or, the History of the Life and Death of . . . William . . . Lord Archbishop of Canterbury*, 2 parts (Dublin, 1719) pt II, p. 36; Wedgwood, *Strafford*, pp. 119-20; Trevor-Roper, *Archbishop Laud*, p. 219.

2. Laud, *Works*, III 214; H.M.C., *Ninth Report*, pt I, p. 307; B.L., Bankes MS. 55/35; Rushworth, II 88-91; Anthony Wood, *History and Antiquities of the Colleges and Halls in the University of Oxford* (Oxford: 1786) pp. 547-8; *CSPD 1629-31*, pp. 394-5; *CSPD 1631-3*, pp. 6, 514.

3. Thomas G. Barnes, 'County Politics and a Puritan *cause célèbre*, Somerset Churchales, 1633', *Transactions of the Royal Historical Society*, 5th ser., IX 103-22; Trevor-Roper, *Archbishop Laud*, pp. 155-8; Gardiner, *History*, VII 318-22.

4. Isabel M. Calder (ed.), *Activities of the Puritan Faction of the Church of England, 1625-33* (London, 1957) pp. vii-xiv, xviii-xxiv, 62-3, 121-4; Christopher Hill, *Society and Puritanism in Pre-Revolutionary England* (New York, 1964) pp. 95-6; Gardiner, *History*, VII 258-9.

5. W.W. MSS., 14(a), no. 42, commission to the Committee for Foreign Plantations, Apr 1634; Evans, *Principal Secretary of State*, pp. 231-2; *APC, Colonial*, I 187, 200-1, 214; *CSPD 1635*, p. 286; Carl Bridenbaugh, *Vexed and Troubled Englishmen, 1590-1642* (New York, 1968) pp. 467-70.

6. W.W. MSS., 13(b), no. 60, Plumleigh to Wentworth, Kinsale, 28 Sep 1633; H.M.C., *Cowper MSS.*, II 21-2, 86; M. Oppenheim, *History of the Administration of the Royal Navy and of Merchant Shipping in Relation to the Navy*, 2nd printing (New York, 1961) pts. II, III *passim*; Evans, *Principal Secretary of State*, p. 326; Cooper, 'Francis Cottington', pp. 69-72; *CSP, Ireland, 1633-47*, pp. 21-2; *CSPD 1631-3*, pp. 74, 100, 119, 151, 195, 440, 459, 509, 515, 545; *CSPD 1636-7*, p. 161.

7. B.M., Egerton MS. 2597, f. 128, Cottington to Carlisle, London, 3 June 1633; ibid., f. 140, Wentworth to ?, Westminster, 25 June 1633; P.R.O., C.115/M.31/8158, John Flower to Scudamore, London, 27 July 1633; P.R.O., P.C. 2/42, 26 Apr 1633; H.M.C., *Cowper MSS.*, II 17; *CSPD 1633-4*, pp. 53, 83; *CSPV 1632-6*, pp. 157, 163; *Forty-Third Annual Report of the Deputy Keeper of Public Records*, Appendix, III 476; Agnes Strickland, *Lives of the Queens of England*, 6 vols. (London, 1901) IV 50.

8. W.W. MSS., Letter Book 3, ff. 52-4, Cottington to Wentworth,

London, 26 Dec 1633; ibid., 13(b), no. 147, same to same, London, 19 Dec 1633; ibid., 14(d), nos. 309, 323, Garrard to Wentworth, London, 1 and 12 Mar 1635; ibid., no. 322, Cottington to Wentworth, London, 12 Mar 1635; ibid., no. 327, Sir John Bingley to Wentworth, Westminster, 13 Mar 1635; ibid., no. 330, Lord Mohun to Wentworth, London, 14 Mar 1635; ibid., no. 336, Conway to Wentworth, London, 17 Mar 1635; ibid., 8, ff. 234-5, Earl of Dorset to Wentworth, London, 12 Mar 1635.

9. P.R.O., Baschet's Paris Transcripts, 31/3/68, f. 145, M. de Pougny to Richelieu, London, 22 Mar 1635; W.W. MSS., 15(b), no. 139, Cottington to Wentworth, London, 6 July 1635; ibid., 15(c), no. 184, same to same, 4 Aug 1635; Gardiner, *History*, VIII 140-1; Heylin, *William Laud*, pt II, pp. 36-7; Aylmer, *King's Servants*, pp. 114-17, 349, and his 'Officers of Exchequer', in F. J. Fisher (ed.), *Essays in the Economic and Social History of Tudor and Stuart England* (Cambridge, 1961) pp. 177-9.

10. H.M.C., *Buccleuch MSS.*, III 369-70, Robert Dixon to Lord Montagu, London, 19 Mar 1635; P.R.O., P.C. 2/54/3; Gardiner, *History*, VII 379; Laud, *Works*, VII 115-16, Laud to Wentworth, London, 27 Mar 1635.

11. B.L., Bankes MS. 51/34, warrant on Mastership of Wards; *Strafforde's Letters*, I 389, Garrard to Wentworth, London, 17 Mar 1635; *CSPD 1634-5*, pp. 562, 607-8; Aylmer, *King's Servants*, pp. 114-17; H. E. Bell, *Introduction to the History and Records of the Court of Wards and Liveries* (Cambridge, 1953) pp. 18-19, 136; H.M.C., *Buccleuch MSS.*, III 369-70, Robert Dixon to Lord Montagu, London, 19 Mar 1635. Dixon said that Naunton 'resigned' his office on 'Friday last', which was 14 Mar, the day following Portland's death.

12. Cottington became Lord Treasurer at Royalist Oxford on 3 Oct 1643, during the civil war, but his appointment was a hollow tribute in the context of the times.

13. Heylin, *William Laud*, pt II, p. 36.

14. W.W. MSS., 15(a), no. 38, Sir Gervase Clifton to Wentworth, London, 28 Apr 1635; B.M., Add. MS. 28,103, f. 30, treasury warrant to Sir Robert Pye and others, 18 May 1635; *Strafforde's Letters*, I 412-13, Garrard to Wentworth, London, 14 Apr 1635; ibid., 415-16, John Coke to Wentworth, London, 1 May 1635; P.R.O., C.115/M.36/8446, Rossingham to Scudamore, London, 23 Jan 1635; Dietz, *English Public Finance*, II 272-6; Aylmer, 'Officers of Exchequer', in Fisher, *Essays*, pp. 166-7, 177-9, and 'Charles I's Commission on Fees, 1627-40', *BIHR*, XXXI 58-67.

15. W.W. MSS., 15(b), no. 108, Cottington to Wentworth, London, 16 June 1635; ibid., 15(c), no. 253, same to same, London, 30 Oct 1635; ibid., Letter Book 3, f. 225, same to same, London, 3 Oct 1635; ibid., ff. 225-6, Wentworth to Cottington, Dublin, 31 Oct 1635.

16. These letters are by Laud to Wentworth, written at Lambeth unless specified otherwise. Laud, *Works*, v 423, 6 July 1635; ibid., vII 108-9, 202-15, 12 Jan, 30 Nov 1635; W.W. MSS., 6, ff. 168-9, 175, 186-7, 191-4, 27 Mar, 28 Apr, 12 May, 12 June 1635; ibid., ff. 228-33, 31 July, 3 Aug 1635, Croydon; ibid., ff. 253-5, 4 Oct 1635, Hampton Court; ibid., f. 281, 16 Nov 1635.

17. I refer to the enclosure of Oatlands Park (Surrey), the prosecution in Star Chamber of Bishop John Williams of Lincoln, the case of Bagg *v.* Pell and the wrangle over the soap monopoly.

18. Trevor-Roper, *Archbishop Laud*, p. 219.

19. H.M.C., *Sixth Report*, Appendix, p. 278, Finet to ?, London, 16 Oct 1635; Laud, *Works*, vI 442, Laud to Wentworth, Lambeth, 16 Nov 1635; W.W. MSS., 8, ff. 271-2, Wentworth to Earl of Newcastle, Dublin, 26 Sep 1635; ibid., f. 329, Conway to ?Wentworth, London, 14 Nov 1635; ibid., Letter Book 3, ff. 235-6, Wentworth to Cottington, Dublin, 19 Dec 1635; ibid., 15(b), no. 139, Cottington to Wentworth, London, 6 July 1635; ibid., 15(c), no. 184, same to same, London, 4 Aug 1635; ibid., no. 206, Garrard to Wentworth, Petworth, 1 Sep 1635.

20. H.M.C., *Portland MSS.*, II 125, Countess of Devonshire to Earl of Newcastle, London, ? Jan 1636; Laud, *Works*, vII 223, 233, Laud to Wentworth, Lambeth, 14 and 23 Jan 1636; W.W. MSS., 15(e), no. 335, Cottington to Wentworth, Westminster, 27 Jan 1636; ibid., Letter Book 3, ff. 242-3, Wentworth to Cottington, Dublin, 13 Feb 1636; *Strafforde's Letters*, I 507, Garrard to Wentworth, Petworth, 8 Jan 1636; *CSPD, Addenda, 1635-49*, p. 742.

21. Laud, *Works*, vII 248, 277, Laud to Wentworth, Lambeth and Croydon, 8 Apr, 22 Aug 1636; ibid., v 148-50, diary entry for 29-30 Aug 1636; *Strafforde's Letters*, II 4, Sir John Temple to Wentworth, London, 18 Apr 1636; ibid., II 2, Garrard to Wentworth, Petworth, 5 Apr 1636; Heylin, *William Laud*, pt II, p. 37; H.M.C., *Cowper MSS.*, II 123-4; Smith, *Life and Letters of Wotton*, II 354; W.W. MSS., 15(e), no. 365, Howell to Wentworth, Westminster, 15 Mar 1636; ibid., 16(c), no. 11, Conway to Wentworth, London, 11 Apr 1636; *CSPD 1637-8*, p. 75; Lysons, *Historical Account of those Parishes . . . not described in the Environs of London*, p. 101.

Chapter 12: Councillor in Crisis

1. Laud, *Works*, vII 273-7, Laud to Wentworth, Croydon, 22 Aug 1636; *Strafforde's Letters*, II 52, Cottington to Wentworth, London, 27 Feb 1637.

2. P.R.O., S.P., Flanders, 77/22/248, John Taylor to Cottington, Brussels, 4 Nov 1632; B.M., Egerton MS. 1820, ff. 1-3, Instructions to

Hopton, 5 Feb 1631; S.P.S., 94/36/252-4, 298, Hopton to Cottington, Madrid, 21 Mar, 27 May 1633; *CSPD 1633-4*, p. 461; Gardiner, *History*, VII 178-87, 343-7, 351-2, 366-9.

3. W.W. MSS., 16(a), no. 61, William Raylton to Wentworth, Oatlands, 19 Sep 1636; H.M.C., *Third Report*, p. 73, Juxon and Cottington to Northumberland, Fulham House, 13 July 1636; ibid., Windebank to Northumberland, Windsor, 17 July 1636; H.M.C., *Cowper MSS.*, II 125, Juxon and Cottington to Customer Braems at Dover, London, 13 July 1636; ibid., 122, 'A particular of the plate transported from the Groyne' by Sir John Coke, 27 July 1636; H.M.C., *Gawdy MSS.*, p. 160, Anthony Mingay to Framlingham Gawdy, Norwich, 14 Sep 1636; *CSPV 1636-9*, pp. 37, 59.

4. M. J. Hawkins (ed.), *Sales of Wards in Somerset, 1603-1641*, Somerset Record Soc., LXVII (Frome, 1965) pp. xv-xvi; C. V. Wedgwood, *The King's Peace, 1637-1641* (New York, 1956) pp. 153-4.

5. James Ley, *Reports of Diverse Resolutions in Law Arising upon Cases in the Court of Wards, etc.* (London, 1659) pp. 1-2; L. Stone, 'Fruits of Office', in Fisher, *Essays*, pp. 100-1; J. Hurstfield, 'Lord Burghley as Master of Wards, 1561-98', *TRHS*, 4th ser., XXXI 99-100; Bell, *Wards and Liveries*, pp. 31-4, 147-8, 193-205.

6. Laud, *Works*, IV 297, 409; Cooper, 'Francis Cottington', pp. 161-3; Hawkins, *Sales of Wards*, pp. xxii-xxiv.

7. K. D. H. Haley, *The First Earl of Shaftesbury* (Oxford, 1968) pp. 17-19; B.M., Add. MS. 33,319, ff. 49-52; *CSPD 1640-1*, pp. 214-40; Bell, *Wards and Liveries*, pp. 33-4; Hawkins, *Sales of Wards*, p. xxiii, Table 4.

8. The figures in this paragraph are net income resulting from gross income minus all deductions, including arrears.

9. Hawkins, *Sales of Wards*, pp. xxi-xxii; *CSPD 1640-1*, pp. 214-40; Cooper, 'Francis Cottington', p. 163; Dietz, *English Public Finance*, II 303; Bell, *Wards and Liveries*, pp. 152-3, and Table A, facing p. 192.

10. B.L., Bankes MS. 39/9, warrant to Farmer Goring and others, 6 Apr 1638; B.L., Ashmole MS. 829, f. 227, Privy Council of Scotland to Charles, Edinburgh, 25 Aug 1637; W.W. MSS., 10(b), ff. 1-2, Northumberland to Wentworth, Sion, 23 July 1638; Gardiner, *History*, VIII 334-46; Dietz, *English Public Finance*, II 334-7; Ashton, *The Crown and the Money Market*, pp. 100-5, 174-7.

11. W.W. MSS., 10(b), ff. 1-2, Northumberland to Wentworth, Sion, 23 July 1638; ibid., ff. 5-7, Wentworth to Northumberland, Dublin, 30 July 1638; B.L., Bankes MS. 55/90, naval preparations, 17 Mar 1637; Laud, *Works*, VII 453-4, Laud to Wentworth, Croydon, 22 June 1638; Turner, *Privy Council*, II 227-8; Trevor-Roper, *Archbishop Laud*, pp. 368-9.

12. Laud, *Works*, VII 412, 426-8, 511, Laud to Wentworth, Lambeth,

17 Feb, 23 May, 29 Dec 1638; W.W. MSS., 10(b), f. 11, Cottington to Wentworth, London, 1 June 1638; ibid., 18(a), no. 10, Percy to Wentworth, London, 3 Apr 1638; ibid., no. 152, Cottington to Wentworth, London, 24 Nov 1638; *Strafforde's Letters*, II 164, Garrard to Wentworth, London, 10 May 1638; *DNB*, XII 360-2.

13. B.L., Clarendon MS. 15, ff. 36, 44, 48, 82, Scottish Committee Minutes, Nov–Dec 1638; H.M.C., *Cowper MSS.*, II 194, same, 10 Sep 1638; H.M.C., *Montagu MSS.*, p. 124, Privy Council to Earl of Exeter, London, 14 Mar 1639; W.W. MSS., 10(b), f. 20, Wentworth to Cottington, Dublin, 17 Oct 1638; ibid., 18(a), no. 77, Privy Council to Wentworth, Westminster, 30 June 1638; ibid., no. 152, Cottington to Wentworth, London, 24 Nov 1638; *CSPD 1639-40*, pp. 60-1; David Masson, *The Life of John Milton: Narrated in Connexion with the Political, Ecclesiastical, and Literary History of His Time*, 7 vols. (New York, 1946 reprint) II 46-7.

14. Laud, *Works*, VII 537, Laud to Wentworth, Lambeth, 22 Mar 1639; H.M.C., *Rutland MSS.*, I 502, Thomas Lyttleton to Rutland, Belvoir, 17 Feb 1639; H.M.C., *Cowper MSS.*, II 223, Cottington to ?, London, 27 Apr 1639; W.W. MSS., 10(b), ff. 70-1, Wentworth to Cottington, Fairwood Park, 16 Apr 1639; ibid., no. 178, Cottington to Wentworth, Hanworth, 5 Mar 1639; *CSPD 1638-9*, p. 81; Turner, *Privy Council*, II 227-8, 302-3.

15. Wedgwood, *Strafford*, pp. 259-60, 265-7; Turner, *Privy Council*, II 302-3; *CSPD 1639-40*, p. 188; Masson, *Life of Milton*, II 127.

16. B.L., Bankes MS. 9/3, warrant to purchase Wimbledon, 16 Jan 1640; ibid., 9/36, Crown jewels, 29 Nov 1639; ibid., 13/21, Petty Farm customs, 20 Nov 1639; H.M.C., *Cowper MSS.*, II 239, Juxon to Coke, London, 29 July 1639; *CSPD 1639-40*, pp. 119, 178, 298, 332-3, 420, 458-9, 471, 529-30, 548-50, 565, 586; W. H. Price, *English Patents of Monopoly* (Boston, 1906) pp. 114-18.

17. V.C.H., *Wiltshire*, V 135; Clarendon, *History*, I 172-3; *CCSP*, II 81; Valerie Pearl, *London and the Outbreak of the Puritan Revolution* (London, 1961) pp. 102-4, 107-8.

18. B.L., Clarendon MS. 18, f. 164, Windebank to Hopton, London, 11 May 1640; Laud, *Works*, III 283-4; *CSPD 1640*, pp. 29-30, 59, 112-13; Trevor-Roper, *Archbishop Laud*, p. 387; Wedgwood, *The King's Peace*, pp. 313-14, 322-3; Bulstrode Whitelocke (ed.), *Memorials of the English Affairs* (London, 1732) p. 33.

19. B.L., Bankes MS. 9/32, 21 June 1640; Gardiner, *History*, IX 189; Pearl, *London and the Outbreak of the Puritan Revolution*, p. 101; Wedgwood, *The King's Peace*, pp. 337-8, 344-8.

20. Rushworth, III 1179, 1216; Notestein, *D'Ewes Journal*, pp. 16, 24; Wallington, *Historical Notices*, I 131; H.M.C., *Seventh Report*, Appendix,

H

p. 251, newsletter, 24 Aug 1640; *CSPD 1640*, pp. 629-30; *CSPD 1640-1*, pp. 85, 129-30, 132, 158, 177, 194. Cottington surrendered the office of Constable on his own initiative on 9 Nov 1640.

21. West. Cath. Arch., A Series, XXIX, f. 340, A. Champney to Bishop of Chalcedon, ?London, 6 Aug 1640; B.L., Bankes MS. 41/78, Lord Lieutenancy of Dorset, 6 June 1640; *CSPD 1640*, pp. 323, 453; *CSPD 1640-1*, pp. 103-6, 363; J. C. Sainty, 'Lieutenants of Counties, 1585-1642', *Bulletin of the Institute of Historical Research*, supplement no. 8 (May 1970) p. 19.

22. William Foster, 'Charles I and the East India Company', *EHR*, XIX 456-63; Ashton, *The Crown and the Money Market*, pp. 178-80; E. B. Sainsbury (ed.), *A Calendar of Court Minutes etc. of the East India Company*, 4 vols. (Oxford, 1907-13) II viii-xiii, 12-13, 23-6, 65-6, 73, 80-3, 185; *CSPD 1640*, pp. 648-9; *CSPD 1640-1*, p. 324.

23. B.L., Clarendon MS. 18, f. 265, Charles I to Windebank, York, 23 Aug 1640; ibid., 19, ff. 11-12, Windebank to Hopton, London, 5 Sep 1640; *CSPD 1640-1*, pp. 3-4, 26, 34-7, 43, 46-8, 55, 60-1, 84-5, 94, 96-8, 128, 137, 146, 159, 169-70.

24. *Letters and Memorials of the Sydney Family*, II 663-4, Northumberland to Leicester, London, 13 and 26 Nov 1640; Rushworth, IV 51, 59-60; *D'Ewes Journal*, pp. 65, 348-9; H.M.C., *Buccleuch MSS.*, III 401, 411; *LJ*, IV 107, 148, 164, 169, 181, 279; Gardiner, *Oxinden Letters, 1607-1642*, pp. 186-7, James Oxinden to Henry Oxinden, London, 27 Nov 1640; *CSPD 1640-1*, pp. 312-15; Trevor-Roper, *Archbishop Laud*, pp. 401-4.

25. David Laing (ed.), *Letters and Journals of Robert Baillie*, 3 vols. (Edinburgh, 1842) I 286, Baillie to Presbytery of Irvine, London, 28 Dec 1640; Bell, *Wards and Liveries*, pp. 148-9; *CSPD 1640-1*, pp. 404-535 *passim*.

26. Masson, *Life of Milton*, II 178-82; H.M.C., *House of Lords MSS.*, *Addenda*, XI 239; H.M.C., *Bath MSS.*, II 75-6, Francis Windebank to Thomas Windebank, Paris, 1 Mar 1641; H.M.C., *Cowper MSS.*, II 267, John Coke the Younger to Sir John Coke, London, 15 Dec 1640; Rushworth, IV 564; *Baillie's Letters*, I 342, Baillie to Presbytery of Irvine, London, Apr 1641; Whitelocke, *Memorials of the English Affairs*, p. 43; Kearney, *Strafford in Ireland, 1633-41*, pp. 203-5; Wedgwood, *Strafford*, pp. 348-50, 384; Mathew, *Social Structure in Caroline England*, p. 125.

27. Clarendon, *History*, I 279-81, 333-4 and n. 1; H.M.C., *Cowper MSS.*, II 280-1, Coke the Younger to ?, London, 28 Apr 1641; ibid., 282-3, 286, same to Sir John Coke, London, 18 May, 2 June 1641; Whitelocke, *Memorials of the English Affairs*, p. 46; Aylmer, *King's Servants*, p. 385; Masson, *Life of Milton*, II 280-1; Cooper, 'Francis Cottington', pp. 186a-7; *CSPD 1641-3*, pp. 284-5.

28. Wallington, *Historical Notices*, I 213; *CSPV 1640-2*, pp. 175-6; *CSPD 1640-1*, pp. 36-41, 54, 90.

Chapter 13: Councillor in War

1. Clarendon, *History*, I 198-9, 279-81, 493 n. I; F. M. G. Higham, *Charles I* (London, 1932) p. 188; John L. Sanford, *Studies and Illustrations of the Great Rebellion* (London, 1858) p. 308. Examples of harsh criticism of Cottington could easily be multiplied.

2. H.M.C., *House of Lords MSS., Addenda, 1514-1714*, XI 256; *CSPD 1641-3*, pp. 31, 284-5; *CSPD, Addenda, 1625-49*, pp. 635, 637-8.

3. V.C.H., *Middlesex*, II 395; H.M.C., *Fifth Report*, Appendix, pp. 43, 62, 70; *CJ*, II 649, III 14; *LJ*, V 289; *CSPD 1641-3*, p. 379.

4. *CJ*, III 243; *LJ*, V 517-18; Clarendon, *History*, III 82-3; H.M.C., *Fifth Report*, Appendix, p. 62.

5. Foster, 'Charles I and the East India Company', *EHR*, XIX 456-7, 460-1; *CSPD 1641-3*, pp. 266-7, 275, 305; Sainsbury, *Calendar of the Court Minutes etc. of the East India Company*, II viii-xi.

6. Ibid., II 242, 269; III 2-4, 20, 40-1, 49, 128, 249, 320, 347, 353; IV xxv-xxviii; Foster, *EHR*, XIX 462-3.

7. J. Waylen, 'The Falstone Day-Book', *Wiltshire Archaeological and Natural History Magazine*, XXVI 357; C. H. Firth (ed.), *Memoirs of Edmund Ludlow . . . 1625-1672*, 2 vols. (Oxford, 1894) I 54; C. H. Firth and R. S. Rait (eds.), *Acts and Ordinances of the Interregnum, 1642-1660*, 3 vols. (London, 1911) II 118, 120, 285, 307, 476, 674.

8. Firth, *Ludlow Memoirs*, I 50-1; B.M., Harley MS. 6852, f. 79; W. H. Black (ed.), *Docquets of Letters Patent* (London, 1837) p. 354.

9. Part of this paragraph is based on I. Roy, 'The Royalist Council of War, 1642-6', *BIHR*, XXXV 150-68.

10. Ibid., pp. 152-3, 157, 161-2, 167-8.

11. Clarendon, *History*, III 154-6; Black, *Docquets of Letters Patent*, pp. 60, 80, 90, 120, 372-3; Bell, *Wards and Liveries*, pp. 152-3; John Varley (ed.), *Mercurius Aulicus. A Diurnall Communicating the Telligence and Affaires of the Kingdome* (Oxford, 1948) p. 68; S. R. Gardiner, *History of the Great Civil War, 1642-1649*, 4 vols. (London, 1894) I 246.

12. B.M., Harley MS. 6852, Council of War Minutes, ff. 92, 133, 183, 193, 204; 6802, f. 165, various dates, 1643-5; 6804, f. 229; 6802, f. 165; B.M., Egerton MS. 2978, ff. 156, 158; *CSPD 1641-3*, pp. 492-4; M. A. E. Green (ed.), *Calendar of the Proceedings of the Committee for Compounding, etc. 1643-1660* (London, 1889-92) p. 1099.

13. Black, *Docquets of Letters Patent*, pp. 67, 73; *CSPD 1644-5*, pp. 279, 448; *CSPD, Addenda, 1625-49*, p. 653; *Mercurius Aulicus*, p. 63;

Harley MS. 6852, ff. 79, 92, 182, 193, 233, 238; 6851, ff. 229-30; B.L., Clarendon MS. 24, ff. 30-2.

14. *Mercurius Aulicus*, pp. 103-4; Gardiner, *History of the Great Civil War*, II 213-14, 236; Whitelocke, *Memorials of the English Affairs*, p. 439.

15. *CJ*, III 394; *Calendar of the Proceedings of the Committee for Advance of Money*, pp. 38, 122, II 578-9; *CSPD 1644-5*, p. 461; J. J. Schroeder, 'War Finance in London, 1642-1646', *The Historian*, XXI 366-7.

16. Andrew Clark (ed.), *The Life and Times of Anthony Wood, Antiquary, of Oxford, 1632-1695*, 2 vols. (Oxford, 1891) I 27-8; Gardiner, *History of the Great Civil War*, III 108.

17. Joshua Sprigge, *Anglia Rediviva. England's Recovery (1647)*, ed. Harry T. Moore (Gainesville, Fla., 1960) pp. 260-83; *Life and Times of Anthony Wood*, I 128. The Royalist delegation included Sir Richard Lane, the Marquis of Hertford, Lord Seymour, Sir Thomas Glemham, Cottington, Nicholas and the Earls of Dorset, Southampton and Chichester.

18. B.M., Egerton MS. 2456, f. 25, 23 June 1646, Garter jewels; Sprigge, *Anglia Rediviva*, p. 261.

19. H.M.C., *Sixth Report*, pp. 133, 142, and Appendix, pp. ix-x.

20. T. D. Whitaker, *The Life and Original Correspondence of Sir George Radcliffe* (London, 1810) p. 285; Masson, *Life of Milton*, III 493-4; *CSPD, Addenda, 1625-49*, pp. 412, 702.

21. B.L., Clarendon MS. 30, f. 42, Hyde to Cottington, Jersey, 29 Aug 1647.

Chapter 14: Exile

1. See H. J. Habakkuk, 'Landowners and the Civil War', *EcHR*, 2nd ser., XVIII 131-51; Paul H. Hardacre, *The Royalists during the Puritan Revolution* (The Hague, 1956) pp. 98-9.

2. See David Underdown, *Royalist Conspiracy in England, 1649-1660* (New Haven, 1960) chap. 1.

3. B.L., Clarendon MS. 31, f. 3, Hyde to Cottington, Jersey, 18 Mar 1648; B.M., Add. MS. 36,996, ff. 95-6, T. F. to Cottington, London, 6 Sep 1648.

4. *CSPD 1648-9*, pp. 40-1; *Acts and Ordinances of the Interregnum*, I 1056-7, 1149-50, II 520-45; *Calendar of the Committee for Compounding*, pp. 146, 487; Whitelocke, *Memorials of the English Affairs*, p. 415; John Tarswell, *The History and Antiquities of Lambeth* (London, 1858) pp. 26-7, 259-60.

5. *Calendar of the Proceedings of the Committee for Advance of Money*, pp. 578-81; 'Notes and Documents concerning Hugh Peters', *New-England Historical and Genealogical Register*, XL 286.

6. B.L., Clarendon MS. 31, ff. 172-3, Ostend, 13 July 1648; ibid., f. 194,

Cottington to Henry de Vic, Terveer, 8 Aug 1648; Clarendon, *History*, IV 23; Gardiner, *History of the Great Civil War*, IV 100-1, 111-14, 133, 146-9, 170, 187-9.

7. B.L., Clarendon MS. 31, f. 195, Cottington and Hyde to Prince Charles, Middelburg, 8 Aug 1648; ibid., f. 206, Hyde to Culpepper, Flushing, 20 Aug 1648; ibid., f. 225, Cottington to Hopton, Flushing, 1 Sep 1648; ibid., f. 239, Prince Charles to Cottington and Hyde, The Hague, 15 Sep 1648.

8. Clarendon, *History*, V 1-3.

9. Ibid., V 2; Turner, *Privy Council*, I 371-2; H.M.C., *Montagu MSS.*, p. 164, Cottington to Sir Robert Winde, The Hague, 30 Nov 1648.

10. H.M.C., *Popham MSS.*, p. 10, '473' to Thomas Kynaston, ?The Hague, 15 Mar 1649; Underdown, *Royalist Conspiracy in England*, pp. 12-15.

11. G. F. Warner (ed.), *Nicholas Papers*, Camden Society, new ser., XL (London, 1886) pp. 124-5, Hyde to Nicholas, The Hague, 6 Apr 1649; Clarendon, *History*, V 32-3.

12. Ibid., V 33-7; S. R. Gardiner, *History of the Commonwealth and Protectorate, 1649-1656*, 4 vols. (London, 1903) I 61-2.

13. Clarendon, *History*, V 36-7; Whitelocke, *Memorials of the English Affairs*, pp. 398, 406; B.L., Clarendon MS. 37, f. 71, Hyde and Cottington to Henrietta Maria, The Hague, 13 Apr 1649; ibid., ff. 94, 118, 121, 136, 140, letters patent and warrants to Cottington and Hyde, 10 and 24 May 1649; *CCSP*, II 481, Cottington's instructions; Julián Paz (ed.), *Catálogo de Documentos Españoles Existentes en al Archivo del Ministerio de Negocios Extranjeros de Paris* (Madrid, 1932) p. 270, Cottington to Don Alonzo de Cardeñas, The Hague, 8 Apr 1649; ibid., pp. 270-1, Cardeñas to Cottington, Brussels, 16 Apr 1649.

14. H.M.C., *Bath MSS.*, II 80, Hyde to Lady Hyde, Brussels, 7 June 1649; Sir Henry Craik, *Life of Edward Earl of Clarendon: Lord High Chancellor of England*, 2 vols. (London, 1911) I 236-7; B.L., Clarendon MS. 137, William Edgeman's 'Journal of the Embassy into Spain', ff. 7-8.

15. M. Guizot, *History of Oliver Cromwell and the English Commonwealth from the Execution of Charles the First to the Death of Cromwell*, 2 vols., trans. A. R. Scoble (London, 1854) I 388-91, quoting: deliberation of Council of State on Cardeñas letters, 6 June 1649; Archduke Leopold to Philip IV, Cambrai, 8 July 1649. Edgeman's Journal, ff. 8-9; Clarendon, *History*, V 49-50.

16. Edgeman's Journal, ff. 9-13; H.M.C., *Bath MSS.*, II 80-3, Hyde to Lady Hyde, Péronne and Saint-Germain, 31 July, 12 Aug, 11 Sep 1649; E. S. de Beer (ed.), *The Diary of Sir John Evelyn*, 6 vols. (Oxford, 1955) II 561; Underdown, *Royalist Conspiracy in England*, pp. 10-11; Philip A. Knachel, *England and the Fronde* (Ithaca, N.Y., 1967) pp. 215-19.

17. Edgeman's Journal, ff. 13-22; H.M.C., *Bath MSS.*, II 83-7, Hyde to Lady Hyde, Paris, Blaye, San Sebastian and Madrid, 24 Sep, 11 and 29 Oct 1649, 2 Mar 1650; B.L., Rawlinson MS. c. 726, f. 3, Cottington to Philip IV, San Sebastian, 21 Oct 1649; ibid., ff. 4, 8, 10, Haro to Cottington, Madrid, 28 Oct, 30 Nov, 19 Dec 1649; ibid., Cottington to Haro, ff. 6, 10-11, Alcobendas and Madrid, 22 Nov, 19 Dec 1649; *CCSP*, II 504; B.L., Clarendon MS. 38, f. 131, Hyde and Cottington to Jermyn, Madrid, 29 Nov 1649. Letters cited hereafter were written in Madrid unless specified otherwise.

18. Clarendon, *History*, v 99-100; Gardiner, *History of the Commonwealth and Protectorate*, I 305-8; B.L., Rawlinson MS. c. 726, f. 13, Torre to Cottington and Hyde, 28 Jan 1650; ibid., Cottington and Hyde to Torre, 13 Jan 1651; ibid., f. 49, same to Haro, 31 Jan 1651.

19. Ibid., ff. 12, 14-15, Cottington and Hyde to Haro, 28 Jan, 26 Feb 1650; B.M., Egerton MS. 2534, f. 16, Cottington to Nicholas, 18 Mar 1650; Knachel, *England and the Fronde*, pp. 116-17.

20. S. R. Gardiner (ed.), *Letters and Papers Illustrating Relations between Charles the Second and Scotland in 1650*, Scottish Record Soc., XVII (Edinburgh, 1894) pp. 127-8, Meynell to Cottington, Rome, 31 July 1650; B.L., Clarendon MS. 38, ff. 50-2, same to same, Rome, 18 Oct 1649.

21. Henry Proger, William Spark, John Guillim (William), Valentine Proger, John Halsal (Halsey) or his brother Edward, and William Arnet.

22. P.R.O., S.P.S., 94/43/19, Ascham to Council of State, London, 22 Oct 1649; S.P.S., 94/43/69-70, Fisher to Council of State, 24 Apr 1650; H.M.C., *Tenth Report*, pt IV, pp. 147-8, Cottington to Edward Proger, 20 Apr 1650; B.L., Clarendon MS. 39, f. 216, Cottington and Hyde to Philip IV, ? May 1650; Irene Coltman, *Private Men and Public Causes* (London, 1962) pp. 209-15; Edgeman's Journal, ff. 26-7; Storey-Maskelyne MSS., Proger Letters (Bassett Down Farm, Wroughton, Wiltshire), Cottington to Proger, 27 Apr 1650. Mr Nigel Arnold-Forster kindly allowed me to read these letters in his home.

23. S.P.S., 94/43/70, Fisher to Council of State, 24 Apr 1651; Masson, *Life of Milton*, IV 234-6; Edgeman's Journal, f. 27; Coltman, *Private Men and Public Causes*, pp. 216-17; Clarendon, *History*, v 138.

24. B.L., Clarendon MS. 41, f. 97, Cottington and Hyde to Haro, 13 Dec 1650; ibid., f. 189, note on 50,000 pieces of eight; B.L., Rawlinson MS. c. 726, ff. 21, 26-7, 32, 43, Cottington to Haro, 30 May, 6 and 17 July, 9 Aug, 4 Nov 1650; Clarendon, *History*, v 140-1, 149-51.

25. B.L., Clarendon MS. 41, f. 125, Hyde to Nicholas, 29 Dec 1650; ibid., f. 182, passes to ambassadors, 10 Feb 1651; ibid., f. 190, Hyde to Father Riley, ? Feb 1651; ibid., f. 203, Cottington to Charles II, 1 Mar 1651; Edgeman's Journal, f. 31.

26. Ibid., f. 31; Edwin Hensen (ed.), *Registers of the English College*

at *Valladolid, 1589-1862*, Catholic Record Soc., xxx (Leeds, 1930) p. xxix.

Chapter 15: Epilogue

1. Storey-Maskelyne MSS., Proger Letters, Cottington to Proger, Valladolid, 7 Apr, 20 June, 21 Nov, 12 Dec 1651, 26 Jan 1652; B.L., Clarendon MS. 42, f. 365, Cottington to Hyde, Valladolid, 16 Feb 1652.

2. Proger Letters, Cottington to Proger, Valladolid, 14 May 1652; *Registers of the English College at Valladolid, 1589-1862*, p. xxix; Wiltshire R.O. (Trowbridge), attested copy of Cottington's will, 16 June 1652; P.C.C., Administrations (Somerset House, London), A.A.1660, f. 192, 3 Dec 1660.

3. Jane was born in 1604 and was still alive in December 1666. Dorothy, a spinster, was buried at Bath on 25 Apr 1690.

4. Wiltshire R.O., Cottington's will; *Registers of the English College at Valladolid, 1589-1862*, p. xxxii.

5. Crisp, *Somersetshire Wills*, IV 107-8; Banks, *Dormant and Extinct Baronage of England*, III 215; Rogers, *Records of Yarlington*, p. 39; *Registers of the English College at Valladolid, 1589-1862*, p. xxxii; H.M.C., *Seventh Report*, Appendix, p. 141; Firth, *Ludlow's Memoirs*, II 255-6.

6. V.C.H., *Wiltshire*, III 90; V.C.H., *Berkshire*, III 281; Crisp, *Somersetshire Wills*, IV 107-8; Middlesex R.O. (London), G.D. Reg. 6/199, indictment for trespass (Apr 1664) against Sir Francis Cottington; *A Refutation of a False and Impious Aspersion cast on the late Lord Cottington* (London, 1681) n.p., no. 45, in a volume marked 'Theology 1879', cc. 15, B.M.; *Notes and Queries for Somerset and Dorset*, IV, pt xxv, p. 2; J. Anthony Williams, *Catholic Recusancy in Wiltshire, 1660-1791*, Catholic Record Soc. Monograph I (Newport, Mon., 1968) pp. 175-7, 189, 246. Mrs Pawlet, present owner of Godminster Farm, and the late Revd. K. Ashcroft, vicar of Pitcombe and Shepton Montague, kindly provided references to lands around Pitcombe sold in 1736-43.

7. Clarendon, *History*, I 155-7.

8. Ibid., 198.

Genealogical Tables

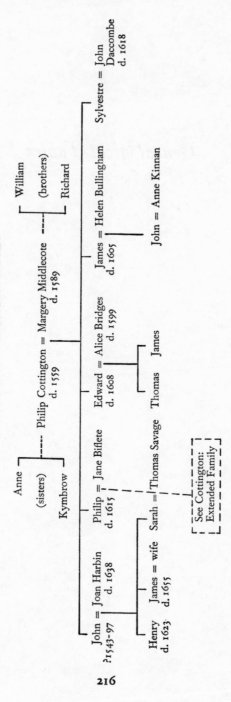

COTTINGTON: PATERNAL FAMILY

COTTINGTON: EXTENDED FAMILY

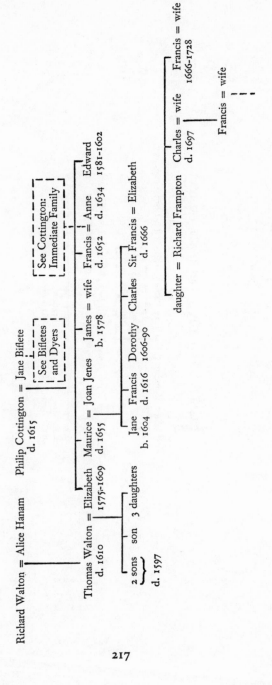

FRANCIS COTTINGTON: IMMEDIATE FAMILY

Sir William Meredith (1) = Jane Palmer = (2) John Lord Vaughan
d. 1605

```
┌ ─ ─ ─ ─ ─ ─ ┐
│ See Palmers and │
│ Merediths       │
└ ─ ─ ─ ─ ─ ─ ┘
```

Sir Robert Brett (1) = Anne Meredith = (2) Francis Lord Cottington
d. 1620   1601–34   1579–1652

Elizabeth	Charles	Frances	Anne	Anne
1626–30	1628–36	1625–30	1632	1634–41?

218

PALMERS AND MEREDITHS

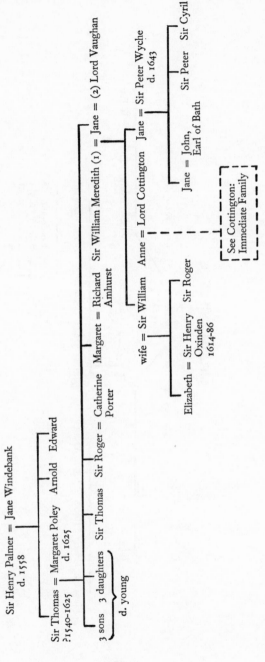

BIFLETES AND DYERS

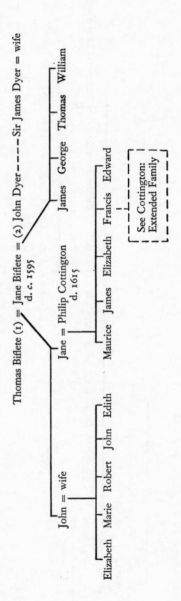

Index